THE **250** BEST
Brownies
Bars &
Squares

THE **250** BEST
Brownies
Bars &
Squares

Robert
ROSE

THE 250 BEST Brownies Bars & Squares

Text copyright © 2001

Photographs copyright © 2001 Robert Rose Inc.

For complete cataloguing information, see page 6.

DESIGN, EDITORIAL AND PRODUCTION:	MATTHEWS COMMUNICATIONS DESIGN INC.
PHOTOGRAPHY:	MARK T. SHAPIRO
ART DIRECTION, FOOD PHOTOGRAPHY:	SHARON MATTHEWS
FOOD STYLISTS:	KATE BUSH & JILL SNIDER
PROP STYLIST:	CHARLENE ERRICSON
MANAGING EDITOR:	PETER MATTHEWS
TEST KITCHEN/RECIPE EDITORS:	JENNIFER MacKENZIE & JUDITH FINLAYSON
INDEX:	BARBARA SCHON
COLOR SCANS:	POINTONE GRAPHICS

We acknowledge the financial support of the Government of Canada through the Book Publishing Industry Development Program (BPIDP) for our publishing activities.

Published by: Robert Rose Inc. • 120 Eglinton Ave. E., Suite 1000

Toronto, Ontario, Canada M4P 1E2 Tel: (416) 322-6552

Printed in Canada

1234567 BP 04 03 02 01

Contents

National Library of Canada Cataloguing in Publication Data

Brody, Esther
   The 250 best brownies, bars and squares

Includes index.
ISBN 0-7788-0035-0

   1. Bars (Desserts) I. Title. II. Title: Two hundred fifty best
brownies, bars and squares.

TX771.B76 2001   641.8'65   C2001-900971-2

To my little granddaughter, Natty (Natalie),
the love of my life,
whose beautiful little face and smile,
head full of curls,
loving hugs and kisses
and treasured moments that she and I, alone,
share with special songs, stories and laughter,
I dedicate this book.

I wish you a lifetime of good health,
happiness and success
in everything you do and hope for,
and may your entire life be filled
with the special love,
smiles and laughter
which you have brought into my life.

I want you always to remember
that Baba loves you
with all her heart.

Introduction

Brownies, bars and squares! Just hearing the words gets the attention of everyone — young and old alike. These are desserts that bring back memories of special times and holidays, with flavors of spices such as cinnamon, nutmeg and ginger, as well as other wonderful ingredients.

Think of nuts — not just old standbys such as walnuts, but other varieties such as pecans, almonds, hazelnuts, cashews and macadamia nuts. Think of rich chocolate and fresh, dried and candied fruits. Put these together with some good-for-you, hearty, nutritious ingredients such as rolled oats, wheat germ, granola and whole-wheat flour, and you have delicious, wholesome treats.

Best of all, brownies, bars and squares are so easy to make. For many recipes, you just mix up the dough, put it into a square or oblong pan, bake, slice and enjoy.

Even multi-layered bars or squares (my personal favorites), are much simpler to prepare than you might think. You just begin with a crumbly mixture for the base. Pour this mixture into your prepared baking pan, spread evenly all over bottom of pan, press down to form a solid crust, and bake if required. Add the filling and spread evenly over top of the crust, then add whatever topping is required in your recipe. Then it's just a matter of following the instructions for baking, cooling and cutting.

Everyone appreciates brownies, bars and squares. There is no greater way of saying "Thanks", "Happy Holidays" or "Welcome to the Neighborhood!" Students at school away from home anxiously await parcels of homemade goodies. They are also perfect for fundraisers, bazaars, wedding or baby showers, and on and on.

In this book, you'll find many familiar recipes, as well as new recipes that are sure to create wonderful memories for your family and friends. Whether you're a novice or a long-time baker, once you start experimenting with various recipes and see the fantastic results, you will be inspired to make baking a part of your everyday life.

Happy Baking!

– Esther Brody

Making great brownies, bars and squares

With brownies, bars and squares, all it takes a little preparation and some easy measuring and mixing. After that, it's just a matter of baking, cooling, slicing – and enjoying!

GETTING STARTED

Before you begin, read the recipe carefully and assemble all the necessary equipment and ingredients. Adjust oven racks to the desired level. Fifteen minutes before you want to bake, preheat the oven to the required temperature.

Be sure to follow the recipe as given. Don't make ingredient substitutions, or double or halve the recipe, unless it states that you can do so.

MAKE SURE ALL YOUR INGREDIENTS ARE FRESH:

- Purchase ground spices in small amounts and store tightly sealed in a cool, dry place. Replace ground spices annually.

- Ensure that leavening agents such as baking soda and baking powder are still functional. Baking soda will keep for up to 1 1/2 years in a glass jar with a tight lid or in its original container.

- Buy seeds and nuts from a bulk food store with rapid turnover and store them in the refrigerator.

- Keep marshmallows in the freezer.

- Check the "best before" date on ingredients such as peanut butter, sour cream and yogurt.

Always use large-size eggs for baking. Since eggs separate more easily when they are cold, separate the yolks from the whites as soon as you take them out of the refrigerator. If you're not using them immediately, cover the yolks with cold water and return to the refrigerator until you're ready to use them. (Drain the water off before using the yolks in a recipe.) If you're beating egg whites, allow them to come to room temperature for 5 to 10 minutes before beating. Do not leave eggs at room temperature for longer than 1 hour.

Remove shortening, butter or margarine from the refrigerator to soften 1 hour before mixing, unless the recipe specifies the use of cold butter. Don't substitute margarine or shortening when the recipe calls specifically for butter.

Prepare pans as required. If the recipe calls for a greased baking pan, coat the bottom and sides of the pan with a thin, even layer of shortening. Don't use too much or the cake will be gummy. If you use too little, it will stick to the pan.

How to toast nuts

Spread nuts out in a single layer on a baking sheet and bake at 350° F (180° C) for about 7 minutes, stirring or shaking the pan once or twice, until lightly browned. After toasting hazelnuts, place them on a clean tea towel and rub together vigorously to remove the skin.

How to melt chocolate

To ensure that chocolate melts quickly and evenly on the stovetop, break it into small pieces (or use chocolate chips) and stir constantly. Chocolate should always be melted over low heat, in a double boiler, or in a bowl set on top of a saucepan of hot (not boiling) water.

Chocolate also melts well in the microwave. Use chocolate chips, squares (each 1 oz [28 g]) or small chunks. Place in a microwaveable bowl, cover tightly with plastic wrap and microwave on High approximately 1 minute per ounce. (Times will vary depending upon the power of your microwave and the quantity of chocolate used.) Remove from oven and stir well.

The trick in melting chocolate is to ensure it doesn't "seize" or solidify into a grainy mass. If chocolate seizes up when melting, add 1 tsp (5 mL) shortening (not butter) for every 2 squares (2 oz [56 g]) of chocolate used, and stir well until the mixture is smooth and creamy.

How to store chocolate

Chocolate should be well wrapped and stored in an airtight container in a cool place. If the storage location is too warm, a gray/white color (called "bloom") will appear on the surface of chocolate. This does not affect the flavor of the chocolate and the chocolate will return to its normal color when melted.

Using honey instead of sugar

You can replace sugar with honey in most recipes. (The reverse does not hold true, however; if a recipe specifically calls for honey, then that is what will work best.) When substituting honey for sugar, add 1/2 tsp (2 mL) baking soda for each 1 cup (250 mL) and reduce the amount of liquid by 1/4 cup (50 mL). Also, reduce the oven temperature by 25° F (about 10° C), since recipes containing honey will brown faster.

Measuring and mixing

Measure ingredients carefully and accurately. Use measuring cups with a flat rim for dry ingredients so they can easily be levelled off. To measure less than 1/4 cup (50 mL), use standard measuring spoons. Fill cups or spoons to overflowing, then level off using a straight-edged knife or spatula. Do not pack or bang on the table.

Unless a recipe calls for "sifted flour" (in which case it should be sifted first, then measured), flour should not be sifted before it is measured. If a recipe calls for sifting dry ingredients together, there is no need to sift the flour prior to measuring. Sift all pre-measured ingredients together and proceed with the recipe.

If a recipe calls for "packed brown sugar", spoon it into a measuring cup, pack it down firmly with the back of a spoon, then level off.

Shortening, butter or margarine that is not sold in stick form should be measured in a cup that holds the exact amount when leveled off. Press firmly into the cup so that no air holes are left. Level off and scoop out.

Before mixing batter or dough, combine dry ingredients (such as flour, baking powder, baking soda and salt) in a bowl and mix thoroughly to ensure they are well blended.

If the recipe calls for a melted ingredient (such as butter, shortening or chocolate) cool slightly before adding eggs. Otherwise, the eggs may curdle.

Don't overbeat cake batter. When adding flour alternately with a liquid, keep the mixing to an absolute minimum, mixing only until the flour and liquid are incorporated into the batter. If using an electric mixer, beat on low speed. Overmixing will make the cake tough.

When pouring batter into a baking pan, spread it evenly in the pan and take care to fill all corners so the baked cake will come out even. Use a spatula to spread the batter gently across the bottom of the pan and into the corners, in a smooth, even layer without touching the sides of the pan.

Once the batter is in the baking pan, bang the pan on the counter 2 or 3 times. This will eliminate any large air pockets that will create holes in the finished product.

Baking, cooling and cutting

Use heavy metal baking pans for best results. If all you have is a glass baking dish, reduce the oven temperature by 25° F (20° C) and decrease the baking time slightly.

For multi-layered bars and squares, with a crust topped by a fluid batter, the crust must be pre-baked before the batter is added to prevent it from becoming soggy. All the recipes in this book have taken this into account and are written accordingly. Follow the recipe instructions.

The position of the baking pan in the oven influences how the product turns out. Center the baking pan on the middle rack of the oven. For best results, bake only one cake at a time. If you are baking multiple cakes, make sure the pans don't touch each other or the sides of the oven. Also, don't place pans directly underneath each other.

Since temperatures (and therefore baking times) can vary dramatically between different ovens, check for doneness a few minutes before the time indicated in the recipe. You will know your cake is done if you insert a tester into the center and it comes out clean and dry. You can also tell that cooking is complete if the cake shrinks slightly from the sides of the pan or the top springs back when touched lightly in the center with a fingertip.

Most brownies, bars and squares should be cooled completely in their baking pan before cutting. To prevent cakes from becoming soggy, cool cakes in their pan on a wire rack. This allows the bottom of the pan to be cooled by circulating air.

Sometimes it is appropriate to cut cakes before they are completely cooled. If the cake has a sticky filling, run a knife around the edge of the pan to loosen it as soon as it comes out of the oven. Crispy bars should be cut while still warm to prevent them from shattering. Then place the pan on a rack to cool.

When cutting brownies, bars and squares, use a sharp knife and a gentle, sawing motion to avoid squashing the cake. Store in a tightly covered container or in their own baking pan, covered tightly with foil. Make sure they are completely cooled before storing.

Brownies, bars and squares can be cut into a variety of sizes, depending upon the size of the pan. If you are trying to stretch the quantity of a recipe, cut smaller sizes. A general rule: the thicker and richer the cake, the smaller each portion should be.

Baking problems (and how to solve them)

If your brownies, bars and squares turn out less than perfect, chances are there's a simple solution to the problem. Here are some common examples.

CAKE EXPANDS OVER THE TOP OF THE PAN.

The pan may be too small. Check the pan size in the recipe. Batter should fill the pan only one-half to three-quarters full, depending upon the cake. If you follow this rule and your cake still expands too much, you might have added too much shortening, sugar or leavening agent to the batter. Check your measurements.

THE TEXTURE OF THE CAKE IS COARSE AND DENSE.

There are a number of possible explanations for this problem. The oven temperature may be too low. Raise the temperature by 25° F (about 10° C) and note the results. Dense cakes also result from not having adequate fat in the batter or from not creaming the shortening or butter well enough. Shortening or butter should be well beaten with sugar, until the mixture is smooth and creamy. Coarse, dense cakes can also result from overbeating the batter after the flour is added.

CAKE IS TOO DRY.

The most common reasons for this problem are overbaking or not having enough fat in the batter. If this isn't the cause, the batter may contain too much leavening agent (such as baking powder) or flour. Also, overbeating egg whites until they are too stiff can dry cakes out.

CRACKS OR BUMPS ON TOP OF CAKE.

This problem results from too much flour in the batter or an oven that is too hot. Check these variables.

CAKE HAS HOLES IN IT.

Chances are the batter was not thoroughly mixed. Another possibility is too much egg in the batter – perhaps the eggs were too large or you used too many. Always use large (never extra-large) eggs unless they are called for in the recipe and never add an extra egg just to use it up. Do not use 2 medium or small eggs as the equivalent of 1 large egg.

CAKE CRUMBLES WHEN SLICED.

There may be too much fat or too much sugar in the batter. Always measure ingredients accurately.

CAKE IS SOGGY OR HAS STREAKS AT THE BOTTOM.

There is too much baking powder or sugar in the batter and it's likely that the ingredients were not mixed thoroughly enough. When mixing, ensure that ingredients are blended.

CRUST ON A MULTI-LAYERED CAKE IS TOO STICKY AND MOIST.

This problem usually results from too much sugar. Check the recipe to make sure you didn't measure the sugar incorrectly.

CAKE RISES HIGHER ON ONE SIDE.

Most likely, the batter was spread unevenly in the pan or the pan is slightly warped. Another possibility is that the pan may have been set too close to another pan or the side of the oven.

CAKE BURNS ON BOTTOM.

This is usually the result of uneven heat distribution in the oven. Because the back of the oven is often slightly hotter than the front, rotate the pan halfway through baking to achieve a more even heat distribution.

wnies **Brownie**

Brownies

Bro

MAKES 16 BROWNIES

The Basic Brownie

3/4 cup	all-purpose flour	175 mL
1/2 tsp	salt	2 mL
1/2 tsp	baking powder	2 mL
2	squares (each 1 oz [28 g]) unsweetened chocolate	2
1/3 cup	shortening or butter, softened	75 mL
1 cup	granulated sugar	250 mL
2	eggs	2
1/2 cup	chopped walnuts or pecans	125 mL
	Cocoa Frosting, optional (see page 180)	
	Confectioner's (icing) sugar, for dusting (optional)	

TIP For a light-textured brownie, beat eggs more thoroughly. For a firmer brownie, beat eggs less.

Preheat oven to 350° F (180° C)
8-inch (2 L) square cake pan, greased

1. In a bowl mix together flour, salt and baking powder.

2. In a large saucepan over low heat, melt chocolate with shortening, stirring until smooth. Remove from heat and set aside to cool slightly.

3. When chocolate mixture has cooled, stir in sugar. Add eggs and beat just until blended. Blend in flour mixture. Stir in nuts.

4. Spread batter evenly in prepared pan. Bake in preheated oven for 30 to 35 minutes or until a tester inserted in the center comes out clean. Place pan on a rack to cool completely, then cut into squares. If desired, frost with Cocoa Frosting or your favorite chocolate frosting. Or sift confectioner's sugar over top.

MAKES 36 BROWNIES

Old-Time Brownies

1 3/4 cups	cake flour, sifted	425 mL
3/4 tsp	baking soda	4 mL
1 tsp	salt	5 mL
1 1/3 cups	granulated sugar	325 mL
5	egg yolks, beaten	5
2 1/2	squares (each 1 oz [28 g]) unsweetened chocolate	2 1/2
1 tsp	vanilla extract	5 mL
1 cup	sour cream	250 mL
1 cup	chopped walnuts	250 mL

TIP If you run out of unsweetened chocolate, substitute 3 level tbsp (45 mL) unsweetened cocoa powder and 1 tbsp (15 mL) butter for every 1 oz (28 g) unsweetened chocolate.

Preheat oven to 400° F (200° C)
Three 12-cup muffin tins, greased or paper-lined

1. In a bowl mix together flour, baking soda and salt.

2. In another bowl, beat sugar and egg yolks until thickened. Blend in melted chocolate. Stir in vanilla.

3. Gradually add flour mixture, alternately with sour cream, stirring until just combined. Stir in nuts.

4. Spoon into prepared tin, filling cups about three-quarters full. Bake in preheated oven for about 15 minutes or until a tester inserted in center of a brownie comes out clean. Place pan on a rack to cool slightly, then remove from cups and cool completely on rack.

MAKES 24 BROWNIES

Caramel Candy Brownies

	Filling	
1	bag (14 oz [397 g]) caramels, unwrapped (about 45 caramels)	1
2 tbsp	milk	25 mL

	Base and Topping	
4	squares (each 1 oz [28 g]) unsweetened chocolate	4
3/4 cup	butter *or* margarine	175 mL
2 cups	granulated sugar	500 mL
3	eggs	3
1 tbsp	milk	15 mL
1 cup	all-purpose flour	250 mL
1 cup	chopped pecans, divided	250 mL

TIP To melt chocolate in a microwave, use chocolate chips, chocolate squares (each 1 oz [28 g]) or small chunks of chocolate. Place in a microwave-safe bowl, cover tightly with plastic wrap and microwave on High approximately 1 minute per ounce (28 g). (Times will vary depending upon the power of your microwave and the quantity of chocolate used.) Remove from microwave and stir until melted and smooth.

Preheat oven to 350° F (180° C)
9-inch (2.5 L) square cake pan, greased

1. **Filling:** In a microwave-safe bowl, on medium power, heat caramels and milk for 3 minutes. Remove from oven and stir until melted and smooth. (Alternately, heat caramels and milk in a saucepan over low heat, stirring until smooth and melted.) Keep warm while preparing brownie batter.

2. **Base and Topping:** In a large saucepan over low heat, melt chocolate and butter, stirring constantly, until smooth. Remove from heat and set aside to cool slightly. When mixture has cooled, stir in sugar. Add eggs and beat until just blended. Stir in milk. Blend in flour. Stir in nuts.

3. Spread half the batter evenly in prepared pan. Spoon filling over batter. Sprinkle 3/4 cup (175 mL) of the nuts over top. Drop remaining batter by spoonfuls over nuts, then sprinkle with remaining nuts. Bake in preheated oven for 30 to 35 minutes or until a tester inserted in the centre comes out clean. Place pan on a rack to cool completely, then cut into squares.

MAKES 36 BROWNIES

Classic Chocolate Nut Brownies

4	squares (each 1 oz [28 g]) unsweetened chocolate	4
3/4 cup	butter *or* margarine	175 mL
2 cups	granulated sugar	500 mL
3	eggs	3
1 tsp	vanilla extract	5 mL
1 cup	all-purpose flour	250 mL
1 1/4 cups	chopped nuts	300 mL
	Frosting (optional)	

Preheat oven to 350° F (180° C)
13- by 9- inch (3.5 L) cake pan, greased

1. In a large saucepan over low heat, melt chocolate and butter stirring until smooth. Set aside to cool slightly.

2. When chocolate mixture has cooled, stir in sugar. Add eggs and vanilla and beat until just combined. Blend in flour. Stir in nuts.

3. Spread batter evenly in prepared pan. Bake in preheated oven for 30 to 35 minutes or until a tester inserted in the center comes out clean. Place pan on a rack to cool completely. If desired, frost, then cut into squares.

MAKES 16 BROWNIES

Cheesecake Swirl Brownies

Filling		
4 oz	cream cheese, softened	125 g
2 tbsp	granulated sugar	25 mL
1	egg	1

Base and Topping		
1 cup	all-purpose flour	250 mL
1/2 cup	unsweetened cocoa powder, sifted	125 mL
3/4 cup	granulated sugar	175 mL
1/2 tsp	baking powder	2 mL
1/2 cup	mini chocolate chips	125 mL
1/4 cup	chopped walnuts	50 mL
1/4 cup	vegetable oil	50 mL
1/4 cup	unsweetened applesauce	50 mL
1/4 cup	milk	50 mL
1 tsp	vanilla extract	5 mL
1	egg	1

Preheat oven to 350° F (180° C)
8-inch (2 L) square cake pan, greased

1. **Filling:** In a bowl, beat cream cheese and sugar until smooth. Beat in egg until incorporated. Set aside.

2. **Base and Topping:** In a separate bowl, mix together flour, cocoa, sugar and baking powder. Stir in chocolate chips and walnuts.

3. In another bowl, whisk together oil, applesauce, milk, vanilla and egg, until well blended. Add to flour mixture and mix until combined. Reserve 1 cup (250 mL) of mixture for topping and spread remainder evenly in prepared pan. Spread cream cheese filling evenly over batter. Drop reserved batter, by spoonfuls, over filling.

4. Run a knife through the batter at 1-inch (2.5 cm) intervals across the width of the pan, to create a marbling effect. Bake in preheated oven for 25 minutes or until a tester inserted in the center comes out clean. Place pan on a rack to cool completely, then cut into squares.

MAKES 24 BROWNIES

Coffee Mocha Brownies

3	squares (each 1 oz [28 g]) unsweetened chocolate	3
1/2 cup	butter	125 mL
2 tsp	instant espresso or coffee powder	10 mL
1 1/4 cups	granulated sugar	300 mL
2	eggs	2
1 tsp	vanilla extract	5 mL
2/3 cup	all-purpose flour	150 mL
1/2 tsp	salt	2 mL
1/2 cup	coarsely chopped bittersweet chocolate	125 mL
1/2 cup	chopped pecans, toasted	125 mL

Preheat oven to 350° F (180°C)
9-inch (2.5 L) square cake pan, lightly greased

1. In a large saucepan over low heat, melt chocolate, butter and coffee, stirring constantly, until mixture is smooth and coffee is dissolved. Set aside to cool slightly.

2. When chocolate has cooled, stir in sugar. Add eggs and vanilla and mix until blended. Blend in flour and salt. Stir in bittersweet chocolate and pecans.

3. Spread evenly in prepared pan. Bake in preheated oven for 25 to 30 minutes or until a tester inserted in the center comes out almost clean but with some moist crumbs. Place pan on a rack to cool completely, then cut into squares.

Cherry Cream Brownies

MAKES 24 BROWNIES

Filling		
3 oz	cream cheese, softened	90 g
1/4 cup	granulated sugar	50 mL
1/2 tsp	vanilla extract	2 mL
1/4 tsp	almond extract	1 mL
1	egg	1
1/3 cup	maraschino cherries, drained and chopped	75 mL

Base and Topping		
1/2 cup	all-purpose flour	125 mL
1/2 tsp	baking powder	2 mL
1/4 tsp	salt	1 mL
1/3 cup	unsweetened cocoa powder	75 mL
1/2 cup	butter or margarine, melted	125 mL
1 cup	granulated sugar	250 mL
2	eggs, beaten	2
1 tsp	vanilla extract	5 mL

Preheat oven to 350° F (180° C)
9-inch (2.5 L) square cake pan, greased

1. **Filling:** In a bowl, beat cream cheese and sugar until smooth. Beat in egg until incorporated. Stir in almond extract, vanilla and cherries and mix until blended.

2. **Base and topping:** In a bowl mix together flour, baking powder and salt.

3. In another bowl, sift cocoa into melted butter and mix until smooth. Stir in sugar. Add eggs and vanilla, beating until just combined. Blend in flour mixture.

4. Spread half the batter evenly in prepared pan. Spread filling over top. Drop remaining batter, by spoonfuls, over filling. Run a knife through the batter and filling to create a marbling effect. Bake in preheated oven for 35 to 40 minutes or until a tester inserted in the centre comes out clean. Place pan on a rack to cool completely, then cut into squares.

Original Fudge Brownies

MAKES 16 BROWNIES

1/2 cup	butter or margarine	125 mL
2	squares (each 1 oz [28 g]) unsweetened chocolate	2
1 cup	granulated sugar	250 mL
2	eggs	2
1/2 tsp	vanilla extract	2 mL
1/2 cup	all-purpose flour	125 mL
Pinch	salt	Pinch
1 cup	chopped walnuts	250 mL

TIP To line a pan with foil, turn the pan upside down, then smooth the foil around the pan to shape it. Turn the pan over and grease the bottom and sides before placing foil inside the pan. This prevents the foil from shifting.

Preheat oven to 350° F (180° C)
8-inch (2 L) square cake pan, greased

1. In a saucepan over low heat, melt butter and chocolate, stirring until smooth. Set aside to cool slightly.

2. When chocolate mixture has cooled, stir in sugar. Add eggs and vanilla and mix just until blended. Blend in flour and salt. Stir in nuts.

3. Spread batter evenly in prepared pan. Bake in preheated oven for 30 minutes or until a tester inserted in the center comes out clean. Place pan on a rack to cool completely, then cut into squares.

Chocolate Butter Pecan Brownies

1 1/2 cups	all-purpose flour	375 mL
1 tsp	baking powder	5 mL
1 tsp	salt	5 mL
1 cup	chopped pecans	250 mL
2/3 cup	butter	150 mL
4	squares (each 1 oz [28 g]) unsweetened chocolate	4
2 cups	granulated sugar	500 mL
4	eggs	4

Frosting		
1/4 cup	butter	50 mL
2 cups	confectioner's (icing) sugar, sifted	500 mL
3 tbsp	whipping (35%) cream	45 mL
2 tsp	vanilla extract	10 mL

Glaze		
1 tbsp	butter	15 mL
1	square (1 oz [28 g]) unsweetened chocolate	1

Preheat oven to 350° F (180° C)
13- by 9-inch (3.5 L) cake pan, greased

1. In a bowl mix together flour, baking powder, salt and pecans.

2. In a saucepan over low heat, melt butter and chocolate, stirring until smooth. Remove from heat and set aside to cool slightly.

3. When butter mixture has cooled, stir in sugar. Add eggs and beat just until blended. Blend in flour mixture.

4. Spread batter evenly in prepared pan. Bake in preheated oven for 30 to 35 minutes or until tester inserted in the center comes out clean. Place pan on a rack to cool completely.

5. **Frosting:** In a saucepan over low heat, melt butter. Remove from heat. Gradually add confectioner's sugar, alternately with cream, beating until smooth. Stir in vanilla. Spread evenly over brownies.

6. **Glaze:** In another saucepan, or in a microwave oven (see Tip, page 17), melt butter and chocolate until smooth. Cool slightly, then drizzle over top of frosting. When cooled, cut into squares.

Low-Fat Brownies

1/2 cup	cake flour	125 mL
1/2 cup	unsweetened cocoa powder	125 mL
1/4 tsp	salt	1 mL
3/4 cup	granulated sugar	175 mL
6 tbsp	unsweetened applesauce	90 mL
1	egg	1
2	egg whites	2
2 tbsp	vegetable oil	25 mL
1 1/2 tsp	vanilla extract	7 mL
1 tbsp	chopped walnuts or pecans	15 mL

Preheat oven to 350° F (180° C)
8-inch (2 L) square cake pan, greased

1. In a bowl sift together flour, cocoa and salt.

2. In another bowl, beat sugar, applesauce, egg, egg whites, oil and vanilla until blended. Blend in flour mixture. Spread batter evenly in prepared pan. Sprinkle walnuts over top. Bake in preheated oven for 25 minutes or until a tester inserted in the center comes out clean. Place pan on a rack to cool completely, then cut into squares.

Chocolate-Mint Dream Brownies

3/4 cup	butter *or* margarine	175 mL
1 2/3 cups	semi-sweet chocolate chips	400 mL
1 1/2 cups	all-purpose flour	375 mL
1/4 tsp	salt	1 mL
1 3/4 cups	granulated sugar	425 mL
6	eggs	6
2 tsp	vanilla extract	10 mL
12	small chocolate-covered mints	12
1/2 cup	white chocolate chips	125 mL
2 tbsp	whipping (35%) cream	25 mL

Preheat oven to 350° F (180° C)

13- by 9-inch (3.5 L) cake pan, greased

1. In a saucepan over low heat, melt butter and chocolate chips, stirring until smooth. Set aside to cool slightly.

2. In a bowl mix together flour and salt.

3. When chocolate mixture has cooled, stir in sugar. Add eggs and vanilla and beat until just blended. Blend in flour mixture.

4. Spread half the batter evenly in prepared pan. Arrange mints evenly over batter, pressing down lightly. Spoon remaining batter over top. Bake in preheated oven for 30 to 35 minutes, or until tester inserted in the center comes out clean. Place pan on a rack to cool completely, then chill for 2 hours.

5. Meanwhile, in a saucepan over low heat, melt white chocolate chips and cream, stirring constantly until smooth. Drizzle mixture over top of chilled brownies and cut into squares.

Ice Cream Chocolate Brownies

1	pkg (15.5 oz [440 g]) Brownie Mix or Brownie Mix with Chocolate Chunks	1
1 cup	peanut brittle, crushed	250 mL
6 cups	softened vanilla ice-cream	1.5 L
1/2 cup	ready-to-serve whipped chocolate frosting	125 mL

TIP To prevent ice crystals from forming on ice-cream after the carton has been opened, fit a piece of plastic wrap snugly on top of the ice cream before resealing the carton.

Preheat oven to 350° F (180° C)

13- by 9-inch (3.5 L) cake pan, greased on bottom only

1. Prepare brownie mix as directed on package. Spread evenly in prepared pan. Bake in preheated oven for 25 to 30 minutes or until tester inserted in the center comes out clean. Place pan on a rack to cool completely.

2. In a clean bowl, fold nut brittle into softened ice-cream. Spread evenly over cooled base. Cut into squares.

3. In a saucepan over low heat, heat frosting until melted, stirring constantly. Drizzle over top of squares in zig-zag lines. Serve immediately. Any leftover brownies can be frozen until firm, then wrapped in plastic and stored in the freezer up to 1 month.

1 1/4 cups	all-purpose flour	300 mL
1/2 tsp	baking powder	2 mL
1 cup	chopped nuts (optional)	250 mL
1 2/3 cups	semi-sweet chocolate chips	400 mL
1/2 cup	butter *or* margarine	125 mL
1 2/3 cups	granulated sugar	400 mL
3	eggs	3
1 tsp	vanilla extract	5 mL

	Topping	
1 cup	semi-sweet chocolate chips	250 mL
3/4 cup	whipping (35%) cream	175 mL
3	eggs	3
1/3 cup	granulated sugar	75 mL
Pinch	salt	Pinch
	Confectioner's (icing) sugar	

Chocolate Mousse Brownies

Preheat oven to 350° F (180° C)
13- by 9-inch (3.5 L) cake pan, greased

1. In a bowl mix together flour, baking powder and nuts, if using.

2. In a large saucepan over low heat, melt chocolate chips and butter, stirring constantly. Set aside to cool slightly.

3. When chocolate mixture has cooled, stir in sugar. Add eggs and vanilla, beating until blended. Blend in flour mixture. Spread batter evenly in prepared pan. Set aside.

4. **Topping:** In a saucepan over low heat, melt chocolate chips in cream, stirring until smooth. Set aside to cool slightly.

5. In a bowl, beat eggs, sugar and salt. Add chocolate mixture and mix well. Spoon topping evenly over batter. Bake in preheated oven for 40 to 45 minutes or until a tester inserted in the center comes out clean. Place pan on a rack to cool completely, then sift confectioner's sugar over top, if desired. Cut into squares.

1 1/2 cups	all-purpose flour	375 mL
1/2 tsp	baking soda	2 mL
Pinch	salt	Pinch
1/2 cup	butter, margarine or shortening, softened	125 mL
1 cup	packed brown sugar	250 mL
1	egg	1
1 1/2 tsp	vanilla extract	7 mL
2	squares (each 1 oz [28 g]) unsweetened chocolate, melted and cooled	2
1/2 cup	milk	125 mL
1 tsp	shortening	5 mL
	Chocolate Butter Frosting (optional, see page 179)	
	Shredded or flaked coconut (optional)	
	Confectioner's (icing) sugar (optional)	

Frypan Brownies

Preheat a medium-size electric frypan to 300° F (150° C) with vent closed

1. In a bowl mix together flour, baking soda and salt.

2. In another bowl, beat butter and brown sugar until smooth and creamy. Beat in egg until incorporated. Stir in vanilla and melted chocolate. Gradually blend in flour mixture alternately with milk until just incorporated.

3. Brush frypan with shortening. Spread batter evenly over pan. Cover and cook in preheated pan for 25 minutes or until top is no longer sticky. Open vent for the last 5 minutes.

4. Using a spatula, loosen cake around the edges, then invert onto a rack. Cool completely, then cut into squares. If desired, frost with Chocolate Butter Frosting, sprinkle with coconut or dust with confectioner's sugar.

Coconut Macaroon Brownies

Preheat oven to 350° F (180° C)
13- by 9-inch (3.5 L) cake pan, greased

Brownie Batter

4	squares (each 1 oz [28 g]) unsweetened chocolate	4
3/4 cup	butter *or* margarine	175 mL
2 cups	granulated sugar	500 mL
3	eggs	3
1 tsp	vanilla extract	5 mL
1 cup	all-purpose flour	250 mL
1 cup	chopped almonds, toasted	250 mL

Coconut Macaroon Batter

8 oz	cream cheese, softened	250 g
2/3 cup	granulated sugar	150 mL
2	eggs	2
2 tbsp	all-purpose flour	25 mL
2 cups	flaked coconut	500 mL
1 cup	chopped almonds, toasted	250 mL

Chocolate Glaze

2	squares (each 1 oz [28 g]) semi-sweet chocolate, melted	2
	Whole almonds (optional)	

TIP To make cutting brownies easy, line the baking pan with greased foil. You can lift out the cooled brownie cake and cut it on a cutting board.

1. **Brownie batter:** In a saucepan over low heat, melt chocolate and butter, stirring constantly until smooth. Set aside to cool slightly.

2. When chocolate mixture has cooled, stir in sugar. Add eggs and vanilla and mix until blended. Blend in flour. Stir in almonds. Spread batter evenly in prepared pan.

3. **Coconut macaroon batter:** In a bowl, beat cream cheese and sugar until smooth. Add eggs, one at a time, beating until incorporated. Blend in flour. Stir in coconut and almonds.

4. Spread coconut macaroon batter evenly over brownie batter and bake for 35 to 40 minutes or until a tester inserted in the center comes out clean. Place pan on a rack to cool completely, then drizzle with melted chocolate. Cut into squares and, if desired, place 1 whole almond on top of each.

Malted Milk Brownies

1 1/2 cups	all-purpose flour	375 mL
1/2 tsp	baking powder	2 mL
1/2 tsp	salt	2 mL
4	squares (each 1 oz [28 g]) semi-sweet chocolate	4
2	squares (each 1 oz [28 g]) unsweetened chocolate	2
3/4 cup	butter or margarine	175 mL
4	eggs, beaten	4
1 1/2 cups	granulated sugar	375 mL
1 tbsp	vanilla extract	15 mL

Topping		
3 tbsp	milk	45 mL
1 tsp	vanilla extract	5 mL
3/4 cup	unsweetened malted milk powder	175 mL
3 tbsp	butter or margarine, softened	45 mL
1 cup	confectioner's (icing) sugar, sifted	250 mL

TIP For an added treat, chop malted milk balls or a malted milk chocolate bar into pieces and sprinkle over top.

Plain brownies freeze well wrapped tightly in a double layer of plastic wrap or foil. To avoid condensation, thaw completely before unwrapping.

Preheat oven to 350° F (180° C)
13- by 9-inch (3.5 L) cake pan, greased

1. In a bowl mix together flour, baking powder and salt.

2. In a saucepan over low heat, melt chocolates and butter, stirring constantly, until smooth. Remove from heat and set aside to cool slightly.

3. When mixture has cooled stir in sugar. Add eggs and vanilla and beat until blended. Blend in flour mixture.

4. Spread batter evenly in prepared pan. Bake in preheated oven for 25 to 30 minutes, until tester inserted in the center comes out clean. Place pan on a rack to cool completely.

5. **Topping:** In a bowl combine milk, vanilla and malted milk powder until blended. In another bowl, cream butter. Gradually add confectioner's sugar, alternately with milk mixture, beating well after each addition until mixture is smooth and spreadable. Spread evenly over cooled brownies. When topping is firm, cut into squares.

Orange Cream Walnut Brownies

MAKES 24 BROWNIES

Base		
1/2 cup	butter or margarine, softened	125 mL
2 tbsp	confectioner's (icing) sugar, sifted	25 mL
1 cup	all-purpose flour	250 mL

Topping		
2 tbsp	all-purpose flour	25 mL
1/2 tsp	baking powder	2 mL
Pinch	salt	Pinch
2	eggs, beaten	2
1 cup	packed brown sugar	250 mL
1/2 cup	flaked coconut	125 mL
1 cup	chopped walnuts	250 mL

Orange Cream Frosting		
1 1/4 cups	confectioner's (icing) sugar, sifted	300 mL
2 tbsp	butter or margarine, melted	25 mL
1 1/2 tsp	grated orange zest	7 mL
1 1/2 tsp	orange juice	7 mL

TIP To get every drop of juice from citrus fruits, bring them to room temperature and roll them on the counter before squeezing.

Preheat oven to 350° F (180° C)
9-inch (2.5 L) square cake pan

1. **Base:** In a bowl, beat butter and confectioner's sugar until smooth and creamy. Gradually add flour, mixing until a soft dough forms. Press evenly into bottom of pan. Bake in preheated oven for 10 minutes or until golden brown. Place pan on a rack to cool for 5 minutes.

2. **Topping:** In a bowl mix together flour, baking powder and salt. Add eggs and brown sugar and beat until just combined. Stir in coconut and nuts. Spoon evenly over baked crust. Bake 25 minutes longer or until top is firm. Place pan on a rack to cool completely, then frost with Orange Cream Frosting.

3. **Frosting:** In a bowl, beat icing sugar, butter and orange juice until blended and smooth. Add zest and mix well. Spread evenly over cooled cake, then cut into squares.

Peanut Butter Brownies

3/4 cup	smooth peanut butter	175 mL
1/4 cup	milk	50 mL
2 cups	brown sugar	500 mL
2	eggs	2
1 cup	all-purpose flour	250 mL

Frosting and Glaze		
3/4 cup	smooth peanut butter, divided	175 mL
4	squares (each 1 oz [28 g]) semi-sweet chocolate	4

Preheat oven to 350° F (180° C)
9-inch (2.5 L) square cake pan, greased

1. In a saucepan over low heat, melt peanut butter in milk, stirring constantly. Remove from heat and set aside to cool slightly.

2. When mixture has cooled, stir in sugar. Add eggs and beat until just combined. Blend in flour. Spread evenly in prepared pan. Bake in preheated oven for 35 to 40 minutes or until a tester inserted in the center comes out clean. Place pan on a rack to cool completely.

3. **Frosting:** In a saucepan over low heat, melt 1/2 cup (125 mL) peanut butter with chocolate, stirring constantly until smooth. Spread evenly over cooled brownies.

4. In another saucepan over low heat, melt remaining peanut butter, stirring until smooth. (Alternately, in a microwaveable bowl, heat peanut butter on High, for about 1 minute, until melted.) Spoon over frosting, then swirl with a knife to create a marble effect. Chill until firm, then cut into squares.

MAKES 36 BROWNIES

Rocky Road Brownies

Base

2 cups	all-purpose flour	500 mL
1 tsp	baking soda	5 mL
1/2 cup	shortening	125 mL
1/2 cup	butter *or* margarine	125 mL
1 cup	strong, brewed coffee	250 mL
1/4 cup	unsweetened cocoa powder, sifted	50 mL
2 cups	granulated sugar	500 mL
2	eggs	2
1 tsp	vanilla extract	5 mL
1/2 cup	buttermilk	125 mL

Frosting

1/4 cup	milk	50 mL
1/2 cup	butter *or* margarine	125 mL
2 tbsp	unsweetened cocoa powder, sifted	25 mL
1 tsp	vanilla extract	5 mL
3 1/2 cups	confectioner's (icing) sugar, sifted	875 mL

Topping

1 cup	white, mini marshmallows	250 mL
1/2 cup	unsalted peanuts	125 mL
3	squares (each 1 oz 28 g]) semi-sweet chocolate, melted	3

Preheat oven to 400° F (200° C)
13- by 9-inch (3.5 L) cake pan, greased

1. **Base:** In a bowl mix together flour and baking soda.

2. In a large saucepan over medium heat, bring shortening, butter, coffee and cocoa to a boil, stirring constantly. Remove from heat and set aside to cool slightly.

3. When mixture has cooled, stir in sugar. Beat in eggs and vanilla. Gradually blend in flour mixture alternately with buttermilk until just incorporated. Spread evenly in prepared pan. Bake in preheated oven for 35 minutes or until a tester inserted in the center comes out clean.

4. **Frosting:** In a saucepan over low heat, heat milk, butter and cocoa, stirring constantly, until steaming (not boiling). Remove from heat. Gradually add confectioner's sugar, beating until mixture is smooth and spreadable. Beat in vanilla. Spread frosting over warm cake.

5. **Topping:** Sprinkle marshmallows and peanuts evenly over cake. Bake 2 to 3 minutes longer, until marshmallows are slightly melted. Drizzle melted chocolate over top. Place pan on a rack to cool completely, then cut into squares.

TIP For fast, easy cleanup when food is stuck to pans, boil a little vinegar and water in the pan before washing. You won't need to do any scrubbing.

Sour Cream Coffee Brownies

Preheat oven to 350° F (180° C)
13- by 9-inch (3.5 L) cake pan, greased

Base		
3/4 cup	all-purpose flour	175 mL
1/2 tsp	baking powder	2 mL
1/4 tsp	salt	1 mL
3/4 cup	butter or margarine, softened	175 mL
6	squares (each 1 oz [28 g]) semi-sweet chocolate	6
1 tbsp	instant coffee powder	15 mL
3/4 cup	packed brown sugar	175 mL
2	eggs	2
1 tsp	vanilla extract	5 mL

Cheesecake Topping		
8 oz	cream cheese, softened	250 g
1/2 cup	granulated sugar	125 mL
2	eggs	2
1 tsp	vanilla extract	5 mL
3 tbsp	coffee liqueur or strong coffee	45 mL
1/2 tsp	ground cinnamon	2 mL
2 tbsp	all-purpose flour	25 mL

Sour Cream Topping		
1 1/2 cups	sour cream	375 mL
1/3 cup	granulated sugar	75 mL

1. **Base:** In a bowl mix together flour, baking powder and salt.

2. In a large saucepan over low heat, heat butter, chocolate and coffee, stirring until mixture is smooth and melted and coffee has dissolved. Set aside to cool slightly.

3. When mixture has cooled, stir in brown sugar. Add eggs and vanilla and beat until combined. Blend in flour mixture. Spread batter evenly in prepared pan.

4. **Cheesecake topping:** In a bowl, beat cream cheese and sugar until smooth. Beat in eggs, one at a time, until incorporated. Stir in vanilla, liqueur and cinnamon until blended. Blend in flour. Spread evenly over base. Bake 20 minutes longer or until top is almost set.

5. **Sour cream topping:** In a bowl mix together sour cream and sugar. Spread carefully over top of brownies. Bake for 10 minutes longer. Place pan on a rack to cool completely, then cut into squares.

Chocolate Fudge Cake Brownies

MAKES 16 BROWNIES

2 cups	cake flour, sifted	500 mL
2 tsp	baking powder	10 mL
1/2 tsp	salt	2 mL
1/2 cup	butter, margarine or shortening, softened	125 mL
1 cup	granulated sugar	250 mL
1	egg	1
2	squares (each 1 oz [28 g]) unsweetened chocolate, melted	2
1 tsp	vanilla extract	5 mL
3/4 cup	milk	175 mL
	No-Cook Fudge Frosting (see recipe, page 181) (optional)	

Preheat oven to 325° F (160° C)
8-inch (2 L) square cake pan, greased

1. In a bowl mix together flour, baking powder and salt.

2. In another bowl, beat butter and sugar until smooth and creamy. Beat in egg, until incorporated. Stir in melted chocolate and vanilla. Gradually blend in flour mixture alternately with milk until just incorporated.

3. Spread batter evenly in prepared pan. Bake in preheated oven for 55 to 60 minutes, or until tester inserted in the center comes out clean. Place pan on a rack to cool completely. If desired frost, then cut into squares.

Chocolate Pecan Brownies

MAKES 24 BROWNIES

1 cup	all-purpose flour	250 mL
Pinch	salt	Pinch
2/3 cup	chopped pecans	150 mL
1/2 cup	butter or margarine, softened	125 mL
1 cup	granulated sugar	250 mL
3	eggs	3
2 tsp	vanilla extract	10 mL
3/4 cup	chocolate-flavored syrup	175 mL
	Whole pecans for garnish (optional)	
	Confectioner's (icing) sugar (optional)	

Preheat oven to 350° F (180° C)
9-inch (2.5 L) square cake pan, greased

1. In a bowl mix together flour, salt and pecans.

2. In another bowl, beat butter and sugar until smooth and creamy. Add eggs, one at a time, beating until incorporated. Stir in vanilla and chocolate syrup. Blend in flour mixture.

3. Spread batter evenly in prepared pan. Bake in preheated oven for 35 to 40 minutes or until a tester inserted in the center comes out clean. Place pan on a rack to cool completely, then cut into squares. Garnish each brownie with a pecan or dust with confectioner's sugar, if desired.

VARIATION Chocolate Walnut

Brownies: Substitute walnuts for the pecans.

Raspberry Cream Cheese Brownies

Filling		
8 oz	cream cheese, softened	250 g
3 tbsp	granulated sugar	45 mL
1	egg	1
1 tsp	vanilla extract	5 mL

Base and Topping		
1/2 cup	butter or margarine, softened	125 mL
3/4 cup + 1 tbsp	granulated sugar	175 mL + 15 mL
1	egg	1
3	squares (each 1 oz [28 g]) semi-sweet chocolate, melted and cooled	3
2	squares (each 1 oz [28 g]) unsweetened chocolate, melted and cooled	2
1 cup	all-purpose flour	250 mL
Pinch	salt	Pinch
1/4 cup	raspberry jam	50 mL

Preheat oven to 350° F (180° C)
8-inch (2 L) square cake pan, greased

1. **Filling:** In a bowl, beat cream cheese and sugar until smooth. Add egg and beat until incorporated. Stir in vanilla. Set aside.

2. **Base and topping:** In another bowl, beat butter and sugar until smooth and creamy. Beat in egg until incorporated. Stir in melted chocolates. Blend in flour and salt. Set aside 1 cup (250 mL) of mixture and spread remainder evenly in prepared pan. Spread filling evenly over batter. Drop reserved batter, by spoonfuls, over filling. Using a teaspoon (5 mL) drop jam on top of batter. Run a knife through the jam and batter to make a zig-zag design.

3. Bake in preheated oven for 35 to 40 minutes or until a tester inserted in the center comes out almost clean, but with just a few moist crumbs. Place pan on a rack to cool completely, then cut into squares.

1-2-3 Brownies

1	pkg (14 oz [425 g]) fudge brownie mix	1
1/3 cup	water	75 mL
1/4 cup	plain yogurt	50 mL

TIP For a quick and easy chocolate frosting, melt a large bittersweet or milk chocolate bar and spread over cake.

Preheat oven to 350° F (180° C)
8-inch (2 L) square cake pan, greased

1. In a bowl mix together brownie mix, water and yogurt until well combined. Spread batter evenly in prepared pan. Bake in preheated oven for 25 minutes or until a tester inserted in the center comes out clean. Place pan on a rack to cool completely, then cut into squares.

Brownies from a Mix

2 1/4 cups	packed Cake Brownie Mix (see recipe, below)	550 mL
2	eggs, beaten	2
1 tsp	vanilla extract	5 mL
1/2 cup	chopped walnuts	125 mL

TIP If you accidentally break an egg on the floor, sprinkle heavily with salt and leave for 5 to 10 minutes. The dried egg will sweep easily into your dustpan.

Preheat oven to 350° F (180° C)
8-inch (2 L) square cake pan, greased

1. In a bowl mix together Cake Brownie Mix, eggs and vanilla until blended. Stir in walnuts.

2. Spread batter evenly in prepared pan. Bake in preheated oven for 30 to 35 minutes or until a tester inserted in the center comes out clean. Place pan on a rack to cool completely, then cut into squares.

Cake Brownie Mix

2 cups	granulated sugar	500 mL
1 cup	all-purpose flour	250 mL
3/4 cup	unsweetened cocoa powder, sifted	175 mL
1 tsp	baking powder	5 mL
3/4 tsp	salt	4 mL
1 cup	shortening, softened	250 mL

1. In a bowl mix together sugar, flour, cocoa, baking powder and salt. Using 2 knives, a pastry blender or your fingers, cut in shortening until mixture resembles coarse crumbs. Store in an airtight container in a cool, dry place.

Chocolate Banana Brownies

1	pkg (15.5 oz [440 g]) chocolate chip brownie mix	1
2/3 cup	finely chopped walnuts	150 mL
1 cup	mashed ripe bananas (2 or 3 bananas)	250 mL
	Chocolate Butter Frosting (see page 179)	

TIP If desired, sprinkle top of brownies with some chopped nuts, or when serving, place 2 or 3 thin slices of fresh banana on top.

To ripen green bananas quickly, wrap them in newspaper.

Preheat oven to 350° F (180° C)
13- by 9-inch (3.5 L) cake pan, greased

1. Prepare mix according to package directions. Add walnuts and bananas and mix until blended. Spread batter evenly in prepared pan. Bake in preheated oven for 25 to 30 minutes or until tester inserted in the center comes out clean. Place pan on a rack to cool completely. Frost with Chocolate Frosting. Cut into squares.

Black Forest Brownies

MAKES 36 BROWNIES

1	pkg (14 oz [425 g]) fudge brownie mix	1
4 oz	cream cheese, softened	125 g
1/4 cup	granulated sugar	50 mL
2	eggs	2
1 tsp	vanilla extract	5 mL
2 tbsp	all-purpose flour	25 mL
1	can (19 oz [540 mL]) cherry pie filling	1
1/4 cup	semi-sweet chocolate chips	50 mL

Preheat oven to 350° F (180° C)
13- by 9-inch (3.5 L) cake pan, greased

1. Prepare brownie mix according to package directions. Spread half the batter evenly in prepared pan. Set remainder aside.

2. In another bowl, beat cream cheese and sugar until smooth. Beat in eggs, one at a time, until incorporated. Stir in vanilla. Blend in flour. Set aside.

3. Spread pie filling evenly over top of batter. Sprinkle chocolate chips evenly across top. Spoon cream cheese mixture over chocolate chips. Drop remaining batter by spoonfuls over cream cheese mixture. Using a knife, lightly draw circles in cream cheese and top layer of fudge batters to create marbling effect. Bake in preheated oven for 45 to 50 minutes or until a tester inserted in the centre comes out clean. Place pan on a rack to cool completely, then cut into squares.

Unbelievable Orange Brownies

MAKES 16 BROWNIES

1	pkg (14 oz [425 g]) fudge brownie mix	1
1	whole orange	1

Preheat oven to 350° F (180° C)
8-inch (2 L) square cake pan, greased

1. Wash orange, cut into quarters and remove the seeds. In a food processor, process until almost smooth.

2. Prepare brownies as directed on package, but substitute the processed orange for the quantity of water in the package instructions.

3. Bake as directed. Place pan on a rack to cool completely, then cut into squares.

CLASSIC CHOCOLATE NUT BROWNIES (PAGE 17) ➤

Broadway Blondies

Preheat oven to 325° F (160° C)
9-inch (2.5 L) square cake pan, greased

Blondies are brownies with a butterscotch rather than a chocolate flavor.

1 1/2 cups	all-purpose flour	375 mL
1 1/2 tsp	baking powder	7 mL
1/2 tsp	salt	2 mL
1/2 cup	butter	125 mL
1 1/2 cups	packed brown sugar	375 mL
2	eggs	2
1 1/2 tsp	vanilla extract	7 mL
3/4 cup	coarsely chopped pecans	175 mL

1. In a bowl mix together flour, baking powder and salt.

2. In a large saucepan over low heat, melt butter. Gradually add sugar, stirring until smooth. Set aside to cool slightly.

3. When butter mixture has cooled, add eggs and vanilla and beat until just blended. Blend in flour mixture. Stir in pecans.

4. Spread batter evenly in prepared pan. Bake in preheated oven for 50 to 60 minutes, or until a tester inserted in the center comes out clean. Place pan on a rack to cool completely, then cut into squares.

Chocolate Chip Blondies

Preheat oven to 350° F (180° C)
13- by 9-inch (3.5 L) cake pan, greased

2 cups	all-purpose flour	500 mL
1 tsp	baking powder	5 mL
1/4 tsp	salt	1 mL
2/3 cup	butter, softened	150 mL
2 cups	packed brown sugar	500 mL
2	eggs	2
1 cup	semi-sweet chocolate chips	250 mL
1 cup	peanut butter chips	250 mL
1/2 cup	coarsely chopped walnuts	125 mL
1/2 cup	coarsely chopped pecans	125 mL

1. In a bowl mix together flour, baking powder and salt.

2. In another bowl, beat butter and brown sugar until smooth and creamy. Add eggs, one at a time, beating until incorporated. Stir in vanilla. Blend in flour mixture. Stir in chocolate and peanut butter chips, walnuts and pecans.

3. Spread batter evenly in prepared pan. Bake in preheated oven for 30 to 35 minutes or until golden brown. Place pan on a rack to cool completely, then cut into squares.

TIP If you can't live without chocolate, add chocolate chips to a blondie batter.

◄ ROCKY ROAD BROWNIES (PAGE 27)

Toffee-Spice Raisin Blondies

2 cups	all-purpose flour	500 mL
1/2 tsp	baking soda	2 mL
1/2 tsp	ground cinnamon	2 mL
1/2 tsp	ground nutmeg	2 mL
1/4 tsp	ground cloves	1 mL
1 1/4 cups	packed brown sugar	300 mL
1 cup	butter or margarine, softened	250 mL
2	eggs	2
2 tbsp	milk	25 mL
1 1/2 cups	raisins	375 mL

Preheat oven to 375° F (190° C)
13- by 9-inch (3.5 L) cake pan, greased

1. In a bowl mix together flour, baking soda, cinnamon, nutmeg and cloves.

2. In another bowl, beat brown sugar and butter until smooth and creamy. Beat in eggs until incorporated. Stir in milk. Gradually blend in flour mixture. Stir in raisins.

3. Spread batter evenly in prepared pan. Bake in preheated oven for 20 minutes or until a tester inserted in the center comes out clean. Place pan on a rack to cool completely, then cut into squares.

Bars Squares

Chocolate Bars and Squares

MAKES 24 BARS

Chocolate Chip Nut Bars

Preheat oven to 350° F (180° C)
9-inch (2.5 L) square cake pan, greased

Base

1 cup	all-purpose flour	250 mL
1/4 cup	granulated sugar	50 mL
1/3 cup	butter *or* margarine	75 mL

Topping

2 tbsp	butter *or* margarine	25 mL
1 cup	semi-sweet chocolate chips	250 mL
1/2 cup	light corn syrup	125 mL
1/2 cup	granulated sugar	125 mL
2	eggs	2
2/3 cup	chopped pecans or walnuts	150 mL

1. **Base:** In a bowl mix together flour and sugar. Using 2 knives, a pastry blender or your fingers, work butter in until mixture resembles coarse crumbs. Press evenly into prepared pan. Bake in preheated oven for 12 to 15 minutes or until golden brown. Place pan on a rack to cool slightly.

2. **Topping:** In a large saucepan, over low heat, melt butter and chocolate chips, stirring until smooth. Remove from heat and set aside to cool slightly. When mixture has cooled beat in sugar and corn syrup. Beat in eggs. Stir in nuts. Spread evenly over base and bake 25 to 35 minutes longer or until topping is set. Place pan on a rack to cool completely, then cut into bars.

MAKES 24 BARS

Chocodamias

Preheat oven to 350° F (180° C)
9-inch (2.5 L) square cake pan, greased

1/4 cup	butter *or* margarine	50 mL
6	squares (each 1 oz [28 g]) semi-sweet chocolate, divided	6
3/4 cup	granulated sugar	175 mL
2	eggs	2
1 tsp	vanilla extract	5 mL
1 1/4 cups	all-purpose flour	300 mL
1/2 tsp	baking powder	2 mL
3/4 cup	chopped macadamia nuts	175 mL

1. In a large saucepan over low heat, melt butter and 3 squares of chocolate, stirring until smooth. Set aside to cool slightly. Chop remaining chocolate into chunks. Set aside.

2. When chocolate mixture has cooled, stir in sugar. Add eggs and vanilla, mixing just until incorporated. Blend in flour and baking powder. Stir in chopped chocolate and nuts. Spread evenly in prepared pan. Bake in preheated oven for 20 to 25 minutes or until a tester inserted in center comes out clean. Place pan on a rack to cool completely, then cut into bars.

TIP Dry ingredients – such as baking powder, baking soda and cocoa – sometimes have a tendency to pack down in their containers, so stir to loosen before measuring.

MAKES 18 BARS

Gooey Caramel-Pecan Chocolate Bars

Preheat oven to 425° F (220° C)
8-inch (2 L) square cake pan, lined with greased foil

Base

1 cup	all-purpose flour	250 mL
1/4 cup	granulated sugar	50 mL
Pinch	salt	Pinch
6 tbsp	cold butter	90 mL
3 tbsp	ice water	45 mL

Filling

3 tbsp	butter	45 mL
1/3 cup	light corn syrup	75 mL
1 1/3 cups	packed brown sugar	325 mL
1/2 cup	whipping (35%) cream	125 mL
1 tsp	white vinegar	5 mL
Pinch	salt	Pinch
1 tsp	vanilla extract	5 mL

Topping

3/4 cup	chopped pecans, toasted	175 mL
3	squares (each 1 oz [28 g]) semi-sweet chocolate	3

TIP To keep salt easy to pour, add a few grains of rice to the salt shaker.

1. **Base:** In a bowl mix together flour, sugar and salt. Using 2 knives, a pastry blender or your fingers, cut butter in until mixture resembles coarse crumbs. Sprinkle water, 1 tbsp (15 mL) at a time, over mixture, mixing lightly after each addition. (Dough should just be moist enough to hold together.) Press evenly into prepared pan. Bake in preheated oven for 15 to 20 minutes or until golden brown. Place pan on a rack to cool completely.

2. **Filling:** In a saucepan over high heat, combine butter, syrup, brown sugar, cream, vinegar and salt. Bring to a boil, reduce heat to low and simmer, stirring constantly, for 5 minutes. Remove from heat and stir in vanilla until bubbling stops (about 20 seconds). Pour filling over cooled base.

3. **Topping:** Sprinkle top with pecans and set aside to cool. In a small saucepan, over low heat, melt chocolate, stirring until smooth. Cool slightly, then drizzle over pecans. Chill until chocolate sets. Using foil to lift, transfer to a cutting board and cut into bars.

Easy Chocolate Delight Bars

Preheat oven to 350° F (180° C)
13- by 9-inch (3.5 L) cake pan, greased

Base		
1 1/4 cups	all-purpose flour	300 mL
1 tsp	baking powder	5 mL
1/2 cup	butter or margarine, melted	125 mL
1 tsp	granulated sugar	5 mL
1	egg yolk	1
2 tbsp	water	25 mL
2 cups	semi-sweet chocolate chips or chunks	500 mL

Topping		
2	eggs	2
3/4 cup	granulated sugar	175 mL
6 tbsp	butter, melted	90 mL
2 tsp	vanilla extract	10 mL
2 cups	finely chopped nuts	500 mL

1. **Base:** In a bowl mix together flour and baking powder.

2. In another bowl, beat butter, sugar, egg yolk and water until blended. Blend in flour mixture. Press mixture evenly into prepared pan. Bake in preheated oven for 10 minutes. Sprinkle chocolate chips over top and bake 1 minute longer or until chocolate begins to melt. Remove from oven and spread chocolate evenly over top of base. Place pan on a rack to cool slightly.

3. **Topping:** Beat eggs, sugar, melted butter and vanilla until smooth and blended. Stir in nuts. Spread over top of chocolate. Bake 30 to 35 minutes longer or until a tester inserted in the center comes out clean.

Fudgey Toffee Bars

Preheat oven to 350° F (180° C)
13- by 9-inch (3.5 L) cake pan, lightly greased

1/2 cup	butter or margarine, melted	125 mL
1 1/2 cups	graham wafer crumbs (about 22 wafers)	375 mL
1	can (10 oz [300 mL]) sweetened condensed milk	1
1 cup	toffee bits	250 mL
1 cup	semi-sweet chocolate chips	250 mL
1 cup	chopped nuts	250 mL

1. In a bowl mix together melted butter and graham wafer crumbs. Press evenly into prepared pan.

2. Pour condensed milk evenly over base. Sprinkle an even layer of toffee bits over milk, then a layer of chocolate chips, then a layer of nuts. Using a spatula, firmly press top layer into base.

3. Bake in preheated oven for 20 to 25 minutes or until lightly browned. Place pan on a rack to cool completely, then cut into bars.

MAKES 36 BARS

Fudgey Chocolate Oatmeal Bars

	Base	
3 cups	quick-cooking oats	750 mL
2 1/2 cups	all-purpose flour	625 mL
1 tsp	baking soda	5 mL
1 tsp	salt	5 mL
1 cup	butter or margarine, softened	250 mL
2 cups	packed brown sugar	500 mL
2	eggs	2
2 tsp	vanilla extract	10 mL

	Topping	
1	can (14 oz [398 mL]) sweetened condensed milk	1
2 cups	semi-sweet chocolate chips	500 mL
2 tbsp	butter *or* margarine	25 mL
1/2 tsp	salt	2 mL
2 tsp	vanilla extract	10 mL
1 cup	chopped walnuts	250 mL

Preheat oven to 350° F (180° C)
13- by 9-inch (3.5 L) cake pan, greased

1. **Base:** In a bowl mix together oats, flour, baking soda and salt.

2. In another bowl, beat butter and brown sugar until smooth and creamy. Beat in eggs until incorporated. Stir in vanilla. Blend in flour mixture. Press two-thirds of mixture evenly into prepared pan. Set remainder aside.

3. **Topping:** In a saucepan over low heat, combine condensed milk, chocolate chips, butter and salt, stirring until chocolate is melted and mixture is smooth. Remove from heat and stir in vanilla and walnuts. Spread evenly over base, then sprinkle top with reserved base mixture. Bake in preheated oven for 25 to 30 minutes or until top is golden brown. Place pan on a rack to cool completely, then cut into bars.

TIP To freshen stale nuts, spread them on a baking sheet and heat in a 250° F (120° C) oven for 5 to 10 minutes.

MAKES 36 BARS

Cherry Pie Cocoa Bars

1 3/4 cup	all-purpose flour	425 mL
1/4 cup	unsweetened cocoa powder, sifted	50 mL
1 cup	granulated sugar	250 mL
1 cup	butter	250 mL
1	egg, lightly beaten	1
1 tsp	almond extract	5 mL
1	can (19 oz [540 mL]) cherry pie filling	1
2 cups	semi-sweet chocolate chips	500 mL
1 cup	chopped almonds	250 mL

Preheat oven to 350° F (180° C)
13- by 9-inch (3.5 L) cake pan, greased

1. In a bowl mix together flour, cocoa and sugar. Using 2 knives, a pastry blender or your fingers, work butter in until mixture resembles coarse crumbs. Add egg and almond extract and mix until blended. Set aside 1 cup (250 mL) of mixture for topping and press remainder evenly into prepared pan. Spoon pie filling evenly over base.

2. In another bowl, combine chocolate chips, almonds and reserved base mixture. Sprinkle over top of filling. Bake in preheated oven for 35 to 40 minutes, until top is golden. Chill for 2 to 3 hours, then cut into bars.

MAKES 36 SQUARES

Buttermilk Chocolate Squares

2	squares (each 1 oz [28 g]) unsweetened chocolate, coarsely chopped	2
1/2 cup	boiling water	125 mL
2 cups	cake flour, sifted	500 mL
2 tsp	baking powder	10 mL
1/2 tsp	baking soda	2 mL
1/2 tsp	salt	2 mL
1/2 cup	shortening, softened	125 mL
2 cups	packed brown sugar	500 mL
2	eggs, separated	2
1 tsp	vanilla extract	5 mL
1/2 cup	buttermilk	125 mL
1/2 cup	water	125 mL
1/2 cup	chopped nuts	125 mL

Cocoa Frosting		
6 tbsp	butter, softened	90 mL
1/2 cup	unsweetened cocoa powder, sifted	125 mL
3 1/2 cups	confectioner's (icing) sugar, sifted	875 mL
1/4 cup	milk (approximate)	50 mL
1 1/2 tsp	vanilla extract	7 mL

TIP When melting chocolate for any recipe, mix a little flour into the remains of melted chocolate. It gets the last bit of chocolate out of the pan and into the batter.

Preheat oven to 350° F (180° C)
13- by 9-inch (3.5 L) cake pan, greased

1. In a saucepan over low heat, stir chocolate with boiling water until chocolate is melted and smooth. Set aside to cool for 10 minutes.

2. In a bowl mix together flour, baking powder, baking soda and salt.

3. In another bowl, beat shortening and brown sugar until smooth and creamy. Beat in egg yolks until incorporated. Stir in vanilla and chocolate mixture. Gradually blend in flour mixture alternately with buttermilk, then water, until just incorporated. Stir in nuts.

4. In a clean bowl, beat egg whites until soft peaks form. Fold into batter, then spread mixture evenly in prepared pan. Bake in preheated oven for 35 to 40 minutes or until a tester inserted in the center comes out clean. Place pan on a rack to cool completely.

5. **Frosting:** In a bowl, beat butter and cocoa until smooth. Gradually add confectioner's sugar alternately with milk, beating until smooth. (Add just enough milk to make the right consistency for spreading.) Beat in vanilla. Spread evenly over cake. Cut into squares.

Chocolate Carrot Nut Squares

MAKES 36 SQUARES

2 cups	all-purpose flour	500 mL
1/3 cup	unsweetened cocoa powder, sifted	75 mL
2 tsp	baking powder	10 mL
2 tsp	ground cinnamon	10 mL
1 1/4 tsp	baking soda	6 mL
1 tsp	salt	5 mL
1 1/2 cups	granulated sugar	375 mL
4	eggs, beaten	4
1 1/2 cups	vegetable oil	375 mL
1 tsp	vanilla extract	5 mL
2 cups	grated carrots	500 mL
1/2 cup	flaked coconut	125 mL
1/2 cup	chopped pecans	125 mL
2 cups	crushed pineapple, drained	500 mL
	Chocolate Butter Frosting (see page 179) or Chocolate Velvet Frosting (see page 180) (optional)	
	Crushed pineapple (optional)	

Preheat oven to 350° F (180° C)
13- by 9-inch (3.5 L) cake pan, greased

1. In a bowl mix together flour, cocoa, baking powder, cinnamon, baking soda and salt. Make a well in the center. Add sugar, eggs, oil and vanilla; mix until blended. Stir in carrots, coconut, pecans and pineapple. Spread evenly in prepared pan.

2. Bake in preheated oven for 50 to 55 minutes or until a tester inserted in the center comes out clean. Place pan on a rack to cool completely. Frost, then spread crushed pineapple over top, if desired. Cut into squares.

Viennese Chocolate Bars

MAKES 36 BARS

	Base	
1 cup	butter, softened	250 mL
1/2 cup	granulated sugar	125 mL
2	egg yolks	2
2 1/2 cups	all-purpose flour	625 mL

	Filling	
1	jar (10 oz [284 mL]) raspberry jam or jelly	1
1 cup	semi-sweet chocolate chips	250 mL

	Topping	
4	egg whites	4
1/4 tsp	salt	1 mL
1 cup	granulated sugar	250 mL
2 cups	finely chopped pecans	500 mL

Preheat oven to 350° F (180° C)
13- by 9-inch (3.5 L) cake pan, greased

1. **Base:** In a bowl, beat butter and sugar until smooth and creamy. Beat in egg yolks until incorporated. Blend in flour. Shape dough into a ball and knead lightly. Press evenly into prepared pan. Bake in preheated oven for 15 to 20 minutes or until lightly browned. Place pan on rack to cool slightly.

2. **Filling:** Stir jam or jelly until smooth, then spread evenly over base. Sprinkle chocolate chips evenly over top. Set aside.

3. **Topping:** In a bowl, beat egg whites with salt until frothy. Gradually beat in sugar until stiff peaks form. Fold in pecans. Spread gently over chocolate chips and bake 25 minutes longer or until lightly browned. Place pan on a rack to cool completely, then cut into bars.

TIP If you have jam, jelly or syrup that has crystallized, place the bottle in a pan of cold water and heat gently. The crystals will disappear.

Mashed Potato Chocolate Squares

2 cups	all-purpose flour	500 mL
3 1/2 tsp	baking powder	17 mL
1 tsp	ground cinnamon	5 mL
1/2 tsp	ground nutmeg	2 mL
1/2 tsp	ground mace	2 mL
1/2 tsp	ground cloves	2 mL
1/2 cup	milk	125 mL
2 cups	granulated sugar	500 mL
2/3 cup	butter or margarine, softened	150 mL
4	eggs	4
1 cup	hot mashed potatoes	250 mL
2	squares (each 1 oz [28 g]) unsweetened chocolate, melted	2
1 cup	chopped nuts	250 mL
	Chocolate Butter Frosting (see recipe, page 179) or Chocolate Velvet Frosting (see recipe, page 180)	

Preheat oven to 350° F (180° C)
13- by 9-inch (3.5 L) cake pan, greased

1. In a bowl mix together flour, baking powder, cinnamon, nutmeg, mace and cloves.

2. In another bowl, beat sugar and butter until smooth and creamy. Beat in eggs, one at a time, until incorporated. Add chocolate and potatoes and mix well. Gradually blend in flour mixture alternately with milk until just incorporated. Stir in nuts. Spread evenly in prepared pan. Bake in preheated oven for 30 to 35 minutes or until a tester inserted in the center comes out clean. Place pan on a rack to cool completely, then frost with a chocolate frosting of your choice. Cut into squares.

Raspberry Chocolate Crumb Squares

Preheat oven to 375° F (190° C)
9-inch (2.5 L) square cake pan, ungreased

Base		
1 1/2 cups	quick-cooking rolled oats	375 mL
1 1/2 cups	all-purpose flour	375 mL
1/2 cup	granulated sugar	125 mL
1/2 cup	packed brown sugar	125 mL
1 tsp	baking powder	5 mL
Pinch	salt	Pinch
1 cup	butter *or* margarine	250 mL

Topping		
1 cup	raspberry jam or preserves	250 mL
1 cup	semi-sweet chocolate chips	250 mL
1/4 cup	chopped almonds	50 mL
3	squares (each 1 oz [28 g]) semi-sweet chocolate, chopped into small pieces	3

1. **Base:** In a bowl mix together oats, flour, sugars, baking powder and salt. Using 2 knives, a pastry blender or your fingers, cut butter in until mixture resembles coarse crumbs. Set aside 1 cup (250 mL) of mixture and press remainder evenly into prepared pan. Bake in preheated oven for 10 minutes. Place pan on rack to cool slightly.

2. **Topping:** Stir jam until smooth and spread evenly over warm base. Sprinkle chocolate chips evenly over jam.

3. In another bowl, combine reserved oat mixture with almonds. Sprinkle evenly over chocolate and gently pat down. Bake 30 to 35 minutes longer or until golden brown. Place pan on a rack to cool completely.

4. In a saucepan over low heat, melt chocolate, stirring until smooth. Set aside to cool slightly. When cake has cooled, drizzle melted chocolate over top. Set aside until chocolate sets, then cut into squares.

Chocolate Macaroon Bars

MAKES 36 BARS

Base		
1/3 cup	butter or margarine, melted	75 mL
1/3 cup	granulated sugar	75 mL
1 1/4 cups	graham wafer crumbs (about 17 or 18 wafers)	300 mL
1/4 cup	unsweetened cocoa powder, sifted	50 mL

Topping		
2 cups	fresh white bread crumbs (about 4 slices)	500 mL
2 2/3 cups	flaked coconut	650 mL
1	can (14 oz [398 mL]) sweetened condensed milk	1
2	eggs, lightly beaten	2
2 tsp	vanilla extract	10 mL
1 cup	semi-sweet mini chocolate chips	250 mL

Preheat oven to 350° F (180° C)
13- by 9-inch (3.5 L) cake pan, lightly greased

1. **Base:** In a bowl mix together butter, sugar, graham crumbs and cocoa until blended. Press evenly into prepared pan. Bake in preheated oven for 10 minutes.

2. **Topping:** In another bowl, mix together bread crumbs, coconut, milk, eggs and vanilla. Stir in chocolate chips. Spread evenly over baked base. Bake 30 minutes longer or until lightly browned. Place pan on a rack to cool completely, then cut into bars. Store, covered, in refrigerator.

Chocolate Chip Dream Bars

MAKES 36 BARS

1/2 cup	butter or margarine, melted	125 mL
1 1/2 cups	graham wafer crumbs (about 22 wafers)	375 mL
1	can (14 oz [398 mL]) sweetened condensed milk	1
1 cup	semi-sweet chocolate chips	250 mL
1 cup	flaked coconut	250 mL
1 cup	chopped nuts	250 mL

TIP For a healthy snack, combine raisins and nuts left over from baking and chop coarsely.

Preheat oven to 350°F (180° C)
13- by 9-inch (3.5 L) cake pan, lightly greased

1. In a bowl mix together butter and graham wafer crumbs. Press evenly into prepared pan. Pour condensed milk over base. Working in layers, sprinkle evenly with chocolate chips, then coconut, then nuts. Using a spatula, press down firmly. Bake in preheated oven for 25 to 30 minutes or until top is golden. Place pan on a rack to cool completely, then cut into bars.

Chocolate Mallow Sensations

Preheat oven to 375° F (190° C)
8-inch (2 L) square cake pan, greased

Filling		
1	square (1 oz [28 g]) unsweetened chocolate	1
2 tbsp	butter *or* margarine	25 mL
1/3 cup	chopped walnuts	75 mL

Base		
3/4 cup	all-purpose flour	175 mL
1 tsp	baking powder	5 mL
1/2 tsp	salt	2 mL
1 1/4 cups	packed brown sugar	300 mL
2	eggs	2
1/2 cup	flaked coconut	125 mL

Topping		
20	large marshmallows, cut in half	20
2 tbsp	butter *or* margarine	25 mL
2	squares (each 1 oz [28 g]) unsweetened chocolate	2
1 cup	confectioner's (icing) sugar, sifted	250 mL
1	egg, lightly beaten	1
1 tsp	vanilla extract	5 mL

TIP To cut sticky foods (like marshmallows, dates or prunes) easily, use kitchen scissors, dipping them frequently in hot water.

1. **Filling:** In a saucepan over low heat, melt chocolate with butter, stirring until smooth. Stir in walnuts. Set aside.

2. **Base:** In a bowl mix together flour, baking powder and salt.

3. In another bowl, beat brown sugar and eggs until smooth and creamy. Blend in flour mixture. Spoon half this batter into a bowl and stir in coconut. Stir filling into remaining batter.

4. Spread coconut batter evenly in prepared pan. Spread chocolate-walnut batter evenly over top. Bake in preheated oven for 25 to 30 minutes until a tester inserted in the center comes out clean.

5. **Topping:** Remove from oven and arrange marshmallow halves on top. Bake 2 minutes longer, until marshmallows are softened. Place pan on rack to cool.

6. In a saucepan over low heat, melt butter and chocolate, stirring until smooth. Cool slightly, then beat in egg and vanilla. Gradually add confectioner's sugar, beating until mixture is smooth. Working quickly, spread topping over marshmallow layer. Place pan on a rack to cool completely, then cut into bars.

MAKES 36 BARS

Rocky Road Bars

1/2 cup	butter or margarine, melted	125 mL
1 1/2 cups	graham wafer crumbs (about 22 wafers)	375 mL
1 1/2 cups	flaked coconut	375 mL
1 1/2 cups	chopped nuts	375 mL
1 1/2 cups	semi-sweet chocolate chips	375 mL
1 1/2 cups	miniature marshmallows	375 mL
1	can (10 oz [300 mL]) sweetened condensed milk	1
3	squares (each 1 oz [28 g]) semi-sweet chocolate, melted	3

Preheat oven to 350° F (180° C)
13- by 9-inch (3.5 L) cake pan, greased

1. In a bowl mix together melted butter and graham wafer crumbs. Press evenly into prepared pan. Working in layers, sprinkle coconut, then nuts, then chocolate chips and, finally, marshmallows evenly over base. Drizzle condensed milk evenly over top.

2. Bake in preheated oven for 25 to 30 minutes or until top is golden brown. Remove from oven. Drizzle with melted chocolate. Place pan on a rack to cool completely, then cut into bars.

MAKES 36 SQUARES

Chocolate Marshmallow Squares

Base		
2	squares (each 1 oz [28 g]) unsweetened chocolate	2
1/2 cup	butter	125 mL
1 cup	all-purpose flour	250 mL
1/2 tsp	baking powder	2 mL
1/4 tsp	baking soda	1 mL
1/4 tsp	salt	1 mL
1 cup	granulated sugar	250 mL
2	eggs	2
1 tsp	vanilla extract	5 mL
1/2 cup	unsweetened applesauce	125 mL

Topping		
2 1/2 cups	miniature, marshmallows divided	625 mL

Glaze		
2 tbsp	butter	25 mL
1/2 cup	granulated sugar	125 mL
2 tbsp	milk	25 mL
1/4 cup	semi-sweet chocolate chips	50 mL

Preheat oven to 350° F (180° C)
13- by 9-inch (3.5 L) cake pan, greased

1. **Base:** In a saucepan over low heat, melt chocolate and butter, stirring until smooth. Set aside to cool slightly.

2. In a bowl mix together flour, baking powder, baking soda and salt.

3. When chocolate mixture has cooled, stir in sugar. Add eggs and vanilla; beat until blended. Stir in applesauce. Blend in flour mixture. Spread evenly in prepared pan. Bake in preheated oven for 20 to 30 minutes or until a tester inserted in the center comes out clean.

4. **Topping:** Set aside 1/2 cup (125 mL) of the marshmallows and sprinkle remainder evenly over cake. Bake for 2 minutes longer or until marshmallows soften.

5. **Glaze:** In a saucepan over medium heat, combine butter, sugar and milk. Stir constantly until mixture comes to a boil, then boil for 1 minute. Remove from heat. Stir in chocolate chips and reserved marshmallows, until melted and smooth. Immediately drizzle over top of warm cake. Place pan on a rack to cool completely, then cut into squares.

MAKES 16 BARS

Grasshopper Cream Cheese Bars

Preheat oven to 350° F (180° C)
8-inch (2 L) square cake pan, ungreased

Base		
3/4 cup	all-purpose flour	175 mL
1/3 cup	unsweetened cocoa powder, sifted	75 mL
1/3 cup	granulated sugar	75 mL
6 tbsp	butter *or* margarine	90 mL

Topping		
8 oz	cream cheese, softened	250 g
1/4 cup	granulated sugar	50 mL
1	egg	1
1/2 tsp	peppermint extract	2 mL
4 or 5	drops green food coloring	4 or 5
1/4 cup	milk	50 mL

1. **Base:** In a bowl mix together flour, cocoa and sugar. Using 2 knives, a pastry blender or your fingers, cut butter in until mixture resembles coarse crumbs. Set aside 1 cup (250 mL) of mixture and press remainder evenly into prepared pan. Bake in preheated oven for 15 minutes or until lightly browned. Place pan on rack to cool slightly.

2. **Topping:** In a bowl, beat cream cheese and sugar until smooth. Beat in egg, peppermint extract and food coloring until blended. Blend in milk. Spread topping evenly over baked base. Sprinkle remaining base mixture over top and bake 20 to 25 minutes longer or until crumbs are golden. Place pan on a rack to cool completely, then cut into bars. Store, covered, in refrigerator.

MAKES 24 BARS

Mocha Cream Cheese Bars

Preheat oven to 350° F (180°C)
9-inch (2.5 L) square cake pan, greased

Base		
1/4 cup	butter or margarine, melted	50 mL
1 1/2 cups	finely crushed chocolate wafers (about 30 wafers)	375 mL

Topping		
8 oz	cream cheese, softened	250 g
2/3 cup	granulated sugar	150 mL
3	eggs	3
3 tbsp	unsweetened cocoa powder, sifted	45 mL
1/4 cup	milk	50 mL
3 tbsp	strong coffee	45 mL

1. **Base:** In a bowl mix together butter and wafers. Press evenly into prepared pan. Set aside.

2. **Topping:** In a bowl, beat cream cheese and sugar until smooth. Beat in eggs, one at a time, until incorporated. Add cocoa, milk and coffee, beating until well blended. Spread mixture evenly over base. Bake in preheated oven for 30 to 35 minutes or until set. Place pan on a rack to cool completely, then cut into bars. Store, covered, in the refrigerator.

TIP If you prefer frostings that are not-too-sweet, combine an 8-oz (250 g) package of softened cream cheese with a 16 oz (500 g) can of prepared frosting and mix until well blended.

MAKES 36 DIAMONDS

Coffee Mocha Cheesecake Diamonds

Preheat oven to 350° F (180° C)
13- by 9-inch (3.5 L) cake pan, greased

Base

6	squares (each 1 oz [28 g]) semi-sweet chocolate	6
3/4 cup	butter *or* margarine	175 mL
1 tbsp	instant coffee powder	15 mL
2	eggs	2
3/4 cup	packed brown sugar	175 mL
3/4 cup	all-purpose flour	175 mL
1/2 tsp	baking powder	2 mL

Cheesecake Layer

8 oz	cream cheese, softened	250 g
1/2 cup	granulated sugar	125 mL
2	eggs	2
2 tbsp	strong coffee *or* coffee liqueur	25 mL
2 tbsp	all-purpose flour	25 mL

Sour Cream Topping

1 1/2 cups	sour cream	375 mL
3 tbsp	granulated sugar	45 mL
	Chocolate-covered almonds or espresso beans (optional)	

1. **Base:** In a saucepan over low heat, melt chocolate and butter, stirring until smooth. Add coffee powder and mix well. Set aside to cool slightly.

2. In a bowl, beat eggs and brown sugar. Add cooled chocolate mixture and mix well. Blend in flour and baking powder. Spread evenly in prepared pan. Chill for 10 minutes.

3. **Cheesecake layer:** In a bowl, beat cream cheese and sugar until smooth. Add eggs, one at a time, beating until incorporated. Stir in coffee until blended. Blend in flour. Spread evenly over base. Bake in preheated oven for 20 minutes or until set.

4. **Sour cream topping:** In a bowl mix together sour cream and sugar. Spread over warm cheesecake. Bake 10 minutes longer. Place pan on a rack to cool completely. When cool, cut cake into 6 long strips, cut strips across on diagonal into diamond shapes. If desired, top each with a chocolate covered almond or espresso bean.

MAKES 24 SQUARES

Marbled Cream Cheese Squares

Preheat oven to 350° F (180° C)
9-inch (2.5 L) square cake pan, greased

Filling		
8 oz	cream cheese, softened	250 g
1/4 cup	granulated sugar	50 mL
1	egg	1
2 tbsp	all-purpose flour	25 mL

Base		
3/4 cup	butter *or* margarine	175 mL
4	squares (each 1 oz [28 g]) unsweetened chocolate	4
1 1/2 cups	granulated sugar	375 mL
3	eggs	3
1 tbsp	milk	15 mL
1 cup	all-purpose flour	250 mL
1 cup	chopped nuts	250 mL

TIP When baking cakes, never open the oven door until the minimum time is up or cakes will collapse.

1. **Filling:** In a bowl, beat cream cheese and sugar until smooth. Beat in egg until incorporated. Blend in flour. Set aside.

2. **Base:** In a saucepan over low heat, melt butter and chocolate, stirring until smooth. Set aside to cool slightly.

3. When mixture has cooled, stir in sugar. Beat in eggs until blended. Stir in milk. Blend in flour. Stir in nuts. Spread half the batter evenly in prepared pan. Spread filling evenly over base. Spread remaining batter evenly over filling. Run a knife through the layers to create a marbling effect. Bake in preheated oven for 35 to 40 minutes or until a tester inserted in the center comes out clean. Cool completely in pan, then cut into squares.

MAKES 36 SQUARES

Chocolate Cookie and Cream Squares

Preheat oven to 350°F (180° C)
13- by 9-inch (3.5 L) cake pan, ungreased

Base		
2 2/3 cups	chocolate cookie crumbs	650 mL
2/3 cup	butter or margarine, melted	150 mL
1/2 cup	granulated sugar	125 mL

Topping		
16 oz	cream cheese, softened	500 g
1 cup	granulated sugar	250 mL
4	eggs	4
2 cups	broken chunks chocolate cookies with white cream filling, divided	500 mL
6	squares (each 1 oz [28 g]) semi-sweet chocolate	6
1/2 cup	whipping (35%) cream	125 mL

1. **Base:** In a bowl mix together cookie crumbs, butter and sugar. Press evenly into pan. Bake in preheated oven for 8 to 10 minutes. Place pan on rack to cool slightly.

2. **Topping:** In a bowl, beat cream cheese and sugar until smooth. Beat in eggs, one at a time, until incorporated. Spread half the mixture evenly over warm base and sprinkle with 1 3/4 cups (425 mL) of cookie chunks. Spread remaining batter over top. Bake 35 to 40 minutes longer or until center is almost set. Place pan on a rack to cool, then chill for at least 3 hours.

3. In a saucepan over low heat, stir chocolate and whipping cream until melted and smooth. Pour over chilled cake. Sprinkle remaining cookie pieces over top. Cut into squares.

Vanilla Fudge Cream Bars

1	pkg (18.25 oz [515 g]) dark chocolate or devil's food cake mix	1
1/2 cup	butter or margarine, melted	125 mL
2	eggs, divided	2
1/2 cup	chocolate fudge sundae sauce	125 mL
1	container (15 oz [450 g]) ready-to-serve vanilla frosting	1
8 oz	cream cheese, softened	250 g

Preheat oven to 350° F (180° C)
13- by 9-inch (3.5 L) cake pan, ungreased

1. In a bowl mix together cake mix, butter, 1 of the eggs and chocolate fudge sauce, until blended. (Mixture will be crumbly.) Press evenly into prepared pan.

2. In another bowl, beat frosting mix with cream cheese until smooth. Set 1 cup (250 mL) of mixture aside and add 1 egg to remainder in bowl. Beat until blended and smooth. Spread evenly over base.

3. Bake in preheated oven for 30 to 35 minutes or until set. Place pan on rack to cool completely, then frost with reserved cream cheese mixture. Cut into bars. Store, covered, in refrigerator.

Bridge Mix Coconut Bars

3 tbsp	butter or margarine, melted	45 mL
Half	pkg (18.25 oz [515 g]) white cake mix	Half
3/4 cup	semi-sweet chocolate chips	175 mL
1 1/2 cups	miniature marshmallows	375 mL
1 cup	flaked coconut	250 mL
1 cup	chopped nuts	250 mL
1 1/4 cups	milk	300 mL

Preheat oven to 350° F (180° C)
13- by 9-inch (3.5 L) cake pan, ungreased

1. Spread melted butter evenly over the bottom of pan. Sprinkle evenly with cake mix, then top with chocolate chips, marshmallows, coconut and nuts. Pour milk evenly over top. Bake in preheated oven for 25 to 30 minutes or until golden brown. Place pan on a rack to cool completely, then cut into bars.

TIP For a richer version of this recipe, substitute 1 can (10 oz [300 mL]) sweetened condensed milk for the regular milk.

To keep freshly baked cakes from sticking to wire cooling racks, spray racks with nonstick cooking spray.

Chocolate Swirl Squares

Base		
2 cups	packaged biscuit mix	500 mL
1/4 cup	granulated sugar	50 mL
1	egg	1
2/3 cup	milk *or* water	150 mL
3 tbsp	melted butter or margarine, divided	45 mL
1/3 cup	semi-sweet chocolate chips or pieces, melted	75 mL
Topping		
1/4 cup	granulated sugar	50 mL
1/3 cup	flaked coconut	75 mL
1/4 cup	chopped nuts	50 mL

Preheat oven to 400° F (200° C)
8-inch (2 L) square cake pan, greased

1. **Base:** In a bowl mix together biscuit mix, sugar, egg, milk and 2 tbsp (25 mL) of the melted butter until blended. Spread evenly in prepared pan. Pour melted chocolate evenly over batter. Run a knife through batter to create a marbling effect.

2. **Topping:** In another bowl, mix together sugar, coconut, nuts and remaining melted butter. Spread mixture evenly over base. Bake in preheated oven for 20 to 25 minutes or until a tester inserted in center comes out clean. Place pan on a rack to cool slightly and serve warm or cool completely then cut into squares.

TIP Don't overbeat cake batter. Overbeating will remove too much air and make finished cakes flat and heavy.

Chocolate Chip Meringue Squares

MAKES 36 SQUARES

2 cups	all-purpose flour	500 mL
1 tsp	baking soda	5 mL
1/2 cup	butter or margarine, softened	125 mL
1/2 cup	granulated sugar	125 mL
1 1/2 cups	packed brown sugar divided	375 mL
2	eggs, separated	2
1 tsp	vanilla extract	5 mL
1 tbsp	water	15 mL
1 cup	semi-sweet chocolate chips or pieces	250 mL

Preheat oven to 325° F (160° C)
13- by 9-inch (3.5 L) cake pan, lightly greased

1. In a bowl mix together flour and baking soda.

2. In another bowl, beat butter and granulated sugar and 1/2 cup (125 mL) of the brown sugar until smooth and creamy. Beat in egg yolks until incorporated. Stir in vanilla and water. Blend in flour mixture. Spread mixture evenly in prepared pan. Sprinkle chocolate chips evenly over top, pressing lightly into the dough.

3. In a clean bowl, beat egg whites until soft peaks form. Gradually beat in remaining brown sugar until stiff peaks form. Spread evenly over dough. Bake in preheated oven for 30 minutes or until meringue is golden brown. Place pan on a rack to cool completely, then cut into squares.

Creole Cake Squares

MAKES 16 SQUARES

3 tbsp	butter or margarine, melted	45 mL
2	squares (each 1 oz [28 g]) unsweetened chocolate, melted	2
1 1/3 cups	cake flour, sifted	325 mL
1 3/4 tsp	baking powder	9 mL
1/4 tsp	salt	1 mL
1 cup	granulated sugar	250 mL
2	eggs	2
1/2 cup	milk	125 mL
	Butter Frosting (see recipe, page 179)	

Preheat oven to 325° F (160° C)
8-inch (2 L) square cake pan, greased

1. In a saucepan over low heat, melt butter and chocolate, stirring until smooth. Set aside to cool slightly.

2. In a bowl mix together flour, baking powder and salt.

3. When chocolate mixture has cooled, stir in sugar. Add eggs and beat until just blended. Gradually blend in flour mixture alternately with milk until just incorporated. Spread evenly in prepared pan. Bake in preheated oven for 45 to 50 minutes or until a tester inserted in the center comes out clean. Place pan on a rack to cool completely, then frost with any flavor of Butter Frosting. Cut into squares.

Polish Chocolate Squares (Mazurek)

MAKES 36 SQUARES

1/3 cup	shortening, softened	75 mL
1 1/2 cups	granulated sugar	375 mL
6	eggs, separated	6
1 1/2 tsp	vanilla extract	7 mL
6	squares (each 1 oz [28 g]) unsweetened chocolate, melted	6
1 2/3 cups	dry bread crumbs, divided	400 mL
	Whipped cream (optional)	

Preheat oven to 350° F (180° C)
13- by 9-inch (3.5 L) cake pan, greased

1. In a bowl, beat shortening and sugar until smooth and creamy. Add egg yolks, one at a time, and beat until incorporated. Stir in vanilla and melted chocolate. Add 1 1/2 cups (375 mL) of the bread crumbs and mix well.

2. In a clean bowl, beat egg whites until soft peaks form. Carefully fold into batter until blended.

3. Dust prepared baking pan with remaining bread crumbs. Spread batter evenly in pan. Bake in preheated oven for 35 minutes. Place pan on a rack to cool completely, then cut into squares. Serve plain or with whipped cream, if desired.

Sour Cream Chocolate Squares

MAKES 16 SQUARES

1 cup	all-purpose flour	250 mL
3/4 tsp	baking soda	4 mL
1/2 cup	milk	125 mL
1/2 cup	sour cream	125 mL
1/4 cup	butter *or* margarine	50 mL
2	squares (each 1 oz [28 g]) unsweetened chocolate, chopped	2
1 cup	granulated sugar	250 mL
1	egg	1
1/2 tsp	vanilla extract	2 mL
Frosting		
2	squares (each 1 oz [28 g]) unsweetened chocolate, melted	2
1/2 cup	sour cream	125 mL
2 1/4 cups	confectioner's (icing) sugar, sifted	550 mL

Preheat oven to 350° F (180° C)
8-inch (2 L) square cake pan, greased

1. In a bowl mix together flour and baking soda. In a cup, combine milk and sour cream.

2. In a saucepan, melt butter and chocolate, stirring until smooth. Remove from heat and set aside to cool slightly.

3. When mixture has cooled, stir in sugar. Add egg and vanilla and beat until blended. Gradually blend in flour mixture alternately milk mixture until just incorporated. Spread evenly in prepared pan. Bake in preheated oven for 25 to 30 minutes or until a tester inserted in center comes out clean. Cool in pan for about 10 minutes, then transfer to a rack to cool completely.

4. **Frosting:** In a bowl, beat melted chocolate and sour cream until smooth and blended. Gradually beat in confectioner's sugar until smooth and spreadable. Spread frosting over cake and cut into squares.

Chocolate-Lover's Banana Squares

Preheat oven to 350° F (180° C)
8-inch (2 L) square cake pan, ungreased

Base		
2 tbsp	butter *or* margarine	25 mL
1/2 cup	mashed ripe banana (1 large banana)	125 mL
1	egg, beaten	1
1 tsp	vanilla extract	5 mL
1/4 cup	water	50 mL
1 cup	all-purpose flour	250 mL
1 tsp	baking powder	5 mL
1/2 cup	granulated sugar	125 mL
3/4 cup	unsweetened cocoa powder, sifted	175 mL
1/2 tsp	salt	2 mL
1/4 tsp	ground cinnamon	1 mL

Topping		
1/2 cup	packed brown sugar	125 mL
1/4 cup	unsweetened cocoa powder, sifted	50 mL
1 1/4 cups	boiling water	300 mL

TIP Score bars or squares that are topped with chocolate as soon as the topping is applied. This prevents the chocolate from cracking later.

1. **Base:** In a saucepan over low heat, melt butter. Remove from heat and stir in banana, egg, vanilla and water until blended. Set aside.

2. In a bowl mix together flour, baking powder, sugar, cocoa, salt and cinnamon. Add banana mixture and mix well (batter will be thick). Spread evenly in prepared pan.

3. **Topping:** In a bowl, beat brown sugar, cocoa and boiling water until smooth and blended. Pour evenly over base. Bake in preheated oven for 35 to 40 minutes or until a tester inserted in the centre of the cake comes out clean (the fudgey sauce on top will be wet). Place pan on a rack to cool for 5 minutes, then cut into squares.

Black and White Chocolate Bars

1 1/4 cups	all-purpose flour, divided	300 mL
1/3 cup	raisins	75 mL
1/2 cup	chopped walnuts	125 mL
1/2 cup	butter *or* margarine	125 mL
6	squares (each 1 oz [28 g]) white chocolate, chopped into small chunks, divided	6
2/3 cup	granulated sugar	150 mL
3	eggs	3
2 tsp	vanilla extract	10 mL
4	squares (each 1 oz [28 g]) bittersweet chocolate, chopped into small chunks	4

Preheat oven to 350°F (180° C)
9-inch (2.5 L) square cake pan, lightly greased

1. In a bowl mix together 2 tbsp (25 mL) of flour, raisins and walnuts. Set aside.

2. In a large saucepan over low heat, melt butter and half the white chocolate chunks, stirring until smooth. Remove from heat and set aside to cool slightly.

3. When mixture has cooled, stir in sugar. Beat in eggs and vanilla just until blended. Blend in remaining flour. Stir in raisin-walnut mixture, remaining white and bittersweet chocolates.

4. Spread evenly in prepared pan. Bake in preheated oven for 30 minutes, or until a tester inserted in center comes out clean. Place pan on a rack to cool completely, then cut into bars.

White Chocolate Dream Bars

Base		
2 1/3 cups	all-purpose flour	575 mL
2 cups	old-fashioned rolled oats	500 mL
1 cup	packed brown sugar	250 mL
1 tsp	baking soda	5 mL
1 cup	butter or margarine, melted	500 mL

Topping		
1 1/2 cups	white chocolate chips	375 mL
1 cup	slivered almonds	250 mL
1 cup	toffee bits	250 mL
1 1/3 cups	caramel sundae sauce	325 mL
1/3 cup	all-purpose flour	75 mL

Preheat oven to 350° F (180° C)
13- by 9-inch (3.5 L) cake pan, greased

1. **Base:** In a bowl mix together flour, oats, brown sugar and baking soda. Add butter and mix thoroughly. Set aside 1 cup (250 mL) of mixture and press remainder evenly into prepared pan. Bake in preheated oven for 12 to 15 minutes or until lightly browned. Place pan on rack to cool slightly.

2. **Topping:** In a bowl combine white chocolate chips, almonds and toffee bits. Sprinkle evenly over base.

3. In a separate bowl, blend caramel sauce with flour. Drizzle over chocolate layer, then sprinkle remaining base mixture over top. Bake 20 to 25 minutes longer or until golden brown. Place pan on a rack to cool completely, then cut into bars.

Raspberry Almond White Triangles

1/2 cup	butter *or* margarine	125 mL
6	squares (each 1 oz [28 g]) white chocolate, chopped	6
1/2 cup	granulated sugar	125 mL
2	eggs	2
1 1/2 tsp	vanilla extract	7 mL
1/4 tsp	salt	1 mL
1 cup	all-purpose flour	250 mL
	Raspberry jam, to taste	
1 1/2 cups	white chocolate chips	375 mL
1/3 cup	sliced almonds	75 mL

TIP Use only the size of pan called for in your recipe. The difference between an 8-inch (2 L) square cake pan and a 9-inch (2.5 L) square cake pan, can mean the difference between a moist, chewy bar or square and an underbaked, heavy failure.

Preheat oven to 325° F (160°C)
9-inch (2.5 L) square cake pan, greased

1. In a large saucepan over low heat, melt butter and chocolate, stirring until smooth. Set aside to cool slightly.

2. When mixture has cooled, stir in sugar. Add eggs and vanilla and beat until just combined. Blend in salt, then flour. Spread half the batter evenly in prepared pan. Bake in preheated oven for 25 minutes or until golden brown. Place pan on a rack to cool for 10 minutes. Stir jam until smooth and spread evenly over top of warm cake.

3. Stir chocolate chips into remaining batter and drop, by spoonfuls, over jam layer. Sprinkle almonds on top. Bake 35 to 40 minutes longer or until lightly browned. Place pan on a rack to cool completely. Cut into 16 squares, then cut each square into 2 triangles.

Bars Bars Sq
res

Coconut Bars and Squares

Makes 16 squares

Southern Coconut Squares

2 cups	all-purpose flour	500 mL
2 1/2 tsp	baking powder	12 mL
1/2 tsp	salt	2 mL
2/3 cup	shortening, softened	150 mL
1 cup	granulated sugar	250 mL
3	eggs	3
1 tsp	almond extract	5 mL
2/3 cup	milk	150 mL
1 cup	flaked coconut	250 mL

Preheat oven to 375° F (190° C)
8-inch (2 L) square cake pan, greased

1. In a bowl mix together flour, baking powder and salt.

2. In another bowl, beat shortening and sugar until smooth and creamy. Beat in eggs, one at a time, until incorporated. Stir in almond extract. Gradually blend in flour mixture alternately with milk until just just incorporated. Stir in coconut. Spread evenly in prepared pan. Bake in preheated oven for 25 minutes or until golden brown. Place pan on a rack to cool completely, then cut into squares.

Makes 36 bars

Double Nut Coconut Bars

	Base	
1/2 cup	butter or margarine, melted	125 mL
1 1/2 cups	finely crushed graham wafer crumbs (about 22 wafers)	375 mL

	Topping	
1	can (14 oz [398 mL]) sweetened condensed milk	1
1 cup	semi-sweet chocolate chips	250 mL
1 1/2 cups	shredded coconut	375 mL
3/4 cup	chopped Brazil nuts	175 mL
3/4 cup	chopped cashews	175 mL

Preheat oven to 350° F (180° C)
13- by 9-inch (3.5 L) cake pan, lined with foil extending over ends

1. **Base:** In a bowl mix together butter and wafer crumbs. Press evenly into prepared pan.

2. **Topping:** Pour condensed milk evenly over crumbs. Working in layers, spread chocolate chips, coconut, Brazil nuts and cashews over crumbs. Using a spatula, press down gently. Bake in preheated oven for 25 to 30 minutes or until coconut is lightly browned. Place pan on a rack to cool completely. Transfer cake with foil to a cutting board and cut into bars.

MAKES 24 BARS

Coconut Bars Supreme

Preheat oven to 375° F (190° C)
9-inch (2.5 L) square cake pan, greased

Base		
1 1/4 cups	all-purpose flour	300 mL
1/4 cup	packed brown sugar	50 mL
1/2 cup	butter, margarine or shortening	125 mL

Topping		
2 tbsp	butter, margarine or shortening, melted	25 mL
1/2 cup	granulated sugar	125 mL
1/2 cup	corn syrup	125 mL
2	eggs	2
1 tsp	vanilla extract	5 mL
1/4 tsp	ground cinnamon	1 mL
1/4 tsp	ground nutmeg	1 mL
2/3 cup	coarsely chopped almonds	150 mL
1/2 cup	flaked coconut	125 mL

1. **Base:** In a bowl mix together flour and brown sugar. Using 2 knives, a pastry blender or your fingers, cut butter in until mixture resembles coarse crumbs. Press evenly into prepared pan. Bake in preheated oven for 15 minutes.

2. **Topping:** In a bowl, beat butter, sugar, syrup, eggs, vanilla, cinnamon and nutmeg, until blended. Stir in almonds and coconut. Spread evenly over base. Bake 20 to 25 minutes longer or until top is set. Place pan on a rack to cool completely, then cut into bars.

TIP To soften brown sugar, place a slice of soft bread in the package or container and close tightly. In a couple of hours, the sugar will be soft again.

MAKES 16 SQUARES

Chewy Coconut Squares

1/4 cup	butter *or* margarine	50 mL
1 cup	packed brown sugar	250 mL
1/2 cup	all-purpose flour	125 mL
1 tsp	baking powder	5 mL
1/2 tsp	salt	2 mL
1	egg, beaten	1
1 tsp	vanilla extract	5 mL
3/4 cup	sweetened shredded coconut	175 mL

Preheat oven to 350° F (180° C)
8-inch (2 L) square cake pan, greased

1. In a saucepan over low heat, melt butter with brown sugar, stirring until sugar dissolves. Remove from heat and cool slightly.

2. In a bowl mix together flour, baking powder and salt. Add egg, vanilla and butter mixture and mix until blended. Stir in coconut. Spread evenly in prepared pan. Bake in preheated oven for 20 to 25 minutes or until golden brown. Place pan on a rack to cool and cut into squares while slightly warm.

TIP If your coconut has dried out, sprinkle it with milk and let stand until it softens.

Golden Butterscotch Triangles

MAKES 16 SQUARES

3/4 cup	all-purpose flour	175 mL
1 tsp	baking powder	5 mL
1/4 tsp	salt	1 mL
1/4 cup	butter *or* margarine	50 mL
1 cup	packed brown sugar	250 mL
1	egg	1
1 tsp	vanilla extract	5 mL
1/3 cup	flaked coconut	75 mL
1/3 cup	chopped nuts	75 mL

Preheat oven to 350° F (180° C)
8-inch (2 L) square cake pan, lightly greased

1. In a bowl mix together flour, baking powder and salt.

2. In another bowl, beat butter and brown sugar until smooth and creamy. Beat in egg until incorporated. Stir in vanilla. Blend in flour mixture. Stir in coconut and chopped nuts. Spread mixture evenly in prepared pan. Bake in preheated oven for 20 to 25 minutes or until lightly browned. Place pan on a rack to cool completely, then cut into squares.

Coconut Dream Squares

MAKES 16 SQUARES

	Base	
1/2 cup	butter or margarine, softened	125 mL
1 tbsp	packed brown sugar	15 mL
1 cup	all-purpose flour	250 mL
Pinch	salt	Pinch

	Topping	
2 tbsp	all-purpose flour	25 mL
1 1/2 tsp	baking powder	7 mL
Pinch	salt	Pinch
1 1/4 cups	packed brown sugar	300 mL
2	eggs, beaten	2
3/4 cup	chopped walnuts	175 mL
1/2 cup	shredded coconut	125 mL
	Butter Frosting (optional, see Tip, below)	

TIP If desired, frost with Butter Frosting (see page 179) flavored with 1 1/2 tsp (7 mL) almond extract, instead of vanilla, before cutting into squares.

To prevent coconut from becoming moldy, toast in a skillet until golden, then store in an airtight container.

Preheat oven to 350° F (180° C)
8-inch (2 L) square cake pan, lightly greased

1. **Base:** In a bowl, beat butter and brown sugar until smooth and creamy. Blend in flour and salt. Press evenly into prepared pan. Bake in preheated oven for 15 minutes or until lightly browned. Place pan on a rack to cool.

2. **Topping:** In a bowl mix together flour, baking powder and salt. Add brown sugar and eggs and mix until blended. Stir in walnuts and coconut. Spread evenly over cooled base. Bake 20 to 25 minutes longer or until golden brown. Place pan on a rack to cool completely, then cut into squares.

MAKES 36 BARS

Coconut Chews

Base		
3/4 cup	butter or shortening, softened	175 mL
3/4 cup	confectioner's (icing) sugar, sifted	175 mL
1 1/2 cups	all-purpose flour	375 mL

Topping		
2 tbsp	all-purpose flour	25 mL
1/2 tsp	baking powder	2 mL
1/2 tsp	salt	2 mL
1 cup	packed brown sugar	250 mL
2	eggs	2
1/2 tsp	vanilla extract	2 mL
1/2 cup	chopped walnuts	125 mL
1/2 cup	flaked coconut	125 mL

Orange-Lemon Frosting (optional)		
2 tbsp	butter or margarine, melted	25 mL
1 1/2 cups	confectioner's (icing) sugar, sifted	375 mL
3 tbsp	orange juice	45 mL
1 tsp	lemon juice	5 mL

TIP To keep freshly baked cakes from sticking to wire cooling racks, spray racks with nonstick cooking spray.

Preheat oven to 350° F (180° C)
13- by 9-inch (3.5 L) cake pan, ungreased

1. **Base:** In a bowl, beat butter and confectioner's sugar until smooth and creamy. Gradually blend in flour until a soft dough forms. Press evenly into pan. Bake in preheated oven for 12 to 15 minutes or until lightly browned.

2. **Topping:** In a bowl mix together flour, baking powder and salt.

3. In another bowl, beat brown sugar, eggs and vanilla until smooth and blended. Blend in flour mixture. Stir in walnuts and coconut. Spread evenly over hot base and bake 20 minutes longer, until top is set. Place pan on a rack to cool slightly.

4. **Frosting (optional):** In a bowl, beat butter, confectioner's sugar, orange juice and lemon juice until smooth and spreadable. Spread frosting over warm cake. When completely cooled, cut into bars.

Coconut Fudge Bars

Base

1 cup	all-purpose flour	250 mL
1/2 cup	chopped walnuts	125 mL
1/4 cup	unsweetened cocoa powder, sifted	50 mL
1 cup	butter or margarine, softened	250 mL
1 1/2 cups	granulated sugar	375 mL
3	eggs	3
1 tsp	vanilla extract	5 mL

Topping

1	can (14 oz [398 mL]) sweetened condensed milk	1
1 cup	shredded coconut	250 mL

Frosting

1/4 cup	unsweetened cocoa powder	50 mL
2 cups	confectioner's (icing) sugar	500 mL
2 tbsp	butter or margarine, melted	25 mL
1/3 cup	evaporated milk	75 mL
1/2 tsp	vanilla extract	2 mL

Preheat oven to 350° F (180° C)
13- by 9-inch (3.5 L) cake pan, greased

1. **Base:** In a bowl mix together flour, walnuts and cocoa.

2. In another bowl, beat butter and sugar, until smooth and creamy. Beat in eggs until incorporated. Stir in vanilla. Blend in flour mixture. Spread evenly in prepared pan. Bake in preheated oven for 30 minutes or until tester inserted in the center comes out clean.

3. **Topping:** In a bowl mix together condensed milk and coconut. Spread evenly over hot base. Bake for 20 minutes longer or until coconut is lightly browned. Place pan on a rack to cool slightly.

4. **Frosting:** In another bowl, sift together cocoa and confectioner's sugar. Beat in butter, evaporated milk and vanilla, until smooth. Spread over warm cake. Chill until cooled completely, then cut into bars.

TIP Fresh milk cannot be used when evaporated milk is called for in a recipe. But evaporated milk, mixed with an equal amount of water, can be substituted for fresh milk.

TIP If a recipes calls for softened butter (at room temperature) and you are short of time, grate butter into a warm bowl. It will soften in no time.

Coco-Nut Crumb Bars

MAKES 36 BARS

Preheat oven to 350° F (180° C)
13- by 9-inch (3.5 L) cake pan, ungreased

Base		
2 cups	chocolate chip cookie crumbs	500 mL
1/4 cup	butter or margarine, melted	50 mL

Toppings		
2 cups	flaked coconut	500 mL
1	can (14 oz [398 mL]) sweetened condensed milk	1
2 cups	semi-sweet chocolate chips	500 mL

1. **Base:** In a bowl mix together cookie crumbs and melted butter. Press evenly into pan. Bake in preheated oven for 10 minutes.

2. **Toppings:** Remove pan from oven and sprinkle coconut over base. Pour condensed milk over coconut. Bake 18 to 20 minutes longer or until coconut begins to brown around the edges of the cake. Place pan on a rack to cool.

3. In a saucepan over low heat, melt chocolate chips, stirring until smooth. Spread melted chocolate evenly over top of coconut. Chill until completely cooled, then cut into bars.

Pineapple Coconut Bars

MAKES 36 BARS

Preheat oven to 350 °F (180°C)
13- by 9-inch (3.5 L) cake pan, greased

Base		
1	pkg (18.25 oz [515 g]) yellow cake mix	1

Filling		
1	pkg (4-serving size) vanilla instant pudding mix	1
1 1/4 cups	milk	300 mL
2 cups	drained crushed pineapple	500 mL

Topping		
1	envelope (1.3 oz [42.5 g]) whipped topping mix	1
3 oz	cream cheese, softened	90 g
1/4 cup	granulated sugar	50 mL
1/2 tsp	vanilla extract	2 mL
1/2 cup	flaked coconut, toasted	125 mL

1. **Base:** Prepare and bake cake mix according to package directions. Place pan on a rack to cool.

2. **Filling:** In a bowl, beat pudding mix and milk. Set aside. When mixture has thickened, fold in pineapple. Spread mixture evenly over cake.

3. **Topping:** In another bowl, prepare whipped topping according to package directions. Set aside.

4. In a bowl, beat cream cheese and sugar until smooth. Stir in vanilla. Add 1 cup (250 mL) of whipped topping and beat until blended. Fold in remaining topping and spread mixture evenly over pudding layer. Sprinkle coconut over top. Cover pan and chill thoroughly (3 to 4 hours), then cut into bars.

MAKES 16 SQUARES

Apple Pie Coconut Squares

Preheat oven to 375° F (190° C)
8-inch (2 L) square cake pan, greased

Base		
1 1/2 cups	all-purpose flour	375 mL
1/4 tsp	salt	1 mL
1/2 cup	butter or margarine, softened	125 mL
1/2 cup	packed brown sugar	125 mL
1 tsp	vanilla extract	5 mL
1 1/3 cups	flaked coconut	325 mL

Topping		
1	can (19 oz [540 mL]) apple pie filling	1
1 tbsp	lemon juice	15 mL
1/2 tsp	ground cinnamon	2 mL
1/4 tsp	ground mace	1 mL

1. **Base:** In a bowl mix together flour and salt.

2. In another bowl, beat butter and brown sugar until smooth and creamy. Stir in vanilla. Blend in flour mixture. Stir in coconut. Spread half the mixture evenly in prepared pan.

3. **Topping:** In a clean bowl, mix apple pie filling, lemon juice, cinnamon and mace until blended. Spoon evenly over base. Top with remaining coconut mixture. Bake in preheated oven for 20 to 25 minutes. Place pan on a rack to cool completely, then cut into squares.

TIP These squares are also delicious served hot with ice cream.

MAKES 16 SQUARES

Maraschino Coconut Squares

Preheat oven to 350° F (180° C)
8-inch (2 L) square cake pan, lightly greased

Base		
1/2 cup	butter, softened	125 mL
3 tbsp	confectioner's (icing) sugar, sifted	45 mL
1 cup	all-purpose flour	250 mL

Topping		
1/4 cup	all-purpose flour	50 mL
1/2 tsp	baking powder	2 mL
1/4 tsp	salt	1 mL
1/2 cup	granulated sugar	125 mL
2	eggs, lightly beaten	2
1 tsp	vanilla extract	5 mL
3/4 cup	chopped walnuts	175 mL
1/2 cup	flaked coconut	125 mL
1/2 cup	maraschino cherries, diced and drained	125 mL

1. **Base:** In a bowl, cream butter and confectioner's sugar. Blend in flour just until dough forms. Press evenly into prepared pan. Bake in preheated oven for 20 minutes or until edges are lightly browned.

2. **Topping:** In another bowl, mix together flour, baking powder and salt. Add sugar, eggs and vanilla and mix well. Stir in walnuts, coconut and cherries until blended. Spread evenly over baked base. Bake 25 minutes longer. Place pan on a rack to cool completely, then cut into squares.

CHOCOLATE CHIP BLONDIES (PAGE 33) ➤

MAKES 36 SQUARES

Lemon Coconut Squares

Base		
1/2 cup	packed brown sugar	125 mL
1/2 cup	butter, softened	125 mL
1 1/2 cups	all-purpose flour	375 mL

Topping		
2 tbsp	all-purpose flour	25 mL
1/2 tsp	baking powder	2 mL
1/4 tsp	salt	1 mL
1 cup	granulated sugar, divided	250 mL
3	eggs, separated	3
2 tbsp	grated lemon zest	25 mL
1/3 cup	lemon juice	75 mL
2 cups	shredded coconut	500 mL

TIP To squeeze a few drops of lemon juice without wasting the rest of the lemon, prick the peel at one end of the lemon with a fork, squeeze out the required quantity, then refrigerate the lemon. It will be fresh enough to use several more times.

Preheat oven to 325° F (160° C)
13- by 9-inch (3.5 L) cake pan, ungreased

1. **Base:** In a bowl, beat brown sugar and butter until smooth and creamy. Gradually add flour, mixing until mixture resembles coarse crumbs. Press evenly into pan. Bake in preheated oven for 10 to 15 minutes or until edges are lightly browned.

2. **Topping:** In another bowl, mix together flour, baking powder, salt and 1/2 cup (125 mL) of the sugar. In another bowl, lightly beat egg yolks, lemon zest and juice. Add to flour mixture and mix until blended. Stir in coconut.

3. In a clean bowl, beat egg whites until frothy. Gradually add remaining sugar and beat until stiff peaks form. Fold into flour mixture until blended. Spread evenly over base. Bake 20 to 25 minutes longer or until nearly set. Place pan on a rack to cool completely, then cut into squares.

MAKES 24 SQUARES

Coconut Nests

Base		
1 cup	packed brown sugar	250 mL
1 cup	butter or margarine, softened	250 mL
1	egg	1
1 tsp	vanilla extract	5 mL
2 cups	all-purpose flour	500 mL
1 tsp	salt	5 mL

Topping		
1/4 to 1/2 cup	raspberry jam	50 to 125 mL
1/2 cup	shredded coconut (approximate)	125 mL

Preheat oven to 350° F (180° C)
9-inch (2.5 L) square cake pan, lightly greased

1. **Base:** In a bowl, beat brown sugar and butter until smooth and creamy. Beat in egg until incorporated. Stir in vanilla. Gradually blend in flour and salt. Press evenly into prepared pan. Bake in preheated oven for 20 to 25 minutes or golden brown. Place pan on rack to cool slightly.

2. **Topping:** Stir jam until smooth and spread over warm base. Sprinkle liberally with coconut until top has a nest-like appearance (you may wish to use more than 1/2 cup (125 mL) of coconut). Place pan on a rack to cool completely, then cut into squares.

◄ COFFEE MOCHA CHEESECAKE DIAMONDS (PAGE 48)

MAKES 36 BARS

Raspberry Coconut Bars

Base		
1 1/2 cups	all-purpose flour	375 mL
1/4 tsp	salt	1 mL
3/4 cup	granulated sugar, divided	175 mL
3/4 cup	shortening	175 mL
2	eggs, separated	2
1/4 tsp	almond extract	1 mL

Topping		
1 cup	raspberry jam or preserves	250 mL
1/2 cup	flaked coconut	125 mL

Preheat oven to 350° F (180° C)
13- by 9-inch (3.5 L) cake pan, ungreased

1. **Base:** In a bowl mix together flour and salt.

2. In another bowl, beat 1/4 cup (50 mL) of the sugar and shortening until smooth and creamy. Beat in egg yolks until incorporated. Stir in almond extract. Blend in flour mixture. Spread evenly in pan. Bake in preheated oven for 15 minutes.

3. **Topping:** Stir jam or preserves until smooth, then spread evenly over hot base. Sprinkle coconut evenly over top. Set aside.

4. In a clean bowl, beat egg whites until foamy. Gradually beat in remaining sugar until stiff peaks form. Spread evenly over top of coconut. Bake for 25 minutes longer, until top is lightly browned. Place pan on a wire rack to cool completely, then cut into bars.

MAKES 24 SQUARES

Coconut Jam Squares

Base		
1 1/4 cups	all-purpose flour	300 mL
1/4 cup	granulated sugar	50 mL
1/2 cup	shortening	125 mL

Topping		
1 cup	raspberry jam	250 mL
2	eggs, beaten	2
2 tsp	vanilla extract	10 mL
1 cup	granulated sugar	250 mL
1/2 tsp	baking powder	2 mL
2 cups	flaked coconut	500 mL

TIP Other flavors of jam such as cherry, strawberry, apricot or peach also work well in this recipe.

Preheat oven to 350° F (180° C)
9-inch (2.5 L) square cake pan, greased

1. **Base:** In a bowl combine flour and sugar. Using 2 knives, a pastry blender or your fingers, cut shortening in until mixture resembles coarse crumbs. Press evenly into prepared pan.

2. **Topping:** Stir jam until smooth and spread evenly over base.

3. In a bowl, beat eggs, vanilla, sugar and baking powder until blended. Stir in coconut. Spread evenly over jam. Bake in preheated oven for 25 to 30 minutes or until golden brown. Place pan on a rack to cool completely, then cut into squares. Or serve warm, topped with whipped cream, if desired.

Chocolate-Coconut-Raspberry Squares

Base		
1/3 cup	granulated sugar	75 mL
1 1/4 cups	all-purpose flour	300 mL
1/2 cup	butter *or* margarine	125 mL
1	egg yolk	1

Topping		
1 1/3 cups	raspberry jam or preserves	325 mL
2 cups	flaked coconut	500 mL
1	can (10 oz [300 mL]) sweetened condensed milk	1
5	squares (each 1 oz [28 g]) semi-sweet chocolate	5
1 tbsp	butter *or* margarine	15 mL

TIP When beating ingredients, 150 strokes by hand are equal to 1 minute of beating with an electric mixer.

Preheat oven to 350° F (180° C)
9-inch (2.5 L) square cake pan, lightly greased

1. **Base:** In a bowl mix together sugar and flour. Using 2 knives, a pastry blender or your fingers, cut in butter until mixture resembles coarse crumbs. Add egg yolk and mix well. Press evenly into prepared pan. Bake in preheated oven for 18 to 20 minutes or until lightly browned.

2. **Topping:** Stir jam until smooth and spread over hot base. In a bowl mix together coconut and condensed milk and spread evenly over jam. Bake 25 minutes longer or until set. Place pan on a rack to cool completely .

3. In a small saucepan over low heat, melt chocolate and butter, stirring until smooth. Spread evenly over coconut and smooth with a spatula. Chill until set, then cut into squares.

Creamy Apricot Coconut Bars

Base		
1	pkg (18.25 oz [515 g]) lemon cake mix	1
1/4 cup	packed brown sugar	50 mL
1/4 cup	butter or margarine, softened	50 mL
2	eggs	2
1/4 cup	water	50 mL
1 cup	flaked coconut	250 mL
1 cup	chopped dried apricots	250 mL

Frosting		
3 oz	cream cheese, softened	90 g
1 tbsp	milk (approximate)	15 mL
Pinch	salt	Pinch
1 tsp	vanilla extract	5 mL
2 1/2 cups	confectioner's (icing) sugar, sifted	625 mL
1/8 tsp	each red and yellow food coloring, mixed to make apricot-orange color	0.5 mL

Preheat oven to 375° F (190° C)
13- by 9-inch (3.5 L) cake pan, greased

1. **Base:** In a bowl mix together half the cake mix, brown sugar, butter, eggs and water until blended and smooth. Stir in remaining cake mix, coconut and apricots. Spread evenly in prepared pan. Bake in preheated oven for 25 to 30 minutes or until a tester inserted in the center comes out clean. Place pan on a rack to cool completely.

2. **Frosting:** In a bowl, beat cream cheese, 1 tbsp (15 mL) of milk, salt and vanilla until smooth and creamy. Gradually beat in confectioner's sugar, adding additional milk, 1 tsp (5 mL) at a time, if necessary, until mixture is smooth and spreadable. Beat in coloring, a bit at a time, until desired shade is achieved. Spread evenly over cake. Cut into bars.

Fruit Bars and Squares

Bars Squares

Apple Cake Bars

MAKES 24 BARS

Topping		
2/3 cup	packed brown sugar	150 mL
1 tsp	ground cinnamon	5 mL

Base		
1 1/3 cups	all-purpose flour	325 mL
3/4 cup	granulated sugar	175 mL
1 tbsp	baking powder	15 mL
1/4 cup	butter *or* margarine	50 mL
1	egg, beaten	1
3/4 cup	milk	175 mL
1 tsp	vanilla extract	5 mL
2 to 4	apples, peeled and sliced	2 to 4

Preheat oven to 350° F (180° C)
8-inch (2 L) square cake pan, greased

1. **Topping:** In a bowl mix together brown sugar and cinnamon. Set aside.

2. **Base:** In another bowl, mix together flour, sugar and baking powder. Using 2 knives, a pastry blender or your fingers, cut butter in until mixture resembles coarse crumbs. Add egg, milk and vanilla and mix well. Spread half evenly in prepared pan. Sprinkle evenly with half the topping mixture. Sprinkle with remaining base mixture.

3. Arrange apple slices over top of cake, pushing them into the batter. Sprinkle with remaining topping. Bake in preheated oven for 50 to 60 minutes or until a tester inserted in the center comes out clean. Place pan on a rack to cool completely, then cut into bars.

Sliced Apple Bars

MAKES 36 BARS

Base		
4 cups	all-purpose flour	1 L
2 cups	granulated sugar	500 mL
1/2 tsp	salt	2 mL
1 cup	butter *or* margarine	250 mL

Topping		
5 cups	sliced peeled tart apples	1.25 L
1 tsp	ground cinnamon	5 mL

TIP To prevent sliced apples from turning brown, soak them for 10 minutes in moderately salted water after slicing.

Preheat oven to 375° F (190° C)
13- by 9-inch (3.5 L) cake pan, greased

1. **Base:** In a bowl mix together flour, sugar and salt. Using 2 knives, a pastry blender, or your fingers, cut butter in until mixture resembles coarse crumbs. Scoop out 1/2 cup (125 mL) of mixture and set aside. Spread half of remainder evenly in prepared pan. Bake in preheated oven for 10 minutes. Place pan on a rack to cool slightly.

2. **Topping:** In a bowl mix together, apples, cinnamon and reserved base mixture. Spread evenly over warm base. Top with the remaining base mixture. Bake in preheated oven for 30 to 35 minutes or until lightly browned. Place pan on a rack to cool completely, then cut into bars.

MAKES 24 BARS

Apple Kuchen Bars

Preheat oven to 375° F (190° C)
9-inch (2.5 L) square cake pan, ungreased

Base

2 cups	all-purpose flour	500 mL
2 tbsp	granulated sugar	25 mL
Pinch	salt	Pinch
3/4 cup	butter	175 mL
1	egg, lightly beaten	1

Filling

1/3 cup	all-purpose flour	75 mL
1/3 cup	packed brown sugar	75 mL
1 tbsp	butter or margarine, softened	15 mL
	Zest of 1 orange	
1/2 tsp	ground cinnamon	2 mL
5	apples, preferably Granny Smith, peeled, cored and thinly sliced	5

Topping

2 tbsp	granulated sugar	25 mL
1/2 tsp	ground cinnamon	2 mL

TIP To make an inexpensive room-freshener, cover orange peels with water in a small saucepan, and simmer over low heat, adding more water as needed. Your house will smell like a citrus grove.

1. **Base:** In a bowl mix together, flour, sugar and salt. Using 2 knives, a pastry blender or your fingers, cut butter in until mixture resembles coarse crumbs. Add egg and mix until a dough forms. Shape into 2 equal balls; wrap dough tightly in plastic wrap and chill for about 1 hour.

2. On a floured work surface, roll out one portion of the dough to fit the bottom of pan. If necessary, cut dough to fit.

3. **Filling:** In another bowl, mix together flour, sugar, butter, zest, cinnamon and apples. Spread evenly over dough. Roll remaining dough out as for first portion and place on top of apple mixture, cutting to fit the pan.

4. **Topping:** In a small bowl, mix together sugar and cinnamon; sprinkle over top of base. Bake in preheated oven for 40 to 50 minutes or until golden brown. Place pan on a rack to cool completely, then cut into bars.

MAKES 36 BARS

Cinnamon Applesauce Bars

2 cups	all-purpose flour	500 mL
1 tsp	baking soda	5 mL
1 tsp	ground cinnamon	5 mL
1/4 tsp	ground nutmeg	1 mL
1/2 cup	butter or margarine, softened	125 mL
1 cup	granulated sugar	250 mL
2	eggs	2
1 tsp	vanilla extract	5 mL
1 1/2 cups	unsweetened applesauce	375 mL
1 cup	raisins	250 mL
1 cup	chopped walnuts or pecans	250 mL
	Confectioner's (icing) sugar	

Preheat oven to 350° F (180° C)
13- by 9-inch (3.5 L) cake pan, greased

1. In a bowl mix together flour, baking soda, cinnamon and nutmeg.

2. In another bowl, beat butter and sugar until smooth and creamy. Beat in eggs until incorporated. Stir in vanilla. Blend in flour mixture. Stir in applesauce, raisins and nuts. Spread evenly in prepared pan. Bake in preheated oven for 30 to 35 minutes or until tester inserted in the center comes out clean. Place pan on a rack to cool completely, then sift confectioner's sugar over top. Cut into bars.

MAKES 36 SQUARES

Cinnamon Applesauce Squares

Base and Topping		
3 cups	all-purpose flour	750 mL
1/4 cup	granulated sugar	50 mL
1 tbsp	baking powder	15 mL
1 1/2 tsp	salt	7 mL
1/3 cup	butter or margarine	75 mL
2	eggs, beaten	2
6 to 8 tbsp	milk	90 to 125 mL

Filling		
2 cups	applesauce	500 mL
	Ground cinnamon	

Glaze		
1	egg yolk	1
1 tbsp	cold water	15 mL
	Granulated sugar	

Preheat oven to 350° F (180° C)
13- by 9-inch (3.5 L) cake pan, greased

1. **Base and Topping:** In a bowl mix together flour, baking powder, sugar and salt. Using 2 knives, a pastry blender or your fingers, cut butter in until mixture resembles coarse crumbs. Add eggs and enough milk to make a dough, mixing lightly with a fork. Form dough into a ball and divide into 2 equal portions.

2. On a floured work surface, roll one portion into a rectangle, just a bit larger than the pan. Ease pastry into the bottom of prepared pan, bringing the dough a bit up the sides.

3. **Filling:** Spread applesauce evenly over dough and sprinkle lightly with cinnamon. Roll out remaining dough, as for first portion and place on top of applesauce mixture. Seal the edges.

4. **Glaze:** Beat egg yolk and water and brush base with the mixture, then sprinkle generously with sugar. Bake in preheated oven for 40 to 45 minutes until well browned. Place pan on a rack and cool completely, then cut into squares. Serve warm or cooled.

MAKES 16 SQUARES

Apricot Crumble Squares

Preheat oven to 400° F (200° C)
8-inch (2 L) square cake pan, ungreased

MAKES 16 SQUARES

Base		
2 cups	all-purpose flour	500 mL
1/2 tsp	baking powder	2 mL
1/4 tsp	salt	1 mL
1/2 cup	butter, softened	125 mL
1/3 cup	granulated sugar	75 mL
1	egg	1
1 tsp	vanilla extract	5 mL

Topping		
2 cups	sliced apricots (drained if canned)	500 mL
1 tsp	granulated sugar	5 mL
1/2 tsp	ground cinnamon	2 mL

TIP To soften cold butter quickly, place a small heated saucepan upside-down over the dish of butter for several minutes.

1. **Base:** In a bowl mix together flour, baking powder and salt.

2. In another bowl, beat butter and sugar until smooth and creamy. Beat in egg and vanilla until incorporated. Blend in flour mixture, just until a dough forms. Spread dough evenly in pan. Bake in preheated oven for 6 to 7 minutes, until lightly browned.

3. **Topping:** Arrange apricots evenly over top of base. Sprinkle with sugar and cinnamon. Bake 10 to 12 minutes longer or until golden brown. Place pan on a rack to cool completely, then cut into squares.

MAKES 36 BARS

Cream Cheese Frosted Banana Bars

Preheat oven to 350° F (180° C)
13- by 9-inch (3.5 L) cake pan, greased

Base		
2 cups	all-purpose flour	500 mL
1 tsp	baking soda	5 mL
Pinch	salt	Pinch
2 cups	granulated sugar	500 mL
1/2 cup	butter or margarine, softened	125 mL
3	eggs	3
1 tsp	vanilla extract	5 mL
1 1/2 cups	mashed ripe bananas (3 or 4 large bananas)	375 mL

Frosting		
8 oz	cream cheese, softened	250 g
1/2 cup	butter or margarine, softened	125 mL
2 tsp	vanilla extract	10 mL
3 1/2 to 4 cups	confectioner's (icing) sugar, sifted	825 mL to 1 L

1. **Base:** In a bowl mix together flour, baking soda and salt.

2. In another bowl, beat sugar and butter until smooth and creamy. Beat in eggs, one at a time, until incorporated. Stir in vanilla, then bananas. Blend in flour mixture. Spread evenly in prepared pan. Bake in preheated oven for 30 to 35 minutes or until a tester inserted in the center comes out clean. Place pan on a rack to cool completely.

3. **Frosting:** In a bowl, beat cream cheese and butter until smooth and creamy. Stir in vanilla. Gradually beat in confectioner's sugar until smooth and spreadable. Spread over top of cooled cake and cut into bars.

Banana Oatmeal Crunch Squares

Preheat oven to 350° F (180° C)
13- by 9-inch (3.5 L) cake pan, greased

Base		
2 cups	all-purpose flour	500 mL
1 cup	old-fashioned rolled oats	250 mL
2 tsp	baking powder	10 mL
1 tsp	baking soda	5 mL
1/2 tsp	salt	2 mL
1/4 tsp	ground nutmeg	1 mL
1/2 cup	shortening, softened	125 mL
1 1/4 cups	granulated sugar	300 mL
2	eggs	2
1 tsp	vanilla extract	5 mL
3/4 cup	buttermilk	175 mL
1 1/2 cups	mashed ripe bananas (4 or 5 bananas)	375 mL

Topping		
1/4 cup	shortening	50 mL
3/4 cup	packed brown sugar	175 mL
1/3 cup	evaporated milk	75 mL
1 1/2 cups	flaked coconut	375 mL
3/4 cup	chopped walnuts	175 mL

TIP Protect the finish on nonstick baking pans by using a plastic knife to cut bars or squares.

1. **Base:** In a bowl mix together flour, oats, baking powder, baking soda, salt and nutmeg.

2. In another bowl, beat shortening and sugar until smooth and creamy. Beat in eggs until incorporated. Stir in vanilla. Blend in flour mixture alternately with buttermilk, then bananas, until just incorporated. Spread evenly in prepared pan. Bake in preheated oven for 35 to 40 minutes or until a tester inserted in the center comes out clean. Place pan on a rack to cool slightly.

3. **Topping:** Preheat broiler. In a saucepan over low heat, melt shortening. Remove from heat and stir in brown sugar, milk, coconut and walnuts. Spread evenly over top of warm cake. Place pan under broiler and broil until top is golden brown. Place pan on a rack to cool completely, then cut into squares.

Blueberry Pie Squares

Preheat oven to 350° F (180° C)
13- by 9-inch (3.5 L) cake pan, greased

1 cup	butter or margarine, softened	250 mL
1 1/2 cups	granulated sugar	375 mL
4	eggs	4
1 tsp	almond extract	5 mL
2 tsp	baking powder	10 mL
2 cups	all-purpose flour	500 mL
1	can (19 oz [540mL]) blueberry pie filling	1

1. In a bowl, beat butter and sugar until smooth and creamy. Beat in eggs, one at a time, until incorporated. Stir in almond extract. Blend in baking powder and flour. Spread evenly in prepared pan. Top with large spoonfuls of pie filling, 4 along the length and 4 across the width.

2. Bake in preheated oven for 45 to 50 minutes or until golden brown. (The blueberry filling will sink into the cake while baking.) Place pan on a rack to cool completely, then cut into squares.

Blueberry Cheesecake Shortbread Bars

MAKES 36 BARS

Base		
2 cups	all-purpose flour	500 mL
1/2 cup	packed brown sugar	125 mL
1/2 tsp	salt	2 mL
3/4 cup	butter	175 mL

Topping		
1 lb	cream cheese, softened	500 g
3/4 cup	granulated sugar	175 mL
2	eggs	2
1 tsp	vanilla extract	5 mL
3/4 cup	blueberry preserves	175 mL

Preheat oven to 350° F (180° C)
13- by 9-inch (3.5 L) cake pan, greased

1. **Base:** In a bowl mix together flour, brown sugar and salt. Using 2 knives, a pastry blender or your fingers, cut butter in until mixture resembles coarse crumbs. Press evenly into prepared pan. Bake in preheated oven for 18 to 20 minutes, until lightly browned.

2. **Topping:** In a bowl, beat cream cheese and sugar until smooth. Add eggs and beat until incorporated. Stir in vanilla.

3. Spread blueberry preserves evenly over hot base. Spread cream cheese mixture evenly over blueberries. Bake 25 to 30 minutes longer or until slightly puffed. Place pan on a rack to cool completely, then cut into bars. Store, covered, in refrigerator.

Cherry Cheesecake Bars

MAKES 24 BARS

Base		
6 tbsp	butter or margarine, melted	90 mL
1 1/2 cups	graham wafer crumbs (about 22 wafers)	375 mL
2 tbsp	granulated sugar	25 mL

Topping		
12 oz	cream cheese, softened	375 g
1/2 cup	granulated sugar	125 mL
2	eggs	2
1 1/2 tsp	vanilla extract	7 mL
1 cup	cherry pie filling	250 mL

Preheat oven to 350° F (180° C)
9-inch (2.5 L) square cake pan, greased

1. **Base:** In a bowl mix together butter, sugar and graham crumbs. Press evenly into prepared pan. Bake in preheated oven for 10 minutes until golden brown. Place pan on a rack to cool.

2. **Topping:** In a bowl, beat cream cheese and sugar until smooth. Beat in eggs until incorporated. Stir in vanilla. Spread evenly over cooled base. Spoon pie filling over cream cheese mixture, then run a knife through the batter to create a marbling effect. Bake 40 to 45 minutes longer or until top is almost set. Place pan on a rack to cool completely, then store in refrigerator until ready to serve. Cut into bars.

MAKES 24 BARS

Crabapple Jelly Bars

Preheat oven to 350° F (180° C)
9-inch (2.5 L) square cake pan, greased

Base		
1 1/2 cups	all-purpose flour	375 mL
1/4 cup	granulated sugar	50 mL
Pinch	salt	Pinch
1 cup	shredded Cheddar cheese	250 mL
1/2 cup	finely chopped pecans	125 mL
3/4 cup	butter *or* margarine	175 mL

Topping		
1 cup	crabapple jelly	250 mL

1. **Base:** In a bowl mix together flour, sugar, salt, cheese and nuts. Using 2 knives, a pastry blender or your fingers, work butter in until mixture resembles coarse crumbs. Press half of mixture evenly into prepared pan.

2. **Topping:** Stir crabapple jelly to loosen; spoon evenly over top. Sprinkle with remaining crumb mixture. Bake in preheated oven for 25 to 30 minutes or until golden brown. Place pan on a rack to cool completely, then cut into bars.

MAKES 36 BARS

Cranberry Streusel Bars

Preheat oven to 350° F (180° C)
13- by 9-inch (3.5 L) cake pan, lightly greased

Base		
1/3 cup	confectioner's (icing) sugar, sifted	75 mL
3/4 cup	butter, softened	175 mL
1 1/2 cups	all-purpose flour	375 mL

Filling		
8 oz	cream cheese, softened	250 g
1	can (10 oz [300 mL]) sweetened condensed milk	1
1/4 cup	lemon juice	50 mL
1 tbsp	packed brown sugar	15 mL
2 tbsp	cornstarch	25 mL
1	can (14 oz [398 mL]) whole-berry cranberry sauce	1

Topping		
1/3 cup	all-purpose flour	75 mL
2 tbsp	packed brown sugar	25 mL
1/4 cup	butter, softened	50 mL
3/4 cup	chopped walnuts	175 mL

1. **Base:** In a bowl, beat confectioner's sugar and butter until smooth and creamy. Gradually blend in flour. Spread evenly in prepared pan. Bake in preheated oven for 15 minutes or until lightly browned. Place pan on a rack to cool slightly.

2. **Filling:** In a bowl, beat cream cheese until smooth. Gradually beat in condensed milk. Stir in lemon juice. Spread mixture evenly over warm base.

3. In another bowl, mix together brown sugar and cornstarch. Add cranberry sauce and mix well. Spread over cream cheese layer.

4. **Topping:** In a clean bowl, mix together flour and brown sugar. Using 2 knives, a pastry blender, or your fingers, cut butter in until mixture resembles coarse crumbs. Stir in nuts. Sprinkle over cranberry layer. Bake 30 to 35 minutes longer or until bubbly and golden brown. Place pan on a rack and cut into bars. Serve warm or cooled.

MAKES 36 BARS

Fig Newton Lattice Bars

Base

3/4 cups	butter, softened	175 mL
1/3 cup	granulated sugar	75 mL
1	egg	1
2 tsp	vanilla extract	10 mL
1/4 tsp	salt	1 mL
2 cups	all-purpose flour	500 mL

Topping

1 cup	water	250 mL
1	pkg (10 oz [300 g]) dried figs, stems cut off	1
1 cup	pitted prunes	250 mL
1/3 cup	packed brown sugar	75 mL
2 tbsp	fresh lemon juice	25 mL

TIP To make a lattice base or top, place half the dough strips parallel to each other at equal intervals. Weave a cross-strip through the center of the pie or cake in the opposite direction by folding back every other strip. Continue to weave remaining strips, folding back alternate strips each time a cross-strip is added. Trim ends if necessary.

Preheat oven to 375° F (190° C)
13- by 9-inch (3.5 L) cake pan, greased

1. **Base:** In a bowl, beat butter and sugar until smooth and creamy. Add egg, vanilla and salt, beating until incorporated. Blend in flour just until a dough forms. Knead lightly, then divide into 2 pieces, one slightly larger than the other. Wrap smaller piece in plastic wrap and refrigerate. Press larger piece evenly into prepared pan and refrigerate until ready to use.

2. **Topping:** In a saucepan over medium heat, combine water, figs, prunes and brown sugar, stirring frequently until mixture thickens and most of the liquid is absorbed, about 10 minutes. Set aside to cool slightly.

3. In a food processor, process fig mixture with lemon juice until almost smooth. Transfer to a bowl and refrigerate until cool.

4. When ready to bake, spread fig mixture over base. On a floured work surface, divide second piece of dough into two pieces, one slightly larger than the other. Cut the larger piece of dough into 10 equal pieces and using your hands, roll each into a rope approximately 13 inches (33 cm) long. Repeat with second piece of dough, rolling the 10 pieces into ropes approximately 9 inches (23 cm) long. Top fig mixture with a lattice pattern made from the ropes of dough. (See Tip, at left.) Trim excess dough.

5. Bake in preheated oven for 40 minutes or until golden brown. Place pan on rack to cool completely in pan, then cut into bars.

MAKES 36 BARS

Fresh Fruit Fiesta Bars

Base		
1 3/4 cups	all-purpose flour	425 mL
1 1/2 cups	old-fashioned rolled oats	375 mL
1/2 tsp	ground cinnamon	2 mL
3/4 cup	butter or margarine, softened	175 mL
1 cup	packed brown sugar	250 mL

Topping		
1	can (10 oz [284 mL]) mandarin oranges, drained	1
1	banana, sliced	1
1 cup	cubed peeled apples	250 mL
1/2 cup	raisins	125 mL
1/4 cup	orange juice	50 mL
1 tsp	ground cinnamon	5 mL

Preheat oven to 375° F (190° C)
13- by 9-inch (3.5 L) cake pan, ungreased

1. **Base:** In a bowl mix together flour, rolled oats, and cinnamon.

2. In another bowl, beat butter and sugar until smooth and creamy. Blend in flour mixture. Set aside 1 1/4 cups (300 mL) of mixture. Press remainder evenly into pan. Bake in preheated oven for 15 minutes.

3. **Topping:** In a bowl mix together oranges, banana, apples, raisins, orange juice and cinnamon. Spread topping evenly over warm base, leaving a space about 1/4 inch (5 mm) from the edges. Sprinkle reserved base mixture over top, patting down gently. Bake 15 to 20 minutes longer or until golden brown. Place pan on a rack to cool completely, then cut into bars.

MAKES 24 BARS

Jam Crumb Bars

Base		
1 3/4 cups	all-purpose flour	425 mL
1/2 cup	finely chopped nuts	125 mL
1/4 cup	butter or margarine, softened	50 mL
1/2 cup	confectioner's (icing) sugar, sifted	125 mL
1/4 tsp	grated lemon zest	1 mL

Topping		
3/4 cup	jam (any flavor)	175 mL
1 tbsp	all-purpose flour	15 mL

Preheat oven to 375° F (190° C)
9-inch (2.5 L) square cake pan, ungreased

1. **Base:** In a bowl mix together flour and nuts.

2. In another bowl, beat butter, confectioner's sugar and lemon zest until smooth and creamy. Blend in flour mixture until crumbly. Set aside one-third of this mixture. Press remainder evenly into pan.

3. **Topping:** Stir jam until smooth, then spread evenly over base.

4. In a bowl mix together reserved base mixture and flour. Sprinkle evenly over jam. Bake in preheated oven for 25 to 30 minutes or until golden brown. Place pan on a rack to cool completely, then cut into bars.

Almond Lemon Bars

Base		
1 3/4 cups	all-purpose flour	425 mL
2 tsp	baking powder	10 mL
1/4 tsp	salt	1 mL
1/2 cup	butter or margarine, softened	125 mL
1 cup	granulated sugar	250 mL
1	egg	1
	Grated zest of 1 lemon	

Topping		
	Milk	
3/4 cup	sliced almonds	175 mL

Glaze		
4 tsp	lemon juice	20 mL
1 cup	confectioner's (icing) sugar, sifted	250 mL

Preheat oven to 325°F (160° C)
2 cookie sheets, ungreased

1. **Base:** In a bowl mix together flour, baking powder and salt.

2. In another bowl, beat butter and sugar until smooth and creamy. Beat in egg and lemon zest until incorporated. Blend in flour mixture.

3. Divide dough into 4 portions. Shape each portion into a log about 12 inches (30 cm) long. Place 2 rolls on each sheet, about 4 inches (10 cm) apart. Using your hand, flatten each roll to a width of about 2 1/2 inches (6.25 cm).

4. **Topping:** Brush rolls with milk. Sprinkle almonds on top and press lightly into dough. Bake 12 to15 minutes longer or until lightly browned. Place pans on racks to cool.

5. **Glaze:** In a bowl, beat lemon juice and confectioner's sugar until smooth and spreadable. Drizzle glaze over top of rolls and set aside until set. Cut diagonally into bars.

Lemon Coconut Tea Squares

Base		
1/2 cup	butter or margarine, softened	125 mL
1/3 cup	confectioner's (icing) sugar, sifted	75 mL
3/4 cup	all-purpose flour	175 mL
1/3 cup	ground almonds	75 mL

Topping		
2	eggs	2
1 cup	granulated sugar	250 mL
1/2 tsp	baking powder	2 mL
1/4 tsp	salt	1 mL
1 tsp	grated lemon zest	5 mL
2 tbsp	lemon juice	25 mL
3/4 cup	flaked coconut	175 mL

Preheat oven to 350° F (180° C)
8-inch (2 L) square cake pan, ungreased

1. **Base:** In a bowl, beat butter and confectioner's sugar until smooth and creamy. Gradually blend in flour just until a soft dough forms. Stir in almonds. Press mixture evenly into pan. Bake in preheated oven for 20 minutes.

2. **Topping:** In a bowl, beat eggs, sugar, baking powder, salt, lemon zest and juice until blended. Stir in coconut. Spread mixture evenly over hot base. Bake 25 to 30 minutes longer or until top is golden brown. Place pan on a rack to cool completely, then cut into squares.

Lemon Blueberry Crumb Bars

Base		
3 cups	all-purpose flour	750 mL
2 cups	old-fashioned rolled oats	500 mL
1 2/3 cups	packed brown sugar	400 mL
1 1/2 tsp	baking powder	7 mL
1 1/4 tsp	ground nutmeg	6 mL
1/2 tsp	salt	2 mL
1 tsp	grated lemon zest	5 mL
1 1/4 cups	butter or margarine, softened	300 mL
1	egg, beaten	1

Topping		
1	egg	1
1	can (14 oz [398 mL]) sweetened condensed milk	1
2 tsp	grated lemon zest	10 mL
1/2 cup	lemon juice	125 mL
2 tbsp	all-purpose flour	25 mL
3 cups	blueberries, thawed if frozen	750 mL

TIP A cake will be less likely to stick to the pan if the pan is placed on a cold wet towel upon removal from the oven.

Preheat oven to 375° F (190° C)
13- by 9-inch (3.5 L) cake pan, greased

1. **Base:** In a bowl mix together flour, oats, brown sugar, baking powder, nutmeg, salt and lemon zest. Using 2 knives, a pastry blender or your fingers, cut butter in until mixture resembles coarse crumbs. Set 2 cups (500 mL) aside. Add egg to remaining mixture and mix until just combined. Spread evenly in prepared pan. Bake in preheated oven for 10 minutes.

2. **Topping:** In another bowl, beat egg, condensed milk and lemon juice until smooth and blended. Blend in flour and lemon zest. Stir in blueberries. Spread evenly over base. Sprinkle with reserved crumb mixture. Bake 40 to 45 minutes longer or until lightly browned. Place pan on a rack to cool completely, then cut into bars.

Lemon Cream Cheese Bars

MAKES 36 BARS

Preheat oven to 350° F (180° C)
13- by 9-inch (3.5 L) cake pan, ungreased

Base		
1	pkg (18.25 oz [515 g]) yellow cake mix	1
1	egg	1
1/3 cup	vegetable oil	75 mL

Topping		
8 oz	cream cheese, softened	250 g
1/3 cup	granulated sugar	75 mL
1	egg	1
1 tsp	lemon juice	5 mL

1. **Base:** In a bowl mix together cake mix, egg and oil until mixture resembles coarse crumbs. Set aside 1 cup (250 mL) of mixture. Press remainder evenly into prepared pan. Bake in preheated oven for 15 minutes.

2. **Topping:** In another bowl, beat cream cheese and sugar until smooth. Add egg and beat until incorporated. Stir in lemon juice. Spread evenly over hot base. Sprinkle with reserved crumb mixture. Bake 15 minutes longer or until lightly browned. Place pan on a rack to cool completely, then cut into bars.

Deluxe Lemon Bars

MAKES 36 BARS

Preheat oven to 350° F (180° C)
13- by 9-inch (3.5 L) cake pan, ungreased

Base		
1 cup	butter or margarine, softened	250 mL
1/2 cup	confectioner's (icing) sugar, sifted	125 mL
2 cups	all-purpose flour	500 mL

Topping		
4	eggs, beaten	4
1 1/2 cups	granulated sugar	375 mL
2 tsp	grated lemon zest	10 mL
1/3 cup	lemon juice	75 mL
1/4 cup	all-purpose flour	50 mL
1/2 tsp	baking powder	2 mL
	Confectioner's (icing) sugar	

1. **Base:** In a bowl, beat butter and confectioner's sugar until smooth and creamy. Gradually blend in flour just until a soft dough forms. Press evenly into pan. Bake in preheated oven for 20 to 25 minutes or until golden brown.

2. **Topping:** In another bowl, beat eggs, sugar, lemon juice and zest until blended. Gradually blend in flour and baking powder. Spread evenly over base. Bake 25 minutes longer. Place pan on a rack to cool completely. Sift confectioner's sugar over top and cut into bars.

TIP Cool bars, squares and brownies thoroughly before slicing. They will cut more easily and keep their shape better.

Lemon Sunburst Bars

MAKES 36 BARS

1 cup	all-purpose flour	250 mL
1 tsp	baking powder	5 mL
1/4 tsp	ground cinnamon	1 mL
1/4 tsp	ground nutmeg	1 mL
1 1/3 cups	packed brown sugar	325 mL
3/4 cup	shortening, softened	175 mL
2	eggs	2
1/2 tsp	vanilla extract	2 mL
1/2 tsp	grated lemon zest	2 mL
2 tbsp	lemon juice	25 mL
1 cup	all-purpose flour	250 mL
1 cup	quick-cooking rolled oats	250 mL
1/2 cup	chopped walnuts	125 mL
	Lemon Glaze (see recipe, page 181) *or* Lemon Butter Frosting (see recipe, page 179) (optional)	

Preheat oven to 350°F (180° C)
13- by 9-inch (3.5 L) cake pan, greased

1. In a bowl mix together flour, baking powder, cinnamon and nutmeg.

2. In another bowl, beat brown sugar and shortening until smooth and creamy. Beat in eggs, one at a time, until incorporated. Stir in vanilla, lemon zest and juice. Blend in flour mixture. Stir in oats and walnuts. Spread evenly in prepared pan. Bake in preheated oven for 20 to 25 minutes or until golden brown. (If desired, top with Lemon Glaze while still warm or allow to cool and frost with Lemon Butter Frosting.) When cool, cut into bars.

Lemon Pecan Diamonds

MAKES 36 BARS

Base		
2 cups	all-purpose flour	500 mL
1/2 cup	chopped pecans	125 mL
1/3 cup	granulated sugar	75 mL
1/4 tsp	salt	1 mL
3/4 cup	shortening	175 mL

Topping		
4	eggs	4
1 1/2 cups	granulated sugar	375 mL
1 tbsp	grated lemon zest	15 mL
1/2 cup	fresh lemon juice	125 mL
1 tsp	baking powder	5 mL
	Confectioner's (icing) sugar (optional)	

Preheat oven to 350° F (180° C)
13- by 9-inch (3.5 L) cake pan, ungreased

1. **Base:** In a food processor, combine flour, pecans, sugar and salt. Pulse twice to combine, then add shortening and process until mixture resembles fine crumbs. Press evenly into pan. Bake in preheated oven for 15 to 18 minutes, until golden brown. Place pan on a rack to cool slightly.

2. **Topping:** In a bowl, beat eggs and sugar until blended and thick. Stir in lemon zest and juice. Add baking powder and mix well. Spread mixture evenly over warm base. Bake 25 minutes longer or until topping sets. Place pan on a rack to cool completely. Sift confectioner's sugar over top, if desired. Cut into diamonds. (For technique, see Coffee Mocha Cheesecake Diamonds, page 48.)

Favorite Glazed Lemon Raspberry Bars

Preheat oven to 350° F (180° C)
13- by 9-inch (3.5 L) cake pan, greased

Base		
1 1/2 cups	all-purpose flour	375 mL
1/2 cup	confectioner's (icing) sugar, sifted	125 mL
3/4 cup	butter	175 mL

Topping		
1/2 cup	raspberry jam	125 mL
4	eggs	4
1 1/2 cups	granulated sugar	375 mL
1/2 cup	lemon juice	125 mL
3 tbsp	all-purpose flour	45 mL
1 tsp	baking powder	5 mL

Glaze		
1/2 cup	confectioner's (icing) sugar, sifted	125 mL
1 tbsp	butter or margarine, melted	15 mL
1 tbsp	lemon juice	15 mL

TIP To sprinkle lemon juice, use a small plastic or glass salt shaker with a non-metallic top.

1. **Base:** In a bowl mix together flour and confectioner's sugar. Using 2 knives, a pastry blender or your fingers, cut butter in until mixture resembles coarse crumbs. Press evenly into prepared pan. Bake in preheated oven for 15 to 18 minutes, until golden brown.

2. **Topping:** Stir jam until smooth and spread evenly over warm base.

3. In a bowl, beat eggs and sugar until thick. Stir in lemon juice. Blend in flour and baking powder. Spread over jam. Bake 20 to 25 minutes longer or until golden brown. Place pan on a rack to cool completely.

4. **Glaze:** In a bowl, beat confectioner's sugar, melted butter and lemon juice until smooth. Spread over cooled cake, then cut into bars.

Sour Cream-Topped Lemon Bars

Base

1 1/2 cups	all-purpose flour	375 mL
1/2 cup	confectioner's (icing) sugar, sifted	125 mL
1 tsp	grated lemon zest	5 mL
1 tsp	grated orange zest	5 mL
3/4 cup	cold butter or margarine, cut into cubes	175 mL

Filling

2 cups	granulated sugar	500 mL
1/4 cup	all-purpose flour	50 mL
1 tsp	baking powder	5 mL
4	eggs, beaten	4
2 tsp	grated lemon zest	10 mL
1/3 cup	lemon juice	75 mL
2 tsp	grated orange zest	10 mL

Topping

1/3 cup	granulated sugar	75 mL
2 cups	sour cream	500 mL
1/2 tsp	vanilla extract	2 mL

TIP Use a pastry brush to dislodge pieces of lemon or orange zest from the holes of a grater before washing.

Preheat oven to 350° F (180° C)
13- by 9-inch (3.5 L) cake pan, greased

1. **Base:** In a food processor, combine flour and confectioner's sugar. Pulse twice to combine. Add zests and butter and process until mixture begins to form a ball. Press evenly into prepared pan. Bake in preheated oven for 12 to 15 minutes or until lightly browned.

2. **Filling:** In a bowl mix together sugar, flour and baking powder. Add eggs, lemon zest and juice and orange zest and mix until blended. Spread mixture evenly over hot base. Bake 14 to 16 minutes longer or until set.

3. **Topping:** In a bowl mix together sugar, sour cream and vanilla. Spread over filling. Bake 8 to 10 minutes longer or until set. Place pan on a rack to cool completely, then store, covered, in refrigerator. Before serving, cut into bars.

MAKES 36 BARS

Lemon Ginger Bars

3 cups	all-purpose flour	750 mL
1 1/2 tsp	baking soda	7 mL
1 1/2 tsp	salt	7 mL
1 tsp	ground cinnamon	5 mL
1 tsp	ground ginger	5 mL
1 cup	shortening, softened	250 mL
1 cup	granulated sugar	250 mL
2	eggs	2
1 cup	fancy molasses	250 mL
1 cup	hot water	250 mL

Lemon Sauce		
1 cup	water	250 mL
1/2 cup	granulated sugar	125 mL
2 tsp	cornstarch	10 mL
Pinch	salt	Pinch
Pinch	ground nutmeg	Pinch
2	egg yolks	2
2 tbsp	butter *or* margarine	25 mL
1/2 tsp	grated lemon zest	2 mL
2 tbsp	lemon juice	25 mL

VARIATION Top each bar with a dollop of whipped cream cheese and spoon lemon sauce over top.

Preheat oven to 350° F (180° C)
13- by 9-inch (3.5 L) cake pan, greased

1. In a bowl mix together flour, baking soda, salt, cinnamon and ginger.

2. In another bowl, beat shortening and sugar until smooth and creamy. Add eggs, one at a time, beating until incorporated. Beat in molasses. Gradually blend in flour mixture alternately with hot water stirring until just incorporated. Spread evenly in prepared pan. Bake in preheated oven for 35 to 40 minutes or until a tester inserted in the center comes out clean. Place pan on a rack to cool completely then cut into bars.

3. **Lemon Sauce:** In a saucepan over medium heat, stir water, sugar, cornstarch, salt and nutmeg until smooth and bubbly. Cook and stir for 2 minutes longer. Remove from heat.

4. In a small bowl, beat egg yolks with 2 tbsp (25 mL) of the cornstarch mixture. Stir into remaining cornstarch mixture and return to heat. Cook over low heat, stirring constantly, for 2 minutes longer. Remove from heat and stir in butter, zest and juice until blended. Serve over warm or cold cake. Store, covered, in refrigerator.

Glazed Lemon Poppyseed Squares

Preheat oven to 350° F (180° C)
8-inch (2 L) square cake pan, greased

Base		
1 1/2 cups	all-purpose flour	375 mL
3/4 tsp	baking soda	4 mL
1 cup + 2 tbsp	granulated sugar, divided	250 mL + 25 mL
3/4 cup	butter, softened	175 mL
3	eggs, separated	3
2 tsp	vanilla extract	10 mL
3/4 cup	sour cream	175 mL
1/4 cup	poppyseeds	50 mL
2 tbsp	grated lemon zest	25 mL

Glaze		
1/4 cup	lemon juice	50 mL
1/2 cup	granulated sugar	125 mL

Topping		
1 cup	whipping (35%) cream	250 mL
2 tbsp	granulated sugar	25 mL
1 tsp	lemon extract	5 mL
	Grated lemon zest (optional)	

TIP For an attractive dessert, cut lemons in half, scoop out the pulp and hollow out shells. Then fill the shells with scoops of lemon sherbet or fresh fruit salad.

1. **Base:** In a bowl mix together flour and baking soda.

2. In another bowl, beat 1 cup (250 mL) of the sugar and butter until smooth and creamy. Beat in egg yolks, one at a time, until incorporated. Stir in vanilla. Gradually blend in flour mixture alternately with sour cream until just incorporated. Stir in poppyseeds and lemon zest.

3. In a clean bowl, beat egg whites until foamy. Add remaining sugar and beat until stiff peaks form. Fold into batter and spread evenly in prepared pan. Bake in preheated oven for 60 to 65 minutes or until a tester inserted in the center comes out clean. Place pan on a rack to cool for 10 minutes, then invert cake onto rack with waxed paper placed underneath.

4. **Glaze:** Mix together lemon juice and sugar until blended. Spoon over warm cake.

5. **Topping:** In a bowl, beat cream until frothy. Add sugar and lemon extract and beat until soft peaks form. Spread evenly over glaze. Sprinkle lemon zest over top, if desired. Cut into squares.

Coconut Crisp Lemon Squares

MAKES 16 SQUARES

Base

1 cup	all-purpose flour	250 mL
3/4 cup	finely crushed saltine crackers (about 18 crackers)	175 mL
1/2 cup	flaked coconut	125 mL
1/2 tsp	baking soda	2 mL
1/2 tsp	salt	2 mL
6 tbsp	butter or margarine, softened	90 mL
3/4 cup	packed brown sugar	175 mL

Topping

1 cup	water	250 mL
3/4 cup	granulated sugar	175 mL
2 tbsp	cornstarch	25 mL
1/4 tsp	salt	1 mL
2	egg yolks, beaten	2
1/2 tsp	grated lemon zest	2 mL
1/2 cup	lemon juice	125 mL

TIP A medium-sized lemon yields about 2 to 3 tbsp (25 to 45 mL) of juice and 1 tbsp (15 mL) grated zest.

Preheat oven to 350° F (180° C)
8-inch (2 L) square cake pan, ungreased

1. **Base:** In a bowl mix together flour, cracker crumbs, coconut, baking soda and salt.

2. In another bowl, beat butter and sugar until smooth and creamy. Blend in flour mixture. Set aside half of mixture and press remainder evenly into prepared pan. Bake in preheated oven for 10 minutes or until lightly browned. Place pan on a rack to cool slightly.

3. **Topping:** In a saucepan over medium heat, stir water, sugar, cornstarch and salt until smooth and bubbly. Cook, stirring constantly, for 2 minutes longer. Remove from heat.

4. In a small bowl, beat egg yolks with 2 tbsp (25 mL) of the cornstarch mixture. Stir into remaining cornstarch mixture and return to heat. Cook over low heat, stirring constantly, for 2 minutes more. Stir in lemon zest and juice. Spread evenly over baked base and sprinkle reserved crumb mixture over top. Bake 30 minutes longer or until golden brown. Place pan on a rack to cool completely, then cut into squares.

Orange Cheesecake Dream Bars

MAKES 36 BARS

Base

6 tbsp	butter or margarine, melted	90 mL
3/4 cup	finely crushed vanilla wafers (16 to 18 wafers)	175 mL

Topping

12 oz	cream cheese, softened	375 g
3/4 cup	granulated sugar	175 mL
2	eggs	2
2 tsp	grated orange zest	10 mL
1/3 cup + 1 tbsp	orange juice	75 mL + 15 mL

TIP For a special touch, cut thin slices of orange in half and arrange evenly over the top of cakes.

Preheat oven to 350° F (180° C)
13- by 9-inch (3.5 L) cake pan, ungreased

1. **Base:** In a bowl mix together melted butter and wafer crumbs until blended. Set aside one-quarter of mixture and press remainder evenly into pan. Bake in preheated oven for 15 minutes, until lightly browned.

2. **Topping:** In a bowl, beat cream cheese and sugar until smooth. Add eggs, one at a time, beating until incorporated. Stir in orange zest and juice. Spread evenly over base. Sprinkle reserved crumb mixture over top. Bake 30 to 35 minutes or until just set. Place pan on a rack to cool completely, then cut into bars.

Lemon-Cocoa Cheesecake Squares

Base		
2 cups	all-purpose flour	500 mL
1/2 cup	packed brown sugar	125 mL
1/4 cup	unsweetened cocoa powder, sifted	50 mL
3/4 cup	butter	175 mL

Topping		
12 oz	cream cheese, softened	375 g
1 cup	granulated sugar	250 mL
4	eggs	4
1/2 cup	fresh lemon juice	125 mL
1 tbsp	vanilla extract	15 mL

Preheat oven to 350° F (180° C)
13- by 9-inch (3.5 L) cake pan, ungreased

1. **Base:** In a bowl mix together flour, brown sugar and cocoa. Using 2 knives, a pastry blender or your fingers, cut butter in until mixture resembles coarse crumbs. Set aside 1 1/2 cups (375 mL) of mixture and press remainder evenly in pan. Bake in preheated oven for 12 to 15 minutes or until lightly browned. Remove from oven and reduce temperature to 325° F (160° C).

2. **Topping:** In a bowl, beat cream cheese and sugar until smooth. Add eggs and beat until incorporated. Stir in lemon juice and vanilla. Spread over hot base and sprinkle remaining crumb mixture evenly over top. Bake 30 to 40 minutes longer or until center appears set. Place pan on a rack to cool completely, then cut into squares. Store, covered, in refrigerator.

Orange, Lemon and Lime Bars

Base		
3/4 cup	butter or margarine, softened	175 mL
1/2 cup	confectioner's (icing) sugar, sifted	125 mL
1 1/2 cups	all-purpose flour	375 mL

Topping		
3	eggs	3
1 cup	granulated sugar	250 mL
1/2 tsp	grated orange zest	2 mL
1/2 tsp	grated lemon zest	2 mL
1/2 tsp	grated lime zest	2 mL
2 tbsp	freshly squeezed orange juice	25 mL
2 tbsp	freshly squeezed lemon juice	25 mL
2 tbsp	freshly squeezed lime juice	25 mL
3 tbsp	all-purpose flour	45 mL
1/2 tsp	baking powder	2 mL
1/2 tsp	salt	2 mL
1 tbsp	confectioner's (icing) sugar	15 mL

Preheat oven to 350° F (180° C)
13- by 9-inch (3.5 L) cake pan, lined with greased foil

1. **Base:** In a bowl, beat butter and confectioner's sugar until smooth and creamy. Gradually blend in flour just until dough forms. Press evenly into prepared pan. Bake in preheated oven for 20 to 25 minutes or until lightly browned.

2. **Topping:** In a bowl, beat eggs, sugar, zests and juices until smooth and blended. Blend in flour, baking powder and salt. Spread mixture evenly over hot base. Bake 15 minutes longer or until topping is just set and golden brown. Sift confectioner's sugar over top. Place pan on a rack to cool completely, then transfer cake, with foil, to a cutting board and cut into bars.

TIP Before squeezing a lemon, lime or orange for juice, grate the peel and freeze it for use in recipes requiring zest.

'Groovy' Raspberry Lemon Bars

Base		
1 cup	butter, softened	250 mL
1/2 cup	confectioner's (icing) sugar, sifted	125 mL
1	egg yolk	1
1 tsp	vanilla extract	5 mL
2 1/2 cups	all-purpose flour	625 mL

Filling		
	Raspberry jam	
1/2 cup	confectioner's (icing) sugar, sifted	125 mL
2 tsp	milk *or* whipping (35%) cream	10 mL
2 tsp	lemon juice	10 mL

Preheat oven to 350° F (180° C)
Cookie sheet, ungreased

1. **Base:** In a bowl, beat butter and confectioner's sugar until smooth and creamy. Beat in egg yolk and vanilla until incorporated. Gradually blend in flour. Wrap dough tightly in plastic wrap and refrigerate for at least 1 hour or up to 4 days.

2. When ready to use, divide dough into 4 portions. Shape each portion into a rope, about 3/4 inches (2 cm) wide and 12 inches (30 cm) long. Place ropes on cookie sheet, about 2 inches apart. With your little finger, press a groove down the center of each rope. Bake in preheated oven for 10 minutes or until firm to the touch.

3. **Filling:** Spoon raspberry jam into the grooves, down each rope. Return to preheated oven and bake for 5 to 10 minutes or until golden brown. Place pan on a rack.

4. In a small bowl, beat confectioner's sugar, milk and lemon juice until smooth and blended. Drizzle over hot strips. Cool slightly then cut, at an angle, into bars. The number of bars will depend on the thickness of the slices.

Lemon Walnut Squares

Base		
1/2 cup	butter	125 mL
1/4 cup	confectioner's (icing) sugar, sifted	50 mL
Pinch	salt	Pinch
1 cup	all-purpose flour	250 mL
1/3 cup	finely chopped walnuts	75 mL

Topping		
3/4 cup	granulated sugar	175 mL
2	eggs	2
1 tbsp	grated lemon zest	15 mL
1/4 cup	lemon juice	50 mL
2 tbsp	all-purpose flour	25 mL
1/2 tsp	baking powder	2 mL
	Confectioner's (icing) sugar (optional)	

Preheat oven to 350° F (180° C)
8-inch (2 L) square cake pan, lightly greased

1. **Base:** In a bowl, beat butter and sugar until smooth and creamy. Add salt and blend well. Gradually blend in flour, mixing until crumbly. Stir in walnuts. Press evenly into prepared pan. Bake in preheated oven for 20 to 25 minutes, or until golden brown. Place pan on a rack to cool slightly.

2. **Topping:** In a bowl, beat sugar, eggs, lemon zest and juice until blended. Blend in flour and baking powder. Spoon over baked base. Bake 25 to 30 minutes longer or until center is set. Place pan on a rack to cool completely. If desired, sift confectioner's sugar lightly over top. Cut into squares.

MAKES 30 SQUARES

Mixed Fruit Squares

Preheat oven to 400° F (200° C)
Cookie sheet, lightly greased

Base		
2 cups	all-purpose flour	500 mL
3/4 tsp	salt	4 mL
1 cup	shortening	250 mL
1	egg	1
1 tbsp	white vinegar	15 mL
2 tbsp	cold water	25 mL

Filling		
1 cup	coarsely chopped dried apricots	250 mL
2	pears, peeled and sliced	2
2	apples, peeled and sliced	2
1 1/2 tbsp	all-purpose flour	22 mL
3/4 cup	water	175 mL
1/4 cup	packed brown sugar	50 mL
1/4 tsp	ground cinnamon	1 mL
1 tsp	grated lemon zest	5 mL
1 tbsp	lemon juice	15 mL
	Confectioner's (icing) sugar	

1. **Base:** In a bowl combine flour and salt. Using 2 knives, a pastry blender or your fingers, cut shortening in until mixture resembles coarse crumbs.

2. In another bowl, beat egg, vinegar and water just until blended. Blend in flour mixture and stir just until a soft dough forms. Divide dough in half, shaping each half into a ball. Wrap tightly in plastic wrap and chill for 15 to 20 minutes.

3. **Filling:** In a saucepan over low heat, combine apricots, pears, apples and flour and stir to blend. Add water, brown sugar, cinnamon, zest and juice. Bring to a boil, stirring frequently, then cover and simmer for 15 minutes or until fruit is tender. Set aside to cool.

4. On a floured work surface, roll out 1 portion of dough, to a 12- by 9-inch (30 by 23 cm) rectangle. Place on prepared cookie sheet. Spoon filling evenly over top, leaving a 1/2 inch (1 cm) border all around. With your fingertips, moisten the edges with a little water.

5. Roll out remaining dough as for the first. Place on top of the fruit and crimp edges together. Using a knife, make some slashes on the top. Bake in preheated oven for 10 minutes, then lower heat to 350° F (180° C) and bake 25 to 30 minutes longer, until golden brown. Place pan on rack to cool slightly and while still warm, sift confectioner's sugar over top and cut into squares.

Velvet Orange Squares

MAKES 16 SQUARES

Base		
1 2/3 cups	all-purpose flour	400 mL
1 tsp	baking powder	5 mL
1/2 tsp	baking soda	2 mL
1/4 tsp	salt	1 mL
1/2 cup	butter or margarine, softened	125 mL
1 cup	granulated sugar	250 mL
2	eggs	2
1 tbsp	grated orange zest	15 mL
1/2 cup	orange juice	125 mL
1/2 tsp	lemon extract	2 mL

Glaze		
1/2 cup	apricot jam	125 mL
1/2 cup	granulated sugar	125 mL
1/3 cup	water	75 mL
2	oranges, thinly sliced	2
	Granulated sugar	

VARIATION If desired, substitute Orange Butter Frosting (see recipe, page 179) or Easy Orange Frosting (see recipe, page 182) for the glaze.

Preheat oven to 350° F (180° C)
8-inch (2 L) square cake pan, greased

1. **Base:** In a bowl mix together flour, baking powder, baking soda and salt.

2. In another bowl, beat butter and sugar until smooth and creamy. Add eggs and beat until incorporated. Stir in orange zest, orange juice juice and lemon extract. Gradually blend in flour mixture. Spread evenly in prepared pan. Bake in preheated oven for 35 to 40 minutes or until a tester inserted in the center comes out clean. Place pan on a rack to cool for 10 minutes. Invert onto rack to cool completely.

3. **Glaze:** In a saucepan over low heat, stir jam for 5 to 10 minutes, until melted and smooth. Set aside to cool slightly. In another saucepan, over low heat, combine sugar and water, stirring constantly until sugar is syrupy. Add orange slices and simmer until softened and translucent. Using a slotted spoon, transfer orange slices onto a sheet of waxed paper. Sprinkle lightly with sugar. Cool just enough to handle, then cut slices into quarters.

4. Spread half the jam over top of cake. Arrange orange pieces evenly over the jam layer, then brush with remaining jam. Chill for at least 1 hour, then cut into squares.

Chocolate Date Nut Bars

Preheat oven to 350° F (180° C)
9-inch (2.5 L) square cake pan, lightly greased

Base		
1/2 cup	semi-sweet chocolate chips or chunks	125 mL
1/2 cup	butter or margarine	125 mL
1/4 cup	granulated sugar	50 mL
1 tbsp	milk	15 mL
1 1/3 cups	all-purpose flour	325 mL

Topping		
1/3 cup	granulated sugar	75 mL
2	eggs	2
2 tbsp	all-purpose flour	25 mL
1/2 tsp	baking powder	2 mL
1 cup	finely chopped pitted dates	250 mL
1/2 cup	chopped walnuts	125 mL

1. **Base:** In a large saucepan over low heat, melt chocolate and butter. Stir in sugar and milk until blended. Blend in flour. Spread evenly in prepared pan. Bake in preheated oven for 10 minutes. Place pan on a rack to cool slightly.

2. **Topping:** In another bowl, beat sugar and eggs until blended. Blend in flour and baking powder. Stir in dates and walnuts. Spread evenly over warm base. Bake 20 to 25 minutes longer or until a tester inserted in the center comes out clean. Place pan on a rack to cool completely, then cut into bars.

Matrimonial Date Bars

Preheat oven to 325° F (160° C)
13- by 9-inch (3.5 L) cake pan, greased

Filling		
2 cups	chopped pitted dates	500 mL
2/3 cup	cold water	150 mL
2 tbsp	packed brown sugar	25 mL
2 tsp	grated orange zest	10 mL
2 tbsp	orange juice	25 mL
1 tsp	lemon juice	5 mL

Base		
1 1/2 cups	all-purpose flour	375 mL
1 tsp	baking powder	5 mL
1/2 tsp	baking soda	2 mL
1/4 tsp	salt	1 mL
1 1/2 cups	old-fashioned rolled oats	375 mL
1 cup	packed brown sugar	250 mL
1 cup	butter or margarine	250 mL

1. **Filling:** In a saucepan combine dates, water, brown sugar and zest. Cook, stirring, over medium heat until thick and smooth. Remove from heat, then stir in orange and lemon juices. Set aside to cool slightly.

2. **Base:** In a bowl mix together flour, baking powder, baking soda and salt. Stir in oats and brown sugar. Using 2 knives, a pastry blender or your fingers, cut butter in until mixture resembles coarse crumbs. Set half aside and press remainder evenly into prepared pan.

3. Spread filling evenly over base. Top with the remaining crumb mixture; smooth lightly with your hands. Bake in preheated oven for 30 to 35 minutes, then increase heat to 350° F (180° C) and bake 5 minutes longer or until lightly browned. Remove from oven and cut into bars while still hot. Place pan on a rack to cool completely.

Double Date-Nut Squares

MAKES 36 SQUARES

2 cups	boiling water	500 mL
2 cups	chopped pitted dates	500 mL
2 tbsp	baking soda	25 mL
2 tbsp	butter or margarine, softened	25 mL
2 cups	granulated sugar	500 mL
2	eggs, beaten	2
2 tsp	vanilla extract	10 mL
2 1/2 cups	cake flour, sifted	625 mL
1/2 cup	chopped walnuts	125 mL
	Date Frosting (see recipe, page 184)	

TIP Keep some vegetable oil in a squeeze bottle for when a small amount is needed.

Preheat oven to 350° F (180° C)
13- by 9-inch (3.5 L) cake pan, greased

1. In a bowl mix together water, dates and baking soda.

2. In another bowl, beat butter, sugar, eggs and vanilla until blended. Add date mixture and mix thoroughly. Blend in flour. Stir in walnuts. Spread evenly in prepared pan. Bake in preheated oven for 45 to 50 minutes or until a tester inserted in the center comes out clean. Place pan on a rack to cool completely. Frost with Date Frosting, then cut into squares.

Full of Prunes Bars

MAKES 36 BARS

Base		
1 cup	chopped pitted prunes	250 mL
2 cups	all-purpose flour	500 mL
1 1/2 cups	granulated sugar	375 mL
1/2 cup	chopped walnuts	125 mL
1 1/4 tsp	baking soda	6 mL
1 tsp	salt	5 mL
1 tsp	ground cinnamon	5 mL
1 tsp	ground nutmeg	5 mL
3	eggs, beaten	3
1/2 cup	vegetable oil	125 mL

Topping		
1/2 cup	granulated sugar	125 mL
2 tbsp	all-purpose flour	25 mL
2 tbsp	butter	25 mL

Preheat oven to 350° F (180° C)
13- by 9-inch (3.5 L) cake pan, greased

1. **Base:** In a covered saucepan, over low heat, simmer prunes, with water to cover, for 15 to 20 minutes or until tender. Drain, reserving 2/3 cup (150 mL) of cooking liquid. (If you do not have sufficient liquid, add required amount of water.)

2. In a bowl mix together flour, sugar, walnuts, baking soda, salt, cinnamon and nutmeg. Make a well in the center. Add eggs, oil, and reserved prune liquid and mix until blended. Stir in prunes. Spread evenly in prepared pan.

3. **Topping:** In a bowl mix together sugar and flour. Using 2 knives, a pastry blender or your fingers, cut butter in until mixture resembles coarse crumbs. Sprinkle evenly over base. Bake in preheated oven for 30 to 35 minutes or until a tester inserted in the center comes out clean. Place pan on a rack to cool completely, then cut into bars.

Spicy Prune Bars

1 1/2 cups	all-purpose flour	375 mL
3/4 cup	granulated sugar	175 mL
1/4 cup	packed brown sugar	50 mL
1 tsp	baking powder	5 mL
1/2 tsp	baking soda	2 mL
1/2 tsp	ground cinnamon	2 mL
1/4 tsp	salt	1 mL
1/4 tsp	ground ginger	1 mL
1	egg, beaten	1
1 tsp	vanilla extract	5 mL
1/2 cup	vegetable oil	125 mL
1/2 cup	cold water	125 mL
1/2 cup	strained prunes (baby food)	125 mL
1/2 cup	chopped walnuts	125 mL

Glaze (optional)		
1 tbsp	light (5%) cream	15 mL
Pinch	ground cinnamon	Pinch
1/2 cup	confectioner's (icing) sugar, sifted	125 mL

Preheat oven to 350° F (180° C)
9-inch (2.5 L) square cake pan, greased

1. In a bowl mix together flour, sugars, baking powder, baking soda, cinnamon, salt and ginger. Make a well in the center. Add egg, vanilla, oil, water and prunes and mix just until incorporated. Spread batter evenly in prepared pan. Sprinkle nuts evenly over top. Bake in preheated oven for 25 to 30 minutes or until a tester inserted in center comes out clean. Place pan on a rack to cool.

2. **Glaze (optional):** In a bowl combine cream and cinnamon. Gradually beat in confectioner's sugar. Drizzle over top of cake. When cool, cut into bars.

Raisin Bars

2 3/4 cups	Make-Ahead Bar Mix (see recipe, page 95)	675 mL
1 cup	raisins	250 mL
1/4 tsp	ground cinnamon	1 mL
1/4 tsp	ground nutmeg	1 mL
2	eggs, beaten	2
1/3 cup	unsweetened applesauce	75 mL
1 tbsp	milk	15 mL
1 tsp	vanilla extract	5 mL
	Frosting (optional)	

TIP To freshen raisins that have dried out, place them in a strainer and steam over hot water.

Preheat oven to 350° F (180° C)
9-inch (2.5 L) square cake pan, greased

1. In a bowl mix together Bar Mix, raisins, cinnamon and nutmeg.

2. In another bowl, beat eggs, applesauce, milk and vanilla. Blend in dry ingredients. Spread evenly in prepared pan. Bake in preheated oven for 20 to 25 minutes or until a tester inserted in the center comes out clean. Place pan on a rack to cool completely. If desired, spread with a frosting, such as Easy Butter Frosting (see recipe, page 179) or Banana Frosting (see recipe, page 178), before cutting into bars.

Mix-Ahead Bar Mix

MAKES ABOUT 8 CUPS (2 L)

4 cups	all-purpose flour	1 L
1 cup	packed brown sugar	250 mL
1 cup	granulated sugar	250 mL
2 tsp	baking powder	10 mL
1 1/2 cups	shortening	375 mL

1. In a bowl mix together flour, brown sugar, sugar and baking powder. Using 2 knives, a pastry blender or your fingers, cut shortening in until mixture resembles coarse crumbs. Store in an airtight container, at room temperature, for up to 6 weeks, or in freezer for up to 6 months.

Strawberry Rhubarb Meringue Bars

MAKES 36 BARS

Base		
1 3/4 cups	all-purpose flour	425 mL
2 tbsp	confectioner's (icing) sugar, sifted	25 mL
1/2 cup	butter *or* margarine	125 mL

Filling		
1 1/2 cups	granulated sugar	375 mL
1/4 cup	all-purpose flour	50 mL
1/4 tsp	salt	1 mL
6	egg yolks	6
1 cup	evaporated milk	250 mL
2 cups	sliced strawberries, thawed if frozen	500 mL
4 cups	sliced rhubarb (1-inch [2.5 cm] thick), thawed if frozen	1 L
1/2 tsp	lemon juice	2 mL

Topping		
6	egg whites	6
1/2 cup	granulated sugar	125 mL

Preheat oven to 350° F (180° C)
13- by 9-inch (3.5 L) cake pan, ungreased

1. **Base:** In a bowl mix together flour and confectioner's sugar. Using 2 knives, a pastry blender or your fingers, cut butter in until mixture resembles coarse crumbs. Press evenly into pan. Bake in preheated oven for 10 to 12 minutes. Place pan on a rack to cool slightly.

2. **Filling:** In a bowl mix together sugar, flour and salt. In another bowl, whisk egg yolks and milk. Add to flour mixture and mix until blended. Stir in strawberries, rhubarb and lemon juice. Spread filling evenly over warm base and bake 55 to 60 minutes longer or until filling is firm.

3. **Topping:** In a clean bowl, beat egg whites until foamy. Gradually add sugar, beating until stiff peaks form. Spread over filling. Bake 10 minutes longer or until meringue is nicely browned. Place pan on a rack to cool completely, then cut into bars.

TIP Use only unsweetened strawberries and rhubarb in this recipe.

Peaches 'n' Cream Dessert Bars

MAKES 36 BARS

Base		
2 cups	graham wafer crumbs	500 mL
1/3 cup	granulated sugar	75 mL
1/2 cup	sliced almonds	125 mL
6 tbsp	butter, melted	90 mL

Filling		
1 1/2 cups	cream cheese, softened	375 mL
1/2 cup	granulated sugar	125 mL
2	eggs	2
1 tsp	vanilla extract	5 mL

Topping		
2 tbsp	all-purpose flour	25 mL
2 tbsp	cold butter, cut into pieces	25 mL
1/4 cup	packed brown sugar	50 mL
1/2 cup	sliced almonds	125 mL
1 cup	peach jam	250 mL

Preheat oven to 350° F (180° C)
13- by 9-inch (3.5 L) cake pan, greased

1. **Base:** In a bowl mix together graham wafer crumbs, sugar, almonds and melted butter. Press evenly into prepared pan. Bake in preheated oven for 10 minutes or until lightly browned. Place pan on a rack to cool slightly.

2. **Filling:** In a bowl, beat cream cheese and sugar until smooth. Beat in eggs until incorporated. Stir in vanilla. Spread filling evenly over warm base. Bake 15 minutes longer until slightly puffed.

3. **Topping:** In a bowl combine flour, butter, brown sugar and almonds and mix together until crumbly. Set aside.

4. Stir jam until smooth, then spread evenly over filling. Sprinkle topping evenly over jam. Bake 15 minutes longer or until hot and bubbly. Place pan on a rack to cool completely.

Oatmeal Peach Crumble Squares

MAKES 16 SQUARES

Base		
4 cups	sliced peeled peaches (about 6 peaches)	1 L
1 cup	granulated sugar	250 mL
2 tbsp	lemon juice	25 mL

Topping		
3 cups	oatmeal muffin mix	750 mL
1/4 tsp	ground nutmeg	1 mL
1/2 cup	butter *or* margarine	125 mL

Preheat oven to 375° F (190° C)
8-inch (2 L) square cake pan, ungreased

1. **Base:** In a bowl mix together peaches, sugar and lemon juice. Spread evenly in pan.

2. **Topping:** In another bowl, combine muffin mix and nutmeg. Using two knives, a pastry blender or your fingers, cut butter in until mixture resembles coarse crumbs. Spoon over fruit. Bake in preheated oven for 40 to 45 minutes or until golden brown. Cool slightly, then cut into squares.

TIP These squares are particularly delicious served warm with ice cream.

For a quick, delicious dessert, fill peach halves with ice-cream, frozen yogurt or whipped topping, and drizzle with chocolate or raspberry sauce.

MAKES 24 BARS

Cinnamon-Nut Pear Bars

Preheat oven to 375° F (190° C)
9-inch (2.5 L) square cake pan, greased

Base

2 cups	packaged biscuit mix	500 mL
1/4 cup	granulated sugar	50 mL
1 tsp	ground cinnamon	5 mL
1	can (28 oz [796 mL]) pears drained, sliced, 1/2 cup (125 mL) of liquid reserved	1
1	egg	1
1/2 tsp	vanilla extract	2 mL

Topping

1/4 cup	packed brown sugar	50 mL
1/4 cup	all-purpose flour	50 mL
2 tbsp	butter	25 mL
1/4 cup	chopped walnuts	50 mL

TIP For an added touch, thinly slice a fresh pear, leaving the skin on and place a slice on top of each bar.

1. **Base:** In a bowl mix together biscuit mix, sugar and cinnamon.

2. In a small bowl, whisk together reserved pear juice, egg and vanilla. Add to biscuit mixture, mixing just until a dough forms. Spread evenly in prepared pan. Arrange pears evenly over top.

3. **Topping:** In a bowl mix together brown sugar and flour. Using 2 knives, a pastry blender or your fingers, cut butter in until mixture resembles coarse crumbs. Stir in walnuts. Spoon evenly over pears. Bake in preheated oven for 30 to 35 minutes or until lightly browned around the edges. Place pan on a rack to cool completely, then cut into bars.

MAKES 12 LARGE BARS

Pineapple Upside-Down Bars

Preheat oven to 350° F (180° C)
8-inch (2 L) square cake pan, ungreased

2 tbsp	butter *or* margarine	25 mL
1/2 cup	packed brown sugar	125 mL
1 1/4 cups	all-purpose flour	300 mL
2 tsp	baking powder	10 mL
1/2 tsp	salt	2 mL
1	can (8 oz [250 mL]) pineapple slices, drained, 1/2 cup (125 mL) juice reserved	1
4	Maraschino cherries	4
1/3 cup	shortening, softened	75 mL
1/2 cup	granulated sugar	125 mL
1	egg	1
1/2 tsp	grated lemon zest (optional)	2 mL

1. In preheated oven, melt butter in baking pan. Remove from oven. Sprinkle brown sugar evenly over pan. Arrange 4 pineapple slices over the sugar and place a cherry in the center of each. Set aside.

2. In a bowl mix together, flour, baking powder and salt.

3. In another bowl, beat shortening and granulated sugar until smooth and creamy. Beat in egg until incorporated. Stir in lemon zest, if using. Gradually blend in flour mixture alternately with reserved pineapple juice until just incorporated.

4. Spread mixture evenly over pineapple. Bake in preheated oven for 30 to 35 minutes or until golden. Let stand for about 10 minutes and then invert onto a platter, leaving pan on top for a few minutes to allow the butter-brown sugar liquid to pour onto the cake. Cool, then cut into bars. Top with whipped cream or ice cream, if desired.

Pineapple Carrot Bars

1/2 cup	all-purpose flour	125 mL
1/2 cup	whole-wheat flour	125 mL
1 tbsp	ground cinnamon	15 mL
1 tsp	baking powder	5 mL
1 tsp	baking soda	5 mL
1/2 cup	packed brown sugar	125 mL
2 tbsp	vegetable oil	25 mL
1	egg, beaten	1
1 tsp	vanilla extract	5 mL
1/4 cup	milk	50 mL
1 cup	finely grated carrots	250 mL
1/2 cup	raisins	125 mL
2/3 cup	crushed unsweetened pineapple, drained	150 mL

Preheat oven to 350° F (180° C)
13- by 9-inch (3.5 L) cake pan, lightly greased

1. In a bowl mix together all-purpose flour, whole wheat flour, cinnamon, baking powder and baking soda. Add sugar, oil, egg, vanilla and milk and mix until just blended. Stir in carrots, raisins, and pineapple. Spread evenly in prepared pan. Bake in preheated oven for 25 minutes, or until top is golden brown. Place pan on a rack to cool completely, then cut into bars. Store, covered, in refrigerator.

Rhubarb Crisp Squares

Filling		
4 cups	chopped rhubarb, thawed if frozen	1 L
1 cup	granulated sugar	250 mL
2 tbsp	cornstarch	25 mL
1 tsp	grated orange zest	5 mL

Base		
1 1/2 cups	all-purpose flour	375 mL
1/2 cup	packed brown sugar	125 mL
1/2 cup	chopped pecans	125 mL
1 tsp	ground cinnamon	5 mL
1/4 tsp	salt	1 mL
1/2 cup	butter or margarine, softened	125 mL

TIP Allow bars, squares and brownies to cool completely before cutting. Then use a sharp knife and a gentle, sawing motion to avoid squashing the cake.

Preheat oven to 350° F (180° C)
8-inch (2 L) square cake pan, greased

1. **Filling:** In a saucepan combine rhubarb, sugar, cornstarch and zest. Cook, over medium heat, stirring constantly, for 5 minutes or until mixture thickens. Set aside to cool.

2. **Base:** In a bowl mix together flour, sugar, pecans, cinnamon and salt. Using 2 knives, a pastry blender or your fingers, cut butter in until mixture resembles coarse crumbs. Set aside 1 cup (250 mL) and press remainder evenly in prepared pan.

3. Spread filling evenly over base and sprinkle reserved flour mixture evenly over top. Bake in preheated oven for 35 to 40 minutes or until golden brown. Place pan on a rack to cool completely, then cut into squares.

MAKES 24 BARS

Strawberry Rhubarb Crisp Bars

Preheat oven to 350 °F (180°C)
9-inch (2.5 L) square cake pan, greased

Base		
1/2 cup	butter or margarine, melted	125 mL
1/4 cup	granulated sugar	50 mL
1 1/2 cups	graham wafer crumbs (about 22 wafers)	375 mL

Topping		
3 cups	chopped rhubarb (1-inch [2.5 cm] pieces), thawed if frozen	750 mL
1 cup	granulated sugar	250 mL
3 tbsp	cornstarch	45 mL
Pinch	ground cinnamon	Pinch
1/2 cup	cold milk	125 mL
1 1/2 tsp	unflavored gelatin	7 mL
8 oz	cream cheese, softened	250 g
2 tbsp	granulated sugar	25 mL
1 cup	sliced fresh strawberries	250 mL

TIP If desired, garnish each bar with sliced strawberries.

1. **Base:** In a bowl mix together butter, sugar and crumbs. Set aside one-quarter of the mixture and press remainder evenly into prepared pan. Bake in preheated oven for 10 minutes or until golden brown. Place pan on a rack to cool slightly.

2. **Topping:** In a saucepan combine rhubarb, sugar, cornstarch and cinnamon. Cook, over low heat, stirring constantly, until sugar dissolves and mixture thickens. Simmer 5 minutes longer until rhubarb is tender. Remove from heat and set aside to cool.

3. In the top of a double boiler, sprinkle gelatin over milk. Let stand for 5 minutes then stir over hot (not boiling) water until gelatin dissolves. Set aside to cool.

4. In a bowl, beat cream cheese and sugar until smooth. Gradually add dissolved gelatin mixture and mix until blended. Stir in rhubarb mixture. Spread evenly over baked base. Sprinkle with reserved crumbs. Chill for at least 1 hour, then cut into bars.

MAKES 24 SQUARES

Scrumptious Strawberry Swirls

Preheat oven to 350° F (180° C)
9-inch (2.5 L) square cake pan, ungreased

Base		
2 1/4 cups	graham wafer crumbs (about 30 wafers)	550 mL
1/2 cup	butter, melted	125 mL

Topping		
2	pkgs (4 servings each) strawberry-flavored gelatin dessert mix	2
1 1/3 cups	boiling water	325 mL
2	pkgs (each 10 oz [300 g]) frozen unsweetened strawberries, thawed	2
5 1/2 cups	miniature marshmallows (1 pkg [10 1/2 oz (300 g)])	1.375 L
1/2 cup	milk	125 mL
1 cup	whipping (35%) cream, whipped	250 mL

TIP If desired, set aside 1/4 cup (50 mL) of graham wafer crumb mixture and sprinkle over top.

1. In a bowl mix together graham crumbs and melted butter. Press evenly into pan.

2. In another bowl, combine gelatin with boiling water and mix until gelatin dissolves. Add strawberries and mix well. Chill until almost set, stirring occasionally.

3. In the top of a double boiler, melt marshmallows in milk, stirring constantly until smooth. Transfer to refrigerator and chill until cold. When gelatin mixture is almost set, fold whipped cream into marshmallow mixture.

4. Alternate layers of marshmallow and gelatin mixtures over base, then run a knife through the layers to create a marbling effect. Refrigerate until ready to serve, then cut into squares.

MAKES 36 BARS

Old-Fashioned Gingerbread Spice Bars

Preheat oven to 350° F (180° C)
13- by 9-inch (3.5 L) cake pan, greased

2 1/2 cups	all-purpose flour	625 mL
2 tsp	baking powder	10 mL
1 tsp	ground cinnamon	5 mL
1 tsp	ground ginger	5 mL
1/2 tsp	baking soda	2 mL
1/2 tsp	salt	2 mL
Pinch	ground cloves	Pinch
1/2 cup	shortening, softened	125 mL
1/2 cup	granulated sugar	125 mL
2	eggs	2
1 cup	fancy molasses	250 mL
1 cup	boiling water	250 mL

1. In a bowl mix together flour, baking powder, cinnamon, ginger, baking soda, salt and cloves.

2. In another bowl, beat shortening and sugar until smooth and creamy. Add eggs, one at a time, beating until incorporated. Beat in molasses. Gradually blend in flour mixture alternately with boiling water until just incorporated. Pour into prepared pan. Bake in preheated oven for 40 to 45 minutes, until a tester inserted in the center comes out clean. Place pan on a rack to cool completely, then cut into bars.

MAKES 36 BARS

Spiced Pumpkin Bars

Preheat oven to 350° F (180° C)
13- by 9-inch (3.5 L) cake pan, greased

Base		
1 cup	all-purpose flour	250 mL
1/2 cup	quick-cooking rolled oats	125 mL
1/2 cup	packed brown sugar	125 mL
1/2 cup	cold butter, cut into cubes	125 mL

Filling		
2 cups	scalded milk	500 mL
3/4 cup	granulated sugar	175 mL
2 cups	pumpkin purée (not pie filling)	500 mL
3	eggs, beaten	3
1 tsp	ground cinnamon	5 mL
1/2 tsp	salt	2 mL
1/2 tsp	ground ginger	2 mL
1/4 tsp	ground cloves	1 mL

Topping		
2 tbsp	all-purpose flour	25 mL
1 cup	packed brown sugar	250 mL
1 cup	chopped nuts	250 mL
1/4 cup	butter, softened	50 mL

1. **Base:** In a bowl mix together flour, oats and sugar. Using 2 knives, a pastry blender or your fingers, cut butter in until mixture resembles coarse crumbs. Press evenly into prepared pan. Bake in preheated oven for 12 to 15 minutes or until golden brown.

2. **Filling:** In a bowl mix together milk, sugar and pumpkin. Add eggs, cinnamon, salt, ginger and cloves and mix until thoroughly blended. Spread evenly over baked base. Bake 15 to 20 minutes longer or until set.

3. **Topping:** In another bowl, mix together flour, brown sugar and nuts. Using 2 knives, a pastry blender or your fingers, cut butter in until mixture is crumbly. Sprinkle evenly over hot cake. Bake 10 to 15 minutes longer or until topping is golden brown. Place pan on a rack to cool completely, then cut into bars.

TIP No time to bake it? Fake it! Surprise guests or your family with the aroma of freshly baked cookies, bars, squares or brownies — without baking! Just heat 2 tsp (10 mL) vanilla and 1/4 cup (50 mL) water in a metal pan, in a warm oven. No one will ever guess your secret.

MAKES 24 BARS

Pumpkin Cheesecake Bars

Preheat oven to 375° F (190° C)
9-inch (2.5 L) square cake pan, lightly greased

Base		
2 tbsp	butter, melted	25 mL
2 tbsp	maple syrup	25 mL
1 1/3 cups	graham wafer crumbs	325 mL

Topping		
1/2 cup	granulated sugar	125 mL
1 1/2 lbs	cream cheese, softened	750 g
4	eggs	4
1/2 cup	maple syrup	125 mL
1 tsp	vanilla extract	5 mL
1 2/3 cups	pumpkin purée (not pie filling)	400 mL
	Whipped cream (optional)	

1. **Base:** In a bowl mix together butter, syrup and wafer crumbs. Press evenly into prepared pan. Bake in preheated oven for 8 to 10 minutes or until lightly browned. Place pan on a rack to cool. Lower oven heat to 350° F (180° C).

2. **Topping:** In a bowl, beat sugar and cream cheese until smooth. Add eggs, one at a time, beating until incorporated. Stir in syrup and vanilla. Blend in pumpkin. Pour over base. Bake 55 to 60 minutes longer or until center is just set. Run a knife around the edge of the cake, then place pan on a rack to cool completely. Chill overnight. When ready to serve, cut into bars. Top with a dollop of whipped cream, if desired.

MAKES 36 BARS

Pumpkin Pie Dessert Bars

Preheat oven to 350° F (180° C)
13- by 9-inch (3.5 L) cake pan, ungreased

Base		
1 1/2 cups	quick-cooking rolled oats	375 mL
1 1/2 cups	packed brown sugar	375 mL
1 1/2 cups	all-purpose flour	375 mL
1/2 tsp	salt	2 mL
3/4 cup	butter	175 mL
1	egg	1

Filling		
3 cups	pumpkin purée (not pie filling)	750 mL
3/4 cup	packed brown sugar	175 mL
1 1/2 tsp	ground cinnamon	7 mL
3/4 tsp	ground nutmeg	4 mL
3/4 tsp	ground ginger	4 mL
3	eggs	3
1 cup	evaporated milk	250 mL
3/4 cup	chopped pecans	175 mL

1. **Base:** In a bowl mix together oats, brown sugar, flour and salt. Using 2 knives, a pastry blender or your fingers, cut butter in until mixture resembles coarse crumbs. Add egg and mix well. Set aside 1 1/2 cups (375 mL) of mixture and press remainder evenly in pan. Bake in preheated oven for 20 minutes or until golden brown. Place pan on a rack to cool slightly.

2. **Filling:** In a bowl combine pumpkin, brown sugar, cinnamon, nutmeg and ginger. Add eggs, one at a time and beat until blended. Gradually stir in milk. Pour evenly over baked base.

3. In small bowl, mix together reserved oat mixture and nuts. Sprinkle evenly over filling. Bake 30 to 35 minutes longer or until center is set. Place pan on a rack to cool completely, then cut into bars.

MAKES 36 BARS

Frosted Carrot Bars

1 1/4 cups	all-purpose flour	300 mL
1 cup	granulated sugar	250 mL
1 tsp	baking soda	5 mL
1 tsp	ground cinnamon	5 mL
1/2 tsp	salt	2 mL
1	jar (7 1/2 oz [213 mL]) strained carrots (baby food)	1
1	jar (7 1/2 oz [213 mL]) strained applesauce (baby food)	1
2 tbsp	vegetable oil	25 mL
2	eggs	2

Frosting		
3 oz	cream cheese, softened	90 g
1 tsp	milk (approximate)	5 mL
1 tsp	vanilla extract	5 mL
2 cups	confectioner's (icing) sugar, sifted	500 mL

Preheat oven to 350° F (180° C)
13- by 9-inch (3.5 L) cake pan, greased

1. In a bowl mix together flour, sugar, baking soda, cinnamon and salt. Add baby foods, oil and eggs and mix until just blended. Spread evenly in prepared pan. Bake in preheated oven for 20 to 25 minutes, or until tester inserted in the center comes out clean. Place pan on a rack to cool completely, then cut into bars.

2. **Frosting:** In a bowl, beat cream cheese, milk and vanilla until smooth. Gradually add confectioner's sugar, beating until smooth and spreadable, adjusting consistency with more milk if necessary. Drop a spoonful of frosting on top of each bar.

MAKES 36 BARS

Carrot Pumpkin Bars

Base		
2 cups	all-purpose flour	500 mL
2 tsp	baking powder	10 mL
1 1/2 tsp	ground cinnamon	7 mL
1 tsp	baking soda	5 mL
1/2 tsp	salt	2 mL
1/2 tsp	ground ginger	2 mL
Pinch	ground cloves	Pinch
1/3 cup	butter or margarine, softened	75 mL
1 cup	granulated sugar	250 mL
1/2 cup	packed brown sugar	125 mL
2	eggs	2
2	egg whites	2
1 cup	finely shredded carrots	250 mL
2 cups	pumpkin, cooked and puréed *or* canned pumpkin purée (not pie filling)	500 mL

Topping		
4 oz	light cream cheese, softened	125 g
1/4 cup	granulated sugar	50 mL
1 tbsp	milk	15 mL

TIP If you prefer, substitute 2 tsp (10 mL) pumpkin pie spice for the cinnamon, ginger and cloves.

To soften brown sugar that has hardened, place sugar in a glass jar with half an apple. Seal tightly and let stand for 1 day. Remove the apple and, using a fork, fluff up sugar. Reseal the jar.

Preheat oven to 350° F (180° C)
13- by 9-inch (3.5 L) cake pan, greased

1. **Base:** In a bowl mix together flour, baking powder, cinnamon, baking soda, salt, ginger and cloves.

2. In another bowl, beat butter, granulated sugar and brown sugar until smooth and creamy. Add eggs and egg whites, beating until incorporated. Stir in carrots and pumpkin. Gradually blend in flour mixture. Spread evenly in prepared pan.

3. **Topping:** In a bowl, beat cream cheese and sugar until smooth. Beat in milk. Drop teaspoonfuls of mixture over top of pumpkin batter. Run a knife through batters to create a marbling effect. Bake in preheated oven for 30 to 35 minutes or until a tester inserted in the center comes out clean. Place pan on a rack to cool completely, then cut into bars.

Raspberry Oat Granola Bars

Base		
1/3 cup	quick-cooking rolled oats	75 mL
17	graham wafers, finely crushed	17
2 tbsp	granulated sugar	25 mL
1	egg white	1
1 tbsp	butter or margarine, melted	15 mL
1 tbsp	fruit juice *or* water	15 mL
1/3 cup	raisins	75 mL

Topping		
1 1/2 cups	raspberry jam	375 mL

Preheat oven to 375° F (190° C)
8-inch (2 L) square cake pan, greased

1. **Base:** In a bowl mix together oats, graham crumbs, sugar, egg white, butter and fruit juice. Set aside 1/4 cup (50 mL) of mixture; stir raisins into the remainder. Spread evenly in prepared pan. Bake in preheated oven for 7 minutes. Place pan on a rack to cool completely.

2. **Topping:** Stir jam until smooth. Spread evenly over cooled base. Sprinkle with reserved crumb mixture. Bake in preheated oven for 30 to 40 minutes or until bubbly. Run a knife around the edges of the pan, then place pan on a rack to cool completely. Cut into bars.

Banana Chip Oatmeal Bars

1 cup	packed brown sugar	250 mL
3/4 cup	butter or margarine, softened	175 mL
1	egg	1
1/2 tsp	salt	2 mL
1 1/4 cups	mashed ripe bananas (4 medium bananas)	300 mL
4 cups	old-fashioned rolled oats	1 L
1/2 cup	chocolate chips	125 mL
1/2 cup	raisins	125 mL

Preheat oven to 350°F (180° C)
13- by 9-inch (3.5 L) cake pan, greased

1. In a bowl, beat brown sugar and butter until smooth and creamy. Beat in egg, salt and bananas until well combined. Stir in oats, chocolate chips and raisins and mix thoroughly. Spread evenly in prepared pan. Bake in preheated oven for 50 to 60 minutes or until a tester inserted in the center comes out clean. Place pan on a rack to cool completely, then cut into bars.

Raisin-Spice Pumpkin Bars

2 cups	all-purpose flour	500 mL
2 cups	granulated sugar	500 mL
2 tsp	baking powder	10 mL
1 tsp	baking soda	5 mL
1 tsp	ground cinnamon	5 mL
1 tsp	ground nutmeg	5 mL
1/2 tsp	salt	2 mL
1/2 tsp	ground cloves	2 mL
4	eggs, beaten	4
1 cup	vegetable oil	250 mL
2 cups	pumpkin purée (not pie filling)	500 mL
1/2 cup	raisins	125 mL
1/2 cup	chopped nuts	125 mL

Frosting (optional)		
4 oz	cream cheese, softened	125 g
1/3 cup	butter or margarine, softened	75 mL
2 tsp	milk	10 mL
1 tsp	vanilla extract	5 mL
2 cups	confectioner's (icing) sugar, sifted	500 mL

TIP Replace ground spices annually; they lose their flavor over time.

Preheat oven to 350° F (180° C)
13- by 9-inch (3.5 L) cake pan, greased

1. In a bowl mix together flour, sugar, baking powder, baking soda, cinnamon, nutmeg, salt and cloves. Make a well in the center. Add eggs, oil and pumpkin and mix until blended. Stir in raisins and nuts. Bake in preheated oven for 30 to 35 minutes or until a tester inserted in the center comes out clean. Place pan on a rack to cool completely.

2. **Frosting (optional):** In a bowl, beat cream cheese and butter until smooth. Beat in milk and vanilla. Gradually add confectioner's sugar, beating until smooth and spreadable. Spread frosting over top of cooled cake. Cut into bars.

MAKES 24 BARS

Wheat Germ Date Bars

1 1/4 cups	chopped pitted dates (8 oz [250 g] package)	300 mL
1 1/4 cups	water	300 mL

Base		
1 cup	wheat germ	250 mL
1 cup	whole-wheat flour	250 mL
1/2 cup	packed brown sugar	125 mL
1/2 cup	butter or margarine, softened	125 mL

Topping		
2/3 cup	whole-wheat flour	150 mL
1/2 cup	granulated sugar	125 mL
1 tsp	baking powder	5 mL
1/2 tsp	salt	2 mL
2	eggs, beaten	2
1/4 tsp	almond extract	1 mL

Preheat oven to 350° F (180° C)
9-inch (2.5 L) square cake pan, greased

1. In a saucepan over medium heat, bring dates and water to a boil. Reduce heat and simmer, uncovered, for 15 to 20 minutes or until water is absorbed and dates thicken. Set aside.

2. **Base:** In a bowl mix together wheat germ, whole-wheat flour and sugar. Using 2 knives, a pastry blender or your fingers, cut butter in until mixture resembles coarse crumbs. Press 2 cups (500 mL) into prepared pan. Set remainder aside. Bake in preheated oven for 10 minutes. Place pan on a rack.

3. **Topping:** In another bowl, mix together whole-wheat flour, sugar, baking powder and salt. Blend in eggs, almond extract and reserved dates. Spread evenly over hot base. Sprinkle reserved crumb mixture evenly over top, pressing down lightly. Bake 25 minutes longer or until topping is set. Place pan on a rack to cool completely, then cut into bars.

MAKES 36 BARS

Glazed Zucchini-Raisin Bars

2 cups	whole-wheat flour (see Tip, below)	500 mL
2 tsp	baking soda	10 mL
3/4 tsp	ground cinnamon	4 mL
1/2 tsp	ground nutmeg	2 mL
1/4 tsp	ground cloves	1 mL
1 cup	raisins	250 mL
1/2 cup	butter or margarine, softened	125 mL
1 1/4 cups	packed brown sugar	300 mL
2	eggs	2
1 tsp	vanilla extract	5 mL
1 1/2 cups	shredded zucchini	375 mL

Lemon Glaze		
2 tbsp	butter or margarine, softened	25 mL
1 to 2 tbsp	lemon juice	15 to 25 mL
1 1/2 cups	confectioner's (icing) sugar, sifted	375 mL

TIP If desired, use 1 cup (250 mL) each of whole wheat and all-purpose flour.

Preheat oven to 350° F (180° C)
13- by 9-inch (3.5 L) cake pan, greased

1. In a bowl mix together flour, baking soda, cinnamon, nutmeg, cloves and raisins.

2. In another bowl, beat butter and brown sugar until smooth and creamy. Beat in eggs, then vanilla until incorporated. Blend in flour mixture. Stir in zucchini. Spread evenly in prepared pan. Bake in preheated oven for 30 to 35 minutes or until a tester inserted in the center comes out clean. Place pan on a rack to cool.

3. **Glaze:** In a bowl, beat butter and lemon juice until smooth. Gradually add confectioner's sugar, beating until smooth and spreadable. Spread over warm cake, then cut into bars. Store, covered, in refrigerator.

Bars

Bar

Squares

Nut and Peanut Butter Bars and Squares

Almond Rocca Bars

Preheat oven to 350° F (180° C)
9-inch (2.5 L) square cake pan, greased

Base		
1 cup	butter, softened	250 mL
1/2 cup	packed brown sugar	125 mL
1/2 cup	granulated sugar	125 mL
2	egg yolks	2
1 tsp	vanilla extract	5 mL
1 cup	all-purpose flour	250 mL
1 cup	old-fashioned rolled oats	250 mL

Topping		
3	milk chocolate bars (each about 1.45 oz [43 g])	3
2 tbsp	butter	25 mL
1/2 cup	finely chopped almonds	125 mL

1. **Base:** In a bowl, beat butter and sugars until smooth and creamy. Beat in egg yolks until incorporated. Stir in vanilla. Blend in flour and oats. Spread evenly in prepared pan. Bake in preheated oven for 30 to 35 minutes or until browned.

2. **Topping:** In the top of a double boiler over hot (not boiling) water, melt chocolate bars and butter, stirring until smooth. Pour over warm base. Sprinkle almonds evenly over top. Place pan on a rack to cool completely, then cut into bars.

Cherry Nut Fingers

Preheat oven to 350° F (180° C)
9-inch (2.5 L) square cake pan, greased

Base		
1 1/4 cups	all-purpose flour	300 mL
1/4 tsp	salt	1 mL
2/3 cup	packed brown sugar	150 mL
1/2 cup	butter, softened	125 mL
2	egg yolks	2
1/2 tsp	vanilla extract	2 mL

Topping		
2	egg whites	2
2 tbsp	all-purpose flour	25 mL
1/2 cup	chocolate sundae topping	125 mL
1/2 cup	shredded coconut	125 mL
1/2 cup	chopped maraschino cherries	125 mL
1/2 cup	chopped nuts	125 mL

1. **Base:** In a bowl mix together flour and salt.

2. In another bowl, beat brown sugar and butter until smooth and creamy. Beat in egg yolks until incorporated. Stir in vanilla. Blend in flour mixture. Spread evenly in prepared pan. Bake in preheated oven for 15 minutes. Place pan on a rack to cool slightly.

3. **Topping:** In a clean bowl, beat egg whites until soft peaks form. Fold in flour, then chocolate topping, coconut, cherries and nuts. Spread evenly over top of warm base. Bake 18 to 20 minutes longer. Place pan on a rack to cool completely, then cut into bars.

TIP Prefer cake with a finer texture? When baking bars or squares, try adding 2 tbsp (25 mL) boiling water to the creamed butter and sugar mixture.

MAKES 24 BARS

Jammin' Almond Bars

Preheat oven to 375° F (190° C)
9-inch (2.5 L) square cake pan, greased

Base		
1 3/4 cups	old-fashioned rolled oats	425 mL
1 cup	all-purpose flour	250 mL
1 cup	packed brown sugar	250 mL
1 tsp	baking powder	5 mL
1/4 tsp	salt	1 mL
3/4 cup	butter or margarine, melted	175 mL

Topping		
3/4 cup	raspberry jam	175 mL
1/2 cup	coarsely chopped almonds	125 mL

1. **Base:** In a bowl mix together oats, flour, brown sugar, baking powder and salt. Add butter and mix until combined. Set aside one-third and press remainder into prepared pan.

2. **Topping:** Stir jam until smooth and spread evenly over base.

3. In a bowl mix together almonds and reserved crumb mixture. Sprinkle over jam layer, pressing down lightly. Bake in preheated oven for 25 to 30 minutes or until golden brown. Place pan on a rack to cool completely, then cut into bars.

MAKES 36 BARS

Coffee Raisin-Nut Bars

Preheat oven to 350° F (180° C)
13- by 9-inch (3.5 L) cake pan, greased

1 1/2 cups	all-purpose flour	375 mL
1/2 tsp	baking powder	2 mL
1/2 tsp	baking soda	2 mL
1/2 tsp	salt	2 mL
1/2 tsp	ground cinnamon	2 mL
1/4 cup	shortening, softened	50 mL
1 cup	packed brown sugar	250 mL
1	egg	1
1/2 cup	hot coffee	125 mL
1/2 cup	raisins	125 mL
1/2 cup	chopped nuts	125 mL
	Coffee Frosting (see recipe, page 181) (optional)	

1. In a bowl mix together flour, baking powder, baking soda, salt and cinnamon.

2. In another bowl, beat shortening and brown sugar until smooth and creamy. Add egg and beat until incorporated. Stir in coffee. Blend in flour mixture. Stir in raisins and nuts. Spread evenly in prepared pan. Bake in preheated oven for 20 to 25 minutes or until golden brown. Place pan on a rack to cool completely. If desired, frost with Coffee Frosting or a frosting of your choice, then cut into bars.

Date Nut Squares

MAKES 16 SQUARES

6 tbsp	all-purpose flour	90 mL
1 tsp	baking powder	5 mL
1/2 tsp	ground cinnamon	2 mL
1 tsp	grated orange zest	5 mL
3/4 cup	packed brown sugar	175 mL
2	eggs	2
1/2 tsp	vanilla extract	2 mL
1 cup	chopped dates	250 mL
1 cup	chopped nuts	250 mL
6	maraschino cherries, chopped	6
	Confectioner's (icing) sugar	

Preheat oven to 325° F (160° C)
8-inch (2 L) square cake pan, greased

1. In a bowl mix together flour, baking powder, cinnamon and orange zest.

2. In another bowl, beat brown sugar, eggs and vanilla until combined. Blend in flour mixture. Stir in dates, nuts and cherries. Spread evenly in prepared pan. Bake in preheated oven for 35 to 40 minutes, or until tester inserted in center comes out clean. Place pan on a rack to cool. Sift confectioner's sugar over top, then cut into squares.

Raspberry Hazelnut Bars

MAKES 36 BARS

Base		
1/3 cup	granulated sugar	75 mL
1/2 cup	butter or margarine, softened	125 mL
1	egg	1
2 cups	all-purpose flour	500 mL

Topping		
3/4 cup	seedless raspberry jam	175 mL
1/2 cup	chopped toasted hazelnuts (see Tip ,below)	125 mL

Preheat oven to 350° F (180° C)
13- by 9-inch (3.5 L) cake pan, lightly greased

1. **Base:** In a bowl, beat sugar and butter until smooth and creamy. Beat in egg until incorporated. Gradually blend in flour just until a dough forms. Spread evenly in prepared pan.

2. **Topping:** Stir jam until smooth and spread over dough, stopping just short of edges. Sprinkle nuts over top of jam. Bake in preheated oven for 20 to 25 minutes or until golden brown. Place pan on a rack to cool completely, then cut into bars.

TIP To toast hazelnuts: Place on a cookie sheet and bake at 325° F (160° C) for about 15 minutes, stirring occasionally. Wrap hot nuts in a clean tea towel or paper towel for 1 to 2 minutes. Using your hands, rub nuts together until skins fall off. Cool, then chop, if desired.

Dutch Jan Hagels

Preheat oven to 350° F (180° C)
13- by 9-inch (3.5 L) cake pan, greased

Base		
1 1/4 cups	all-purpose flour	300 mL
1/2 cup	granulated sugar	125 mL
1/2 tsp	ground cinnamon	2 mL
1/2 cup	butter or margarine, softened	125 mL
1	egg yolk	1

Topping		
1	egg white	1
1/4 cup	granulated sugar	50 mL
1/2 cup	sliced almonds	125 mL

1. **Base:** In a bowl mix together flour, sugar and cinnamon. Using 2 knives, a pastry blender or your fingers, cut butter in until mixture resembles coarse crumbs. Mix in egg yolk until dough forms. Press evenly into prepared pan.

2. **Topping:** Beat egg white slightly and brush over dough. Sprinkle sugar and almonds over top and press down into dough. Bake in preheated oven for 18 to 20 minutes or until golden brown. Place pan on a rack to cool slightly, then cut into bars. Cool completely before removing from pan.

Macadamia Nut Triangles

Preheat oven to 425° F (220° C)
9-inch (2.5 L) square cake pan, greased

Base		
1 cup	all-purpose flour	250 mL
1/4 cup	granulated sugar	50 mL
Pinch	salt	Pinch
6 tbsp	butter or margarine	90 mL
3 tbsp	water	45 mL

Topping		
1 1/4 cups	macadamia nuts, divided	300 mL
2/3 cup	packed brown sugar	150 mL
1	egg	1
2 tsp	vanilla extract	10 mL

1. **Base:** In a bowl mix together flour, sugar and salt. Using 2 knives, a pastry blender, or your fingers, cut butter in until mixture resembles coarse crumbs. Sprinkle with water, 1 tbsp (15 mL) at a time, mixing lightly with a fork until dough is just moist enough to hold together. (You may not need to use all the water.) Press evenly into prepared pan and bake in preheated oven for 15 to 20 minutes or until golden brown. Place pan on a rack to cool and reduce oven temperature to 375° F (190° C).

2. **Topping:** Coarsely chop 1/2 cup (125 mL) of the nuts and set aside. In food processor, combine remaining nuts with brown sugar and process until nuts are finely ground. Add egg and vanilla and pulse to blend.

3. Spread topping evenly over base. Sprinkle reserved nuts over top. Bake 20 minutes longer or until topping is set. Place pan on a rack to cool completely, then cut into 4 long strips. Cut each strip into 4 squares. Cut each square in half on the diagonal to form triangles.

MAKES 36 BARS

Pecan Pie Bars

Base		
2 cups	all-purpose flour	500 mL
1/2 cup	granulated sugar	125 mL
3/4 cup	butter *or* margarine	175 mL

Topping		
1/4 cup	butter or margarine, melted	50 mL
1 cup	granulated sugar	250 mL
1 cup	corn syrup	250 mL
4	eggs	4
1 2/3 cups	butterscotch chips (10 oz [300 g] package)	400 mL
1 1/3 cups	coarsely chopped pecans	325 mL

TIP These bars are particularly delicious served warm, like pecan pie, with ice cream. If you don't like pecans, use a different kind of nut.

Preheat oven to 350° F (180° C)
13- by 9-inch (3.5 L) cake pan, lightly greased

1. **Base:** In a bowl mix together flour and sugar. Using 2 knives, a pastry blender or your fingers, cut butter in until mixture resembles coarse crumbs. Spread evenly in prepared pan. Bake in preheated oven for 15 to 18 minutes or until golden brown.

2. **Topping:** In a bowl, beat butter, sugar, syrup and eggs until blended. Stir in butterscotch chips and pecans. Spread evenly over base. Bake 30 minutes longer or until set and golden brown. Serve warm or cool completely, then cut into bars.

MAKES 36 BARS

Caramel Oatmeal Bars

Base		
1 1/2 cups	all-purpose flour	375 mL
3/4 cup	packed brown sugar	175 mL
1/2 cup	quick-cooking rolled oats	125 mL
1/2 cup	butter *or* margarine	125 mL
1	egg, beaten	1
1/2 cup	chopped pecans	125 mL

Topping		
1 1/4 cups	milk or sweetened condensed milk	300 mL
25	soft caramels, unwrapped	25
1/4 cup	butter *or* margarine	50 mL

Preheat oven to 350° F (180° C)
13- by 9-inch (3.5 L) cake pan, greased

1. **Base:** In a bowl mix together flour, brown sugar and oats. Using 2 knives, a pastry blender or your fingers, cut butter in until mixture resembles coarse crumbs. Add egg and mix until blended. Stir in pecans. Set aside 1 1/2 cups (375 mL) and press remainder evenly into prepared pan. Bake in preheated oven for 15 to 18 minutes or until lightly browned. Place pan on a rack to cool slightly.

2. **Topping:** In a saucepan over low heat, melt caramels with milk, stirring constantly until smooth. Pour over baked base. Sprinkle reserved crumb mixture evenly over top. Bake 20 to 25 minutes longer, until bubbly and golden brown. Place pan on a rack to cool completely, then cut into bars.

Makes 16 squares

Chocolate Nut Squares

Base		
1 cup	all-purpose flour	250 mL
1/4 tsp	salt	1 mL
1/2 cup	butter, softened	125 mL
2 tbsp	confectioner's (icing) sugar, sifted	25 mL
1	egg yolk	1

Topping		
2 tbsp	all-purpose flour	25 mL
1/4 tsp	salt	1 mL
1/2 cup	packed brown sugar	125 mL
3	eggs	3
2/3 cup	corn syrup	150 mL
1 tbsp	lemon juice	15 mL
1 cup	chocolate chips	250 mL
1 cup	chopped pecans or walnuts	250 mL

Preheat oven to 350° F (180° C)
8-inch (2 L) square cake pan, lightly greased

1. **Base:** In a bowl mix together flour and salt.

2. In another bowl, beat butter and confectioner's sugar until smooth and creamy. Beat in egg yolk until incorporated. Blend in flour mixture. Press evenly into prepared pan. Bake in preheated oven for 15 minutes or until golden brown. Place pan on a rack to cool slightly.

3. **Topping:** In a bowl mix together flour and salt. In another bowl, beat brown sugar, eggs, corn syrup and lemon juice until blended. Blend in flour mixture. Stir in chocolate chips and nuts. Spread evenly over top of warm base. Bake 35 to 40 minutes longer or until top is set. Place pan on a rack to cool completely, then cut into squares.

Makes about 36 bars

Carrot Walnut Bars with Cream Cheese Frosting

1 1/2 cups	all-purpose flour	375 mL
1 cup	packed brown sugar	250 mL
1 tsp	baking powder	5 mL
1 tsp	ground cinnamon	5 mL
1/2 tsp	baking soda	2 mL
2/3 cup	vegetable oil	150 mL
2	eggs, beaten	2
1 tsp	vanilla extract	5 mL
1/2 cup	shredded coconut	125 mL
1/2 cup	finely shredded carrots	125 mL
3/4 cup	chopped walnuts	175 mL

Cream Cheese Frosting		
2 tbsp	butter or margarine, softened	25 mL
3 oz	cream cheese, softened	90 g
1 tsp	vanilla extract	5 mL
2 1/4 cups	confectioner's (icing) sugar, sifted	550 mL

Preheat oven to 350° F (180° C)
13- by 9-inch (3.5 L) cake pan, greased

1. In a bowl mix together flour, brown sugar, baking powder, cinnamon and baking soda. Make a well in the center. Add oil, eggs and vanilla and mix just until incorporated. Stir in coconut, carrots and walnuts. Spread batter evenly in prepared pan. Bake in preheated oven for 20 to 25 minutes or until a tester inserted in the center comes out clean. Place pan on a rack to cool completely.

2. **Frosting:** In a bowl, beat butter, cream cheese and vanilla until smooth and creamy. Gradually add confectioner's sugar, beating until smooth. Spread frosting over top of cooled cake. Cut into bars. Store, covered, in refrigerator.

Glazed Walnut Jam Bars

Preheat oven to 350° F (180° C)
9-inch (2.5 L) square cake pan, greased

Base		
1 cup	all-purpose flour	250 mL
1 tsp	baking powder	5 mL
1/2 cup	shortening, softened	125 mL
1 tbsp	milk	15 mL
1	egg	1

Topping		
1/2 cup	raspberry jam	125 mL
2 tbsp	all-purpose flour	25 mL
1/4 tsp	salt	1 mL
1/4 tsp	baking powder	1 mL
1 cup	packed brown sugar	250 mL
2	eggs, beaten	2
1 tsp	vanilla extract	5 mL
1/2 cup	flaked coconut	125 mL
1 cup	chopped walnuts	250 mL

Glaze		
1 1/2 cups	confectioner's (icing) sugar, sifted	375 mL
1 1/2 tbsp	lemon juice	22 mL
1 to 2 tbsp	milk or light (5%) cream	15 to 25 mL

1. **Base:** In a bowl mix together flour and baking powder. Using 2 knives, a pastry blender or your fingers, cut shortening in until mixture resembles coarse crumbs. Add milk and eggs; mix just until incorporated. Press evenly into prepared pan.

2. **Topping:** Stir jam until smooth and spread over base.

3. In a bowl mix together flour, salt and baking powder. In another bowl, beat brown sugar, eggs and vanilla until blended. Blend in flour mixture. Stir in coconut and walnuts. Spread evenly over jam and bake in preheated oven for 35 to 40 minutes or until set and golden brown. Place pan on a rack to cool.

4. **Glaze:** In a bowl combine confectioner's sugar and lemon juice. Stir in enough milk to make a spreadable consistency. Spread over warm cake. Cool completely, then cut into bars.

Chinese Nut Chews

Preheat oven to 350° F (180° C)
13- by 9-inch (3.5 L) cake pan, greased

1 cup	granulated sugar	250 mL
3/4 cup	all-purpose flour	175 mL
1 tsp	baking powder	5 mL
1/4 tsp	salt	1 mL
3	eggs, beaten	3
1 cup	chopped dates	250 mL
1 cup	chopped walnuts	250 mL
	Confectioner's (icing) sugar	

1. In a bowl mix together sugar, flour, baking powder and salt. Add eggs, dates and walnuts and mix well. Spread evenly in prepared pan. Bake in preheated oven for 20 minutes, or until top is golden brown. Place pan on a rack and cut into bars. Cool completely, then sift confectioner's sugar over top.

Peanut-Butterscotch Bars

MAKES 36 BARS

Preheat oven to 350° F (180° C)
13- by 9-inch (3.5 L) cake pan, ungreased

Base

1/2 cup	packed brown sugar	125 mL
1/2 cup	butter or margarine, softened	125 mL
1 1/3 cups	all-purpose flour	325 mL

Topping

2/3 cup	light corn syrup	150 mL
2/3 cup	granulated sugar	150 mL
3/4 cup	butterscotch chips	175 mL
1/2 cup	chunky peanut butter	125 mL
2 cups	corn flakes cereal	500 mL

1. **Base:** In a bowl, beat brown sugar and butter until smooth and creamy. Blend in flour just until crumbly. Press evenly into prepared pan. Bake in preheated oven for 15 minutes. Place pan on a rack to cool slightly.

2. **Topping:** In a saucepan over low heat, stir together corn syrup and sugar until dissolved. Increase heat and bring to a boil. Remove from heat and stir in butterscotch chips and peanut butter, until chips are melted and mixture is smooth. Stir in corn flakes. Spread evenly over baked base. Cool completely, then cut into bars.

Caramel Peanut Cup Bars

MAKES 36 BARS

Preheat oven to 350° F (180° C)
13- by 9-inch (3.5 L) cake pan, greased

Base

1	pkg (18.25 oz [515 g]) yellow cake mix	1
1/2 cup	butter or margarine, softened	125 mL
1	egg	1
20	miniature peanut butter cups, chopped	20

Topping

2 1/2 cups	caramel sundae sauce	625 mL
2 tbsp	cornstarch	25 mL
1/4 cup	peanut butter	50 mL
1 cup	chopped salted peanuts, divided	250 mL
1	container (15 oz [450 g]) ready-to-serve chocolate frosting	1

1. **Base:** In a bowl mix together cake mix, butter and egg, until smooth. Fold in peanut butter cups. Spread mixture evenly in prepared pan. Bake in preheated oven for 18 to 20 minutes or until lightly browned. Place pan on a rack to cool slightly.

2. **Topping:** In a saucepan over low heat, stir together caramel sauce, cornstarch and peanut butter. Increase heat and bring to a boil; cook, stirring constantly, for 2 minutes until smooth. Remove from heat. Stir in 1/2 cup (125 mL) of the peanuts and spread evenly over warm base. Bake 6 to 8 minutes longer or until almost set. Place pan on a rack to cool completely. Spread frosting over top. Sprinkle with remaining peanuts. Chill at least 1 hour before cutting into bars.

TIP To determine if an egg is fresh, place it in a large bowl filled with water. A fresh egg will sink; a stale one will float.

Chocolate-Drizzled Peanut Butter Bars

1 1/2 cups	all-purpose flour	375 mL
1 tsp	baking powder	5 mL
1/4 tsp	salt	1 mL
1 cup	packed brown sugar	250 mL
1/2 cup	granulated sugar	125 mL
1/2 cup	butter or margarine, softened	125 mL
1/4 cup	smooth peanut butter	50 mL
2	eggs	2
1 tsp	vanilla extract	5 mL
1/2 cup	chopped unsalted peanuts	125 mL
24	miniature peanut butter cups, cut into quarters	24
Chocolate Drizzle		
1/4 cup	semi-sweet chocolate chips	50 mL
1 tsp	butter *or* margarine	5 mL

Preheat oven to 350° F (180° C)
13- by 9-inch (3.5 L) cake pan, lightly greased

1. In a bowl mix together flour, baking powder and salt.

2. In another bowl, beat sugars, butter and peanut butter until smooth. Beat in eggs, one at a time, until incorporated. Stir in vanilla. Blend in flour mixture. Stir in peanuts. Spread evenly in prepared pan. Sprinkle pieces of peanut butter cups over batter and press down slightly. Bake in preheated oven for 20 to 25 minutes or until a tester inserted in the center of cake comes out clean. Place pan on a rack to cool slightly.

3. **Chocolate drizzle:** In the top of a double boiler over hot (not boiling) water, melt chocolate chips with butter, stirring until smooth. Drizzle over top of warm cake. Cool completely, then cut into bars.

Nutty Mix Bars

1	pkg (18.25 oz [515 g]) yellow cake mix	1
1/2 cup	chunky peanut butter	125 mL
1 2/3 cups	milk	400 mL
3	eggs	3
Nutty Frosting		
4 3/4 cups	confectioner's (icing) sugar, sifted	1.2 L
1/2 cup	unsweetened cocoa powder, sifted	125 mL
1/4 tsp	salt	1 mL
1/3 cup	butter *or* margarine	75 mL
1/4 cup	chunky peanut butter	50 mL
1 tsp	vanilla extract	5 mL
1/3 cup	boiling water	75 mL

Preheat oven to 350° F (180° C)
13- by 9-inch (3.5 L) cake pan, greased

1. In a bowl, beat cake mix, peanut butter, milk and eggs until blended and smooth. Spread evenly in prepared pan. Bake in preheated oven for 35 to 40 minutes or until a tester inserted in the center comes out clean. Place pan on a rack to cool completely.

2. **Frosting:** In a bowl mix together confectioner's sugar, cocoa and salt. In another bowl, beat butter, peanut butter and vanilla until smooth and creamy. Beat in boiling water. Gradually add sugar mixture, beating until mixture is smooth and spreadable. Spread frosting on cooled cake, then cut into bars.

Peanut Butter Marshmallow Treats

MAKES 36 BARS

Preheat oven to 325° F (160° C)
13- by 9-inch (3.5 L) cake pan, greased

Base		
1 1/2 cups	packed brown sugar	375 mL
1/2 cup	butter, softened	125 mL
1/2 cup	peanut butter (smooth or crunchy)	125 mL
2	eggs	2
1 tsp	vanilla extract	5 mL
1 1/2 cups	quick-cooking rolled oats	375 mL
1 cup	all-purpose flour	250 mL

Topping		
3 cups	miniature marshmallows	750 mL

Frosting		
1/4 cup	smooth peanut butter	50 mL
1/4 cup	butter or margarine, softened	50 mL
2 tbsp	milk	25 mL
1 tsp	vanilla extract	5 mL
1 1/3 cups	confectioner's (icing) sugar, sifted	325 mL

1. **Base:** In a bowl, beat brown sugar, butter and peanut butter until smooth. Beat in eggs, then vanilla until blended. Blend in oats and flour. Press evenly into prepared pan. Bake in preheated oven for 25 to 30 minutes or until lightly browned around the edges.

2. **Topping:** Sprinkle marshmallows evenly over base. Bake 1 to 2 minutes longer or until marshmallows puff up slightly. Place pan on a rack to cool completely.

3. **Frosting:** In a bowl, beat peanut butter, butter, milk and vanilla until smooth and creamy. Gradually add confectioner's sugar, beating until mixture is smooth and spreadable. Spread evenly over marshmallow layer, then cut into bars.

TIP To freshen up stale marshmallows, store them in an airtight container with a slice of fresh bread.

Oatmeal Chip Peanut Squares

MAKES 16 SQUARES

Preheat oven to 350° F (180° C)
8-inch (2 L) square cake pan, greased

1/2 cup	packed brown sugar	125 mL
1/2 cup	corn syrup	125 mL
1/2 cup	butter or margarine, softened	125 mL
1 tsp	vanilla extract	5 mL
3 cups	quick-cooking rolled oats	750 mL
1/2 cup	semi-sweet chocolate chips	125 mL
1/4 cup	smooth peanut butter	50 mL

1. In a bowl, beat sugar, syrup, butter and vanilla until blended and smooth. Stir in oats. Press evenly into prepared pan. Bake in preheated oven for 25 to 30 minutes or until lightly browned. Place pan on a rack to cool for 5 minutes.

2. Sprinkle chocolate chips evenly over top, then drop small spoonfuls of peanut butter over top of the chips. Let stand for about 5 minutes, until chips and peanut butter have softened, then, run a knife through the topping to create a marbling effect. Chill for 15 to 20 minutes, until topping is firm, then cut into squares.

MAKES 36 BARS

Chocolate Raisin Peanut Bars

1 cup	all-purpose flour	250 mL
1 1/2 tsp	baking powder	7 mL
1/2 cup	butter *or* margarine	125 mL
1/2 cup	smooth peanut butter	125 mL
1 1/2 cups	granulated sugar	375 mL
2	eggs	2
1 tbsp	vanilla extract	15 mL
1 1/2 cups	raisins	375 mL
2	squares (each 1 oz [28 g]) semi-sweet chocolate, melted	2

TIP If you have forgotten to remove eggs from the refrigerator to allow them to come to room temperature, place them in a bowl of warm water for several minutes.

Preheat oven to 350° F (180° C)
13- by 9-inch (3.5 L) cake pan, greased

1. In a bowl mix together flour and baking powder.

2. In a large saucepan, over medium heat, stir butter and peanut butter until melted. Remove from heat. Beat in sugar until blended. Add eggs and vanilla and beat until smooth. Blend in flour mixture. Stir in raisins. Spread evenly in prepared pan. Bake in preheated oven for about 25 minutes or until a tester inserted in the center comes out clean. Place pan on a rack to cool completely.

3. Drizzle melted chocolate over the top. Allow chocolate to set, then cut into bars.

MAKES 36 BARS

Savannah Cake Bars

1	pkg (18.25 oz [515 g]) yellow cake mix	1
1/2 cup	butter *or* margarine	125 mL
1 cup	packed brown sugar	250 mL
1/2 cup	crunchy peanut butter	125 mL
1 1/4 cups	flaked coconut	300 mL
1/3 cup	half-and-half (10 %) cream	75 mL

Preheat oven to 350° F (180°C)
13- by 9-inch (3.5 L) cake pan, greased

1. Prepare and bake cake mix according to package directions. Place pan on a rack.

2. In a saucepan over low heat, melt butter. Remove from heat and add brown sugar, peanut butter, coconut and cream, mixing until well blended. Spread evenly over cake.

3. Preheat broiler. Place cake about 5 to 6 inches (12.5 to 15 cm) from heat and broil for 1 to 2 minutes or just until frosting bubbles. Place pan on a rack to cool completely, then cut into bars.

MAKES 16 SQUARES

Grandma's Traditional Almond Squares

1 cup	ground almonds	250 mL
3/4 cup	all-purpose flour	175 mL
1/4 tsp	salt	1 mL
1 cup	granulated sugar	250 mL
1 cup	butter, softened	250 mL
6	egg yolks	6
16	whole blanched almonds	16

TIP To blanch almonds, cover shelled nuts with boiling water. Let stand for a few minutes, then rinse under cold water. Almonds will pop out of their skins.

Preheat oven to 350° F (180° C)
8-inch (2 L) square cake pan, greased

1. In a bowl mix together ground almonds, flour and salt.

2. In another bowl, beat sugar and butter until smooth and creamy. Beat in egg yolks, one at a time, until incorporated. Gradually add flour mixture, mixing until blended. Spread evenly in prepared pan. Lightly mark off 16 squares and place an almond in the center of each. Bake in preheated oven for 30 to 35 minutes or until golden brown. Place pan on a rack to cool slightly, then cut into squares.

MAKES 16 SQUARES

Banana Cream Walnut Squares

Base		
1 cup	granulated sugar	250 mL
1	egg, beaten	1
1 cup	chopped walnuts	250 mL

Topping		
1	pkg (4-serving size) vanilla instant pudding mix	1
1 cup	milk	250 mL
1 cup	sour cream	250 mL
2	medium bananas, sliced	2

TIP To toast nuts, spread them in a single layer on a baking sheet. Bake at 350° F (180° C) for 5 to 10 minutes, stirring occasionally until lightly browned.

Preheat oven to 350° F (180° C)
Baking sheet, greased
8-inch (2 L) square cake pan, ungreased

1. **Base:** In a bowl mix together sugar, egg and nuts until blended. Spread a thin layer on prepared baking sheet. Bake in preheated oven for 18 to 20 minutes or until golden brown. Place pan on a rack to cool. When cooled, crush into crumbs. Set aside half and spread remainder evenly in cake pan.

2. **Topping:** In a bowl, beat pudding mix, milk and sour cream until well blended. Fold in bananas. Pour over base and sprinkle with reserved crumbs. Chill for 3 to 4 hours, then cut into squares.

MAKES 16 SQUARES

Caramel Double-Nut Squares

3/4 cup	all-purpose flour	175 mL
1 tsp	baking powder	5 mL
1/4 tsp	salt	1 mL
1 cup	packed brown sugar	250 mL
1/4 cup	butter	50 mL
1	egg	1
1 tsp	vanilla extract	5 mL
1 cup	shredded coconut	250 mL
1/2 cup	ground pecans	125 mL
1/2 cup	chopped walnuts	125 mL

Preheat oven to 350° F (180° C)
8-inch (2 L) square cake pan, greased

1. In a bowl mix together flour, baking powder and salt.

2. In a saucepan over medium heat, melt brown sugar and butter, stirring until smooth and blended. Set aside to cool, then beat in egg and vanilla. Gradually blend in flour mixture. Stir in coconut, pecans and walnuts. Spread evenly in prepared pan. Bake in preheated oven for 25 to 30 minutes or until golden brown. Place pan on a rack to cool, then cut into squares.

MAKES 24 BARS

Marbled Pistachio Bars

1/2 cup	butter or margarine	125 mL
3	eggs	3
1 1/2 cups	granulated sugar	375 mL
1/2 tsp	vanilla extract	2 mL
1/4 tsp	almond extract	1 mL
1 cup	cake flour, sifted	250 mL
1/4 cup	finely chopped pistachio nuts	50 mL
Half	square (1 oz [28 g]) semi-sweet chocolate, grated	Half
	Confectioner's (icing) sugar (optional)	
	Vanilla Frosting (optional) (see recipe, page 183)	

Preheat oven to 350° F (180°C)
9-inch (2.5 L) square cake pan, greased

1. In a saucepan over low heat, melt butter. Set aside to cool.

2. In a bowl, beat eggs until foamy. Gradually beat in sugar, beating continually until mixture has tripled in volume, about 15 minutes. Beat in vanilla and almond extract. Fold flour into egg mixture, alternately, with cooled butter just until combined. Spread half evenly in prepared pan. Sprinkle half the nuts and half the grated chocolate evenly over top. Spoon remaining batter over top and sprinkle with the remaining nuts and grated chocolate. Run a knife through the batters to create a marbling effect.

3. Bake in preheated oven for 25 to 30 minutes or until a tester inserted in the center comes out clean. Place pan on a rack to cool for 5 minutes, then transfer cake from pan to rack to cool completely. Sift confectioner's sugar lightly over top or frost with Vanilla Frosting. Cut into bars.

MAKES 36 BARS

Orange Nut Oatmeal Bars

Preheat oven to 350° F (180° C)
13- by 9-inch (3.5 L) cake pan, greased

Base		
1 1/4 cups	boiling water	300 mL
1 cup	quick-cooking rolled oats	250 mL
1 3/4 cups	all-purpose flour	425 mL
1 tsp	baking powder	5 mL
1 tsp	baking soda	5 mL
1/2 tsp	salt	2 mL
1/2 tsp	ground cinnamon	2 mL
1/2 cup	butter or margarine, softened	125 mL
1/2 cup	packed brown sugar	125 mL
1 cup	granulated sugar	250 mL
2	eggs	2
1 tsp	vanilla extract	5 mL
1/4 cup	frozen orange juice concentrate, thawed	50 mL

Topping		
1/2 cup	packed brown sugar	125 mL
1/4 cup	butter or margarine	50 mL
2 tbsp	frozen orange juice concentrate, thawed, undiluted	25 mL
1 cup	flaked coconut	250 mL
1/2 cup	chopped walnuts	125 mL

1. **Base:** In a bowl combine boiling water and oats. Set aside.

2. In another bowl, mix together flour, baking powder, baking soda, salt and cinnamon.

3. In a separate bowl, beat butter and sugars until smooth and creamy. Beat in eggs, one at a time, until incorporated. Stir in vanilla and orange juice concentrate. Gradually blend in flour mixture alternately with oat mixture. Spread evenly in prepared pan. Bake in preheated oven for 40 minutes or until a tester inserted in the center comes out clean. Place pan on a rack to cool.

4. **Topping:** Preheat broiler. In a saucepan over low heat, stir together brown sugar, butter and orange juice concentrate until dissolved. Increase heat and bring to a boil, stirring constantly; cook for 1 minute. Remove from heat and stir in coconut and nuts. Spread evenly over top of cooled cake and place pan under broiler for 1 to 2 minutes or until golden brown. Place pan on a rack to cool slightly, then cut into bars.

TIP To toast nuts in a skillet, stir often over medium heat until nuts become golden brown.

Raisin-Nut Coffee Cake Bars

MAKES 24 BARS

Base

2 cups	all-purpose flour	500 mL
1 1/2 tsp	baking powder	7 mL
1 tsp	baking soda	5 mL
1/4 tsp	salt	1 mL
1 cup	granulated sugar	250 mL
1/2 cup	butter or margarine, softened	125 mL
2	eggs	2
1 tsp	vanilla extract	5 mL
1 cup	sour cream	250 mL

Filling

1 cup	chopped walnuts	250 mL
1/2 cup	granulated sugar	125 mL
1 tsp	ground cinnamon	5 mL
1 1/2 cups	raisins	375 mL

TIP To toast nuts in the microwave, spread the nuts out on a paper plate or a shallow dish. Cook on High 1 1/2 minutes for 1/2 cup (125 mL) nuts and 2 minutes for 1 cup (250 mL) nuts. Stir, then microwave for 2 minutes longer or until golden.

Preheat oven to 350° F (180° C)
9-inch (2.5 L) square cake pan, greased

1. **Base:** In a bowl mix together flour, baking powder, baking soda and salt.

2. In another bowl, beat sugar and butter until smooth and creamy. Beat in eggs until incorporated. Stir in vanilla and sour cream. Blend in flour mixture. Set half aside and spread remainder evenly in prepared pan.

3. **Filling:** In a bowl mix together nuts, sugar and cinnamon. Sprinkle half evenly over batter in pan. Sprinkle raisins evenly over top. Top with remaining batter. Sprinkle remaining nut mixture evenly over top of batter.

4. Bake in preheated oven for 35 to 40 minutes or until a tester inserted in the center comes out clean. Place pan on a rack to cool slightly, then cut into bars. Serve warm.

Walnut Squares

MAKES 16 SQUARES

Base

1 cup	all-purpose flour	250 mL
1/2 cup	butter or margarine, softened	125 mL

Topping

2	eggs, beaten	2
1 cup	packed brown sugar	250 mL
1 tbsp	all-purpose flour	15 mL
1/2 tsp	baking powder	2 mL
1 cup	chopped walnuts	250 mL
1/2 cup	flaked coconut	125 mL
	Butter Frosting (see recipe, page 179) (optional)	

Preheat oven to 325° F (160° C)
8-inch (2 L) square cake pan, greased

1. **Base:** In a bowl mix together flour and butter. Press evenly into prepared pan. Bake in preheated oven for 8 to 10 minutes or until lightly browned. Place pan on a rack to cool slightly.

2. **Topping:** In a bowl, beat eggs, brown sugar, flour and baking powder until blended. Stir in nuts and coconut. Spread evenly over warm base. Bake 20 to 25 minutes longer or until golden brown. Place pan on a rack to cool completely, then cut into squares. If desired, frost with your favorite Butter Frosting.

Raspberry Nut Meringue Bars

MAKES 24 BARS

Base		
1/2 cup	butter or margarine, softened	125 mL
1/2 cup	confectioner's (icing) sugar, sifted	125 mL
2	egg yolks	2
1 1/4 cups	all-purpose flour	300 mL

Filling		
3/4 cup	raspberry jam	175 mL

Topping		
2	egg whites	2
Pinch	cream of tartar	Pinch
1/2 cup	granulated sugar	125 mL
1 cup	ground toasted pecans	250 mL

TIP Always use large-size eggs for baking, unless a recipe states otherwise.

VARIATIONS Strawberry Nut
Meringue Bars: Substitute 3/4 cup (175 mL) strawberry jam for the raspberry.

Apricot Nut Meringue Bars: Substitute 3/4 cup (175 mL) apricot jam for the raspberry.

Preheat oven to 350° F (180° C)
9-inch (2.5 L) square cake pan, greased

1. **Base:** In a bowl, beat butter and confectioner's sugar until smooth and creamy. Beat in eggs yolks until incorporated. Blend in flour. Press evenly into prepared pan. Bake in preheated oven for 10 to 12 minutes or until golden brown. Place pan on a rack to cool slightly.

2. **Filling:** Stir jam until smooth and spread evenly over warm base.

3. **Topping:** In a clean bowl, beat egg whites and cream of tartar until soft peaks form. Gradually add sugar, beating until stiff peaks form. Fold in nuts. Spread evenly over jam. Bake 20 to 25 minutes longer or until lightly browned. Place pan on a rack to cool completely, then cut into bars.

Sour Cream Coffee Cake Bars

Base		
1 1/2 cups	all-purpose flour	375 mL
1 1/2 tsp	baking powder	7 mL
1 tsp	baking soda	5 mL
Pinch	salt	Pinch
1/2 cup	granulated sugar	125 mL
1/2 cup	butter or margarine, softened	125 mL
2	eggs	2
1 tsp	vanilla extract	5 mL
1 cup	sour cream	250 mL

Topping		
1/4 cup	granulated sugar	50 mL
1/4 cup	chopped walnuts	50 mL
2 tsp	ground cinnamon	10 mL

TIP A wet knife does a smoother job of cutting fresh bars, squares or brownies.

Preheat oven to 350° F (180° C)
9-inch (2.5 L) square cake pan, lightly greased

1. **Base:** In a bowl combine flour, baking powder, baking soda and salt.

2. In another bowl, beat sugar and butter until smooth and creamy. Add eggs and beat until incorporated. Stir in vanilla. Gradually blend in flour mixture, alternately with sour cream. Spread half in prepared pan. Set remainder aside.

3. **Topping:** In a bowl mix together sugar, nuts and cinnamon . Sprinkle half evenly over base. Spread reserved batter over nut mixture. Sprinkle remaining topping evenly over batter. Bake in preheated oven for 40 minutes or until a tester inserted in the center comes out clean. Place pan on a rack to cool completely, then cut into squares.

Walnut Cheesecake Bars

Base		
2 cups	all-purpose flour	500 mL
2/3 cup	packed brown sugar	150 mL
1/2 tsp	salt	2 mL
1 cup	finely chopped walnuts	250 mL
2/3 cup	cold butter or margarine, cut into cubes	150 mL

Topping		
1 lb	cream cheese, softened	500 g
1/2 cup	granulated sugar	125 mL
2	eggs	2
1/4 cup	milk	50 mL
1 tsp	vanilla extract	5 mL

Preheat oven to 350° F (180° C)
13- by 9-inch (3.5 L) cake pan, greased

1. **Base:** In a bowl mix together flour, brown sugar, salt and walnuts. Using 2 knives, a pastry blender or your fingers, cut butter in until mixture resembles coarse crumbs. Set half aside and press remainder evenly in prepared pan. Bake in preheated oven for 10 to 15 minutes or until lightly browned. Place pan on a rack to cool slightly.

2. **Topping:** In a bowl, beat cream cheese and sugar until smooth. Beat in eggs until incorporated. Stir in milk and vanilla. Spread evenly over warm base. Sprinkle reserved base mixture over top. Bake 20 to 25 minutes longer or until just set. Place pan on a rack to cool completely, then cut into bars. Store, covered, in refrigerator.

MAKES 30 SQUARES

Butterscotch Peanut Butter Krunchies

Base

1 1/3 cups	all-purpose flour	325 mL
1/2 cup	packed brown sugar	125 mL
1/2 cup	butter *or* margarine	125 mL

Topping

2/3 cup	granulated sugar	150 mL
2/3 cup	light corn syrup	150 mL
1/2 cup	crunchy peanut butter	125 mL
1 cup	butterscotch chips	250 mL
2 cups	corn flakes cereal	500 mL

TIP Whenever I make anything flavored with butterscotch, I replace vanilla with almond extract. It seems to enhance the flavor.

Preheat oven to 350° F (180° C)
13- by 9-inch (3.5 L) cake pan, ungreased

1. **Base:** In a bowl mix flour and brown sugar. Using 2 knives, a pastry blender or your fingers, cut butter in until mixture resembles coarse crumbs. Press evenly into pan. Bake in preheated oven for 15 minutes or until lightly browned. Place pan on a rack to cool slightly.

2. **Topping:** In a saucepan over low heat, stir together sugar and syrup until dissolved. Increase heat and bring to boil. Remove from heat. Add peanut butter and butterscotch chips, stirring until chips are melted and mixture is smooth. Stir in corn flakes until blended. Spread evenly over baked base. Place pan on a rack to cool completely, then cut into squares.

MAKES 16 SQUARES

Chocolate Chip Peanut Butter Squares

1 cup	all-purpose flour	250 mL
1 tsp	baking powder	5 mL
1/4 tsp	salt	1 mL
1/2 cup	smooth peanut butter	125 mL
1/3 cup	butter or margarine, softened	75 mL
1/2 cup	packed brown sugar	125 mL
1/2 cup	granulated sugar	125 mL
2	eggs	2
1 tsp	vanilla extract	5 mL
1 cup	semi-sweet chocolate chips	250 mL

Peanut Butter Frosting (optional)

1 tbsp	butter or margarine, softened	15 mL
3 tbsp	smooth peanut butter	45 mL
1/2 tsp	vanilla extract	2 mL
2 cups	confectioner's (icing) sugar, sifted	500 mL
1 to 2 tbsp	half-and-half (10%) cream	15 to 25 mL

Preheat oven to 350° F (180° C)
8-inch (2 L) square cake pan, lightly greased

1. In a bowl mix together flour, baking powder and salt.

2. In another bowl, beat peanut butter, butter and sugars until smooth and creamy. Beat in eggs until incorporated. Stir in vanilla. Gradually blend in flour mixture. Stir in chocolate chips. Spread evenly in prepared pan. Bake in preheated oven for 30 to 35 minutes until golden brown. Place pan on a rack to cool completely.

3. **Frosting (optional):** In a medium bowl, beat butter and peanut butter until smooth. Beat in vanilla. Gradually add confectioner's sugar, beating until smooth. Slowly add just enough cream to make the frosting spreadable. Spread over cake, then cut into squares.

TIP Allow cakes to cool completely before frosting, then cut into squares.

Next time you buy cooking oil, don't pull off the silver seal. Instead, cut a small slit in it. It makes it much easier to pour without spilling.

Makes 16 squares

Chunky-Style Peanut Squares

1 1/4 cups	packed brown sugar, divided	300 mL
1 cup	all-purpose flour	250 mL
2 tsp	baking powder	10 mL
1/2 tsp	salt	2 mL
1/3 cup	crunchy peanut butter	75 mL
1/2 cup	milk	125 mL
2 tbsp	vegetable oil	25 mL
1 tsp	vanilla extract	5 mL
1 1/2 cups	hot water	375 mL

Preheat oven to 350° F (180° C)
8-inch (2 L) square cake pan, greased

1. In a bowl mix together 3/4 cup (175 mL) of the brown sugar, flour, baking powder and salt. Make a well in the center. Add peanut butter, milk, oil and vanilla and mix just until incorporated. Spread evenly in prepared pan. Sprinkle remaining brown sugar over top and slowly pour hot water over all. Bake in preheated oven for 45 minutes or until golden brown. Place pan on a rack to cool slightly, then cut into squares. Serve warm.

Makes 36 bars

Peanut Butter Chip Bars

	Base	
1 1/3 cups	graham wafer crumbs (about 18 wafers)	325 mL
1 1/4 cups	all-purpose flour	300 mL
1/2 cup	granulated sugar	125 mL
1 cup	butter or margarine, melted	250 mL

	Topping	
3/4 cup	unsweetened cocoa powder	175 mL
1 1/4 cups	sweetened condensed milk	300 mL
10 oz	peanut butter chips (1 package)	300 g
1 cup	flaked coconut	250 mL
3/4 cup	chopped peanuts, divided	175 mL

Preheat oven to 350° F (180° C)
13- by 9-inch (3.5 L) cake pan, ungreased

1. **Base:** In a bowl combine crumbs, flour and sugar. Add butter and mix well. Press evenly into prepared pan. Bake in preheated oven for 15 to 20 minutes or until golden brown. Place pan on a rack.

2. **Topping:** In a bowl sift cocoa. Gradually stir in condensed milk until blended. Add peanut butter chips, coconut and 1/2 cup (125 mL) of the peanuts and mix well. Spread evenly over hot base. Sprinkle remaining peanuts over top. Bake 20 to 25 minutes longer or until topping is set. Place pan on a rack to cool completely, then cut into bars.

TIP Most bars, squares and brownies should be cooled completely before cutting. But when the filling is sticky, you should run a knife around the edge of the pan as soon as you remove it from the oven.

Cinnamon Applesauce Squares (Page 72) ➤

MAKES 16 SQUARES

Peanut Butter Chews

Base		
1/2 cup	butter or margarine, softened	125 mL
1/2 cup	packed brown sugar	125 mL
1 cup	all-purpose flour	250 mL

Filling		
1/2 cup	semi-sweet chocolate pieces	125 mL

Topping		
1 cup	smooth peanut butter	250 mL
5 cups	miniature marshmallows	1.25 L
1/2 cup	packed brown sugar	125 mL
1/4 cup	table (18%) cream	50 mL
1/4 cup	halved maraschino cherries	50 mL
4 cups	dry chow mein noodles	1 L

Preheat oven to 350° F (180° C)
9-inch (2.5 L) square cake pan, greased

1. **Base:** In a bowl, beat butter and brown sugar until smooth and creamy. Blend in flour. Press evenly into prepared pan. Bake in preheated oven for 15 to 20 minutes or until golden brown. Place pan on a rack.

2. **Filling:** Sprinkle chocolate pieces evenly over hot base.

3. **Topping:** In the top of a double boiler, over low heat, melt peanut butter and marshmallows. Add brown sugar and cream, stirring constantly until melted and blended. Remove top of double boiler from heat. Stir in cherries and noodles. Spread evenly over chocolate layer. Place pan on a rack to cool completely, then cut into squares.

MAKES 24 BARS

Honey Double-Peanut Bars

Base		
2 cups	packaged biscuit mix	500 mL
2 tbsp	granulated sugar	25 mL
2/3 cup	milk	150 mL
1	egg, lightly beaten	1
1/4 cup	smooth peanut butter	50 mL
1/4 cup	liquid honey	50 mL

Topping		
1/2 cup	packaged biscuit mix	125 mL
1/2 cup	packed brown sugar	125 mL
1/2 tsp	ground cinnamon	2 mL
2 tbsp	butter or margarine, softened	25 mL
2 tbsp	smooth peanut butter	25 mL
1/4 cup	chopped peanuts	50 mL

Preheat oven to 400° F (200° C)
9-inch (2.5 L) square cake pan, greased

1. **Base:** In a bowl mix together biscuit mix, sugar, milk and egg. Add peanut butter and honey and mix just until blended. (Mixture will not be smooth.) Spread evenly in prepared pan. Set aside.

2. **Topping:** In another bowl, mix together biscuit mix, brown sugar and cinnamon. Stir in butter and peanut butter until mixture resembles coarse crumbs. Stir in peanuts. Sprinkle evenly over top of batter. Bake in preheated oven for 20 to 25 minutes or until a tester inserted in the center comes out clean. Place pan on a rack to cool completely, then cut into bars.

◄ RHUBARB CRISP SQUARES (PAGE 98)

Makes 36 bars

Peanut Butter 'n' Jelly Bars

Preheat oven to 350° F (180° C)
13- by 9-inch (3.5 L) cake pan, greased

Base		
2 cups	all-purpose flour	500 mL
1 tbsp	baking powder	15 mL
1 tsp	salt	5 mL
1 1/2 cups	granulated sugar	375 mL
1/3 cup	shortening, softened	75 mL
2	eggs	2
1/3 cup	peanut butter	75 mL
1 cup	milk	250 mL

Topping		
1 cup	redcurrant jelly	250 mL
1	container (15 oz [450 g]) vanilla ready-to-serve frosting or Vanilla Frosting (see recipe, page 183)	1
1/2 cup	chopped peanuts	125 mL

1. **Base:** In a bowl mix together flour, baking powder and salt.

2. In another bowl, beat sugar and shortening until smooth and creamy. Add eggs and beat until incorporated. Beat in peanut butter. Gradually blend in flour mixture, alternately with milk, just until incorporated. Spread evenly in prepared pan. Bake in preheated oven for 45 to 50 minutes, until a tester inserted into center comes out clean. Place pan on a rack to cool.

3. **Topping:** Stir jelly until smooth and spread evenly over top of cake. When cake has cooled completely, frost. Sprinkle chopped peanuts over top and cut into bars.

Makes 16 squares

Shortbread Peanut Butter Favorites

Preheat oven to 350° F (180° C)
9-inch (2.5 L) square cake pan, lightly greased

2 cups	cake flour, sifted	500 mL
1/2 tsp	baking powder	2 mL
Pinch	salt	Pinch
1/2 cup	crunchy peanut butter	125 mL
3/4 cup	confectioner's (icing) sugar, sifted	175 mL
3/4 cup	unsalted butter, softened	175 mL
1	egg	1
1/2 tsp	vanilla extract	2 mL
1/2 cup	coarsely chopped salted peanuts	125 mL

1. In a bowl mix together flour, baking powder and salt.

2. In another bowl, beat peanut butter, confectioner's sugar and butter until blended. Beat in egg until incorporated. Stir in vanilla. Gradually blend in flour mixture. Spread evenly in prepared pan. Press peanuts into the surface of the batter. Bake in preheated oven for 25 to 30 minutes or until a tester inserted in the center comes out clean. Place pan on a rack to cool completely, then cut into squares.

Buttermilk Nut Squares

Base		
1 cup	all-purpose flour	250 mL
1/2 tsp	baking powder	2 mL
1/2 tsp	ground cinnamon	2 mL
1/4 tsp	baking soda	1 mL
1/3 cup	butter or margarine, softened	75 mL
1/2 cup	granulated sugar	125 mL
1/4 cup	packed brown sugar	50 mL
1	egg	1
1/2 cup	buttermilk	125 mL

Topping		
1/4 cup	packed brown sugar	50 mL
1/4 cup	finely chopped pecans	50 mL
1/4 tsp	ground cinnamon	1 mL
Pinch	ground nutmeg	Pinch

TIP To prevent freshly-baked brownies, bars or squares from sticking to a serving plate, sprinkle a thin layer of sugar evenly over the plate before adding the cake

Preheat oven to 350° F (180° C)
8-inch (2 L) square cake pan, greased

1. **Base:** In a bowl mix together flour, baking powder, cinnamon and baking soda.

2. In another bowl, beat butter and sugars until smooth and creamy. Beat in egg until incorporated. Blend in flour mixture alternately with the buttermilk, just until incorporated. Spread evenly in prepared pan.

3. **Topping:** In a bowl mix together brown sugar, pecans, cinnamon and nutmeg. Sprinkle evenly over base. Bake in preheated oven for 40 to 45 minutes or until a tester inserted in the center comes out clean. Place pan on a rack to cool completely, then cut into squares.

Chocolate Chip Granola Bars

3 cups	old-fashioned rolled oats	750 mL
1 cup	raisins	250 mL
1 cup	sunflower seeds	250 mL
1 cup	chopped peanuts	250 mL
1 cup	semi-sweet chocolate chips	250 mL
1	can (14 oz [398 mL]) sweetened condensed milk	1
1/2 cup	butter or margarine, melted	125 mL

Preheat oven to 325° F (160° C)
13- by 9-inch (3.5 L) cake pan, lined with greased foil

1. In a bowl mix together oats, raisins, sunflower seeds, peanuts and chocolate chips. Add condensed milk and mix thoroughly. Stir in melted butter until blended. Spread evenly in prepared pan. Bake in preheated oven for 25 to 30 minutes or until top is lightly browned. Place pan on a rack to cool slightly, then transfer cake, with foil, to a cutting board and cut into bars.

es Bars Square

Bars Squares

Specialty Bars and Squares

Blueberry Graham Cheesecake Bars

Base		
1 1/4 cups	graham wafer crumbs (about 16 wafers)	300 mL
1/2 cup	butter or margarine, softened	125 mL
1/4 cup	granulated sugar	50 mL

Filling		
8 oz	cream cheese, softened	250 g
1/2 cup	granulated sugar	125 mL
2	eggs	2
1 tsp	vanilla extract	5 mL
	Ground cinnamon	

Topping		
2 tbsp	cornstarch	25 mL
1/2 cup	granulated sugar	125 mL
1	can (19 oz [540 mL]) blueberry pie filling	1
2 tbsp	lemon juice	25 mL

Preheat oven to 300° F (150° C)
9-inch (2.5 L) square cake pan, ungreased

1. **Base:** In a bowl mix together crumbs, butter and sugar. Press evenly into prepared pan. Set aside.

2. **Filling:** In another bowl, beat cream cheese and sugar until smooth. Beat in eggs and vanilla until blended. Spread evenly over base. Bake in preheated oven for 30 minutes. Sprinkle cinnamon over top and place pan on a rack to cool.

3. **Topping:** In a bowl mix together blueberry pie filling and lemon juice. Spread over warm cake. Chill thoroughly, then cut into bars.

Coffee Lover's Bars

MAKES 24 BARS

2 tsp	instant coffee powder	10 mL
2 tbsp	boiling water	25 mL
1/2 cup	all-purpose flour	125 mL
1/2 cup	unsweetened cocoa powder, sifted	125 mL
1/2 cup	butter or margarine, softened	125 mL
1 cup	granulated sugar	250 mL
2	eggs	2
1 tsp	vanilla extract	5 mL

Frosting		
2 tbsp	butter or margarine, softened	25 mL
4 oz	cream cheese, softened	125 g
2 tsp	instant coffee powder	10 mL
1 tsp	vanilla extract	5 mL
1 1/2 cups	confectioner's (icing) sugar, sifted	375 mL
	Unsweetened cocoa powder	

Preheat oven to 350° F (180° C)
9-inch (2.5 L) square cake pan, greased

1. In a cup mix instant coffee with boiling water until dissolved. Set aside.

2. In a bowl mix together flour and cocoa.

3. In another bowl, beat butter and sugar, until smooth and creamy. Beat in eggs and vanilla just until blended. Blend in flour mixture. Spread evenly in prepared pan. Bake in preheated oven for 20 to 25 minutes or until tester inserted in center comes out clean. Place pan on a rack to cool completely.

4. **Frosting:** In a bowl, beat butter, cream cheese, instant coffee and vanilla until smooth and blended. Gradually add confectioner's sugar, beating until frosting is smooth and spreadable. Spread evenly over cake. Sift cocoa lightly over top, then cut into bars.

Cola Honey Cake Bars

MAKES 36 BARS

4 cups	all-purpose flour	1 L
2 tsp	baking powder	10 mL
1 tsp	ground cinnamon	5 mL
1/2 tsp	baking soda	2 mL
1/2 tsp	ground cloves, nutmeg or allspice	2 mL
4	eggs	4
1 cup	granulated sugar	250 mL
1/2 cup	vegetable oil	125 mL
1 1/2 cups	liquid honey	375 mL
1 cup	cola	250 mL
1/2 cup	raisins (optional)	125 mL

Preheat oven to 325° F (160° C)
13- by 9-inch (3.5 L) cake pan, greased

1. In a bowl mix together flour, baking powder, cinnamon, baking soda and cloves.

2. In a bowl, beat eggs, sugar, oil and honey until smooth and blended. Gradually blend in flour mixture, alternately with cola, just until incorporated. Stir in raisins, if using. Spread evenly in prepared pan. Bake in preheated oven for 50 to 60 minutes or until tester inserted in center comes out clean. Place pan on a rack to cool completely, then cut into bars.

TIP To keep honey or molasses from sticking to a measuring cup, grease the cup first — or, if the recipe calls for oil, measure that before measuring the sticky ingredient.

Lebkuchen (Honey Cake Bars)

Preheat oven to 350° F (180° C)
Two 9-inch (2.5 L) square cake pans, greased

2 cups	all-purpose flour	500 mL
1 1/2 tsp	ground cinnamon	7 mL
1/2 tsp	baking soda	2 mL
1/2 tsp	ground ginger	2 mL
1/2 tsp	ground nutmeg	2 mL
1/4 tsp	salt	1 mL
1/4 tsp	ground cloves	1 mL
1/2 cup	raisins	125 mL
1/2 cup	chopped blanched almonds	125 mL
1 cup	liquid honey	250 mL
3/4 cup	packed brown sugar	175 mL
1	egg	1
3 tbsp	lemon juice, divided	45 mL
1 tsp	grated lemon zest	5 mL
1 cup	confectioner's (icing) sugar, sifted	250 mL
	Candied red cherries, halved	

TIP If you prefer, substitute 1 tbsp (15 mL) pumpkin pie spice for the cinnamon, ginger, nutmeg and cloves.

1. In a bowl mix together flour, cinnamon, baking soda, ginger, nutmeg, salt and cloves. Stir in raisins and almonds.

2. In a saucepan over medium heat, bring honey and brown sugar to a boil, stirring constantly, until sugar dissolves. Allow to cool, then beat in egg, 1 tbsp (15 mL) lemon juice and the lemon zest. Blend in flour mixture. Chill overnight.

3. Divide dough in half and spread evenly in prepared pans. Bake in preheated oven for 30 minutes or until firm. Place pans on racks, score into bars and press a cherry half, cut side down, in the center of each bar.

4. Meanwhile in a bowl, beat confectioner's sugar with remaining 2 tbsp (25 mL) of lemon juice until smooth and blended. Drizzle glaze over top of cake. Cool completely, then cut into bars.

Dainty Petit-Four Bars

MAKES 36 BARS

2 cups	cake flour	500 mL
1 tbsp	baking powder	15 mL
1/4 tsp	salt	1 mL
1/4 cup	shortening, softened	50 mL
1/4 cup	butter or margarine, softened	50 mL
1 1/4 cups	granulated sugar, divided	300 mL
1/2 tsp	vanilla extract	2 mL
1/4 tsp	almond extract	1 mL
3/4 cup	milk	175 mL
6	egg whites	6

Frosting		
1 1/2 cups	hot water	375 mL
3 cups	granulated sugar	750 mL
1/4 tsp	cream of tartar	1 mL
1 tsp	vanilla extract	5 mL
2 1/4 cups	confectioner's (icing) sugar, sifted	550 mL

TIP For a special touch, tint the frosting with food coloring and place a nut or candy decoration on top of each bar.

Don't waste milk that is just about to pass its "best before" date. Pour the milk into an ice-cube tray and freeze. These cubes can be added to hot liquids such as coffee or hot chocolate.

Preheat oven to 350° F (180° C)
13- by 9-inch (3.5 L) cake pan, lightly greased

1. In a bowl sift together flour, baking powder and salt.

2. In another bowl, beat shortening, butter and 1 cup (250 mL) of the sugar until smooth and creamy. Beat in vanilla and almond extracts. Blend in flour mixture, alternately with milk, just until incorporated.

3. In a clean bowl, beat egg whites until foamy. Gradually add remaining sugar beating until stiff peaks form. Fold into batter. Bake in preheated oven for 35 to 40 minutes or until a tester inserted in center comes out clean. Place pan on a rack to cool for 5 minutes, then remove cake and cool completely on rack.

4. **Frosting:** In a saucepan over low heat, stir together water, sugar and cream of tartar until mixture resembles a thin syrup. Cool until lukewarm, then beat in vanilla and confectioner's sugar until smooth and spreadable. Cut cake into bars or diamond shapes. Spoon frosting over cakes.

Powdered Poppyseed Squares

MAKES 16 SQUARES

1 cup	poppyseeds	250 mL
1 cup	milk	250 mL
2 cups	all-purpose flour	500 mL
2 tsp	baking powder	10 mL
1/2 tsp	salt	2 mL
1/2 cup	butter, softened	125 mL
1 cup	granulated sugar	250 mL
2	eggs, separated	2
1/2 tsp	almond extract	2 mL
	Confectioner's (icing) sugar	

Preheat oven to 350° F (180° C)
8-inch (2 L) square cake pan, greased

1. In a bowl combine poppyseeds and milk. Let stand for 1 hour.

2. In another bowl, mix together flour, baking powder and salt.

3. In a separate bowl, beat butter and sugar until smooth and creamy. Beat in egg yolks until incorporated. Stir in almond extract. Gradually blend in flour mixture alternately with poppyseed mixture, just until incorporated.

4. In a clean bowl, beat egg whites until soft peaks form. Fold into batter. Spread evenly in prepared pan. Bake in preheated oven for 40 to 45 minutes or until a tester inserted in the center comes out clean. Place pan on a rack to cool completely, then sift confectioner's sugar over top. Cut into squares.

Raisin-Spice Hermit Bars

MAKES 36 BARS

2 cups	all-purpose flour	500 mL
2/3 cup	packed brown sugar	150 mL
2 tsp	ground cinnamon	10 mL
1 1/2 tsp	ground ginger	7 mL
1/2 tsp	baking soda	2 mL
1/2 tsp	salt	2 mL
6 tbsp	butter or margarine, melted	90 mL
2	eggs	2
2/3 cup	fancy molasses	150 mL
2 tsp	vanilla extract	10 mL
3/4 cup	dark seedless raisins	175 mL

Preheat oven to 375° F (190° C)
13- by 9-inch (3.5 L) cake pan, lined with greased foil

1. In a bowl mix together flour, brown sugar, cinnamon, ginger, baking soda and salt.

2. In another bowl, beat butter, eggs, molasses and vanilla until blended. Blend in flour mixture. Stir in raisins. Spread evenly in prepared pan. Bake in preheated oven for 20 to 25 minutes or until edges are golden brown. Place pan on a rack to cool completely. Transfer cake, with foil, to a cutting board and cut into bars.

TIP To plump raisins, soak them in orange juice and store in refrigerator.

Rice Pudding Bars

MAKES 24 BARS

2	eggs	2
1/3 cup	packed brown sugar	75 mL
1/2 tsp	ground cinnamon	2 mL
1/2 tsp	vanilla extract	2 mL
1 cup	milk	250 mL
1 cup	cooked rice	250 mL
1/4 cup	raisins	50 mL

Preheat oven to 325° F (160° C)
9-inch (2.5 L) square cake pan, greased

1. In a bowl, beat eggs, brown sugar, cinnamon, vanilla and milk until well blended. Stir in rice and raisins. Spread evenly in prepared pan.

2. Bake in preheated oven for 40 to 45 minutes or until firm. Place pan on a rack and cut into bars. Serve warm or cool.

Strawberry Cheesecake Bars

MAKES 36 BARS

Base		
3/4 cup	butter or margarine, softened	175 mL
1/3 cup	light corn syrup	75 mL
1/4 cup	granulated sugar	50 mL
2 cups	all-purpose flour	500 mL
1/2 tsp	salt	2 mL

Topping		
1 lb	cream cheese, softened	500 g
3	eggs	3
2 tsp	vanilla extract	10 mL
1 cup	light corn syrup	250 mL
3/4 cup	strawberry jam	175 mL

Preheat oven to 375° F (190° C)
13- by 9-inch (3.5 L) cake pan, greased

1. **Base:** In a bowl, beat butter, corn syrup and sugar until smooth. Blend in flour and salt until a dough forms. Press evenly into prepared pan.

2. **Topping:** In another bowl, beat cream cheese, eggs and vanilla until smooth and creamy. Beat in corn syrup. Spread evenly over dough. Bake in preheated oven for 35 to 40 minutes or until lightly browned and topping is set. Place pan on a rack.

3. Stir jam until smooth. Spread evenly over hot topping. Cool for 30 minutes then chill 3 hours, or overnight, before cutting into bars. Store, covered, in the refrigerator.

MAKES 16 SQUARES

Trail Mix Squares

1 cup	all-purpose flour	250 mL
1 tsp	baking powder	5 mL
3/4 cup	packed brown sugar	175 mL
1/2 cup	butter or margarine, softened	125 mL
2	eggs	2
1 tsp	vanilla extract	5 mL
1/2 cup	trail mix, chopped	125 mL
1/2 cup	semi-sweet chocolate chips	125 mL

Preheat oven to 325°F (160° C)
8-inch (2 L) square cake pan, greased

1. In a bowl mix together flour and baking powder.

2. In another bowl, beat brown sugar and butter until smooth and creamy. Beat in eggs until incorporated. Stir in vanilla. Blend in flour mixture. Stir in trail mix and chocolate chips. Spread evenly in prepared pan. Bake in preheated oven for 30 to 35 minutes or until a tester inserted in the center comes out clean. Place pan on a rack to cool completely, then cut into squares.

MAKES 24 SQUARES

Orange-Nut Dessert Layers

	Base	
1 1/2 cups	all-purpose flour	375 mL
1/2 cup	packed brown sugar	125 mL
1/4 tsp	salt	1 mL
1 tbsp	grated orange zest	15 mL
1/2 cup	butter *or* margarine	125 mL

	Filling	
1 cup	semi-sweet chocolate chips	250 mL

	Topping	
1/4 cup	all-purpose flour	50 mL
1/2 tsp	baking powder	2 mL
1/4 tsp	salt	1 mL
2	eggs, beaten	2
1 cup	packed brown sugar	250 mL
1 tsp	vanilla extract	5 mL
1 1/2 cups	chopped walnuts	375 mL

Preheat oven to 375° F (190° C)
13- by 9-inch (3.5 L) cake pan, ungreased

1. **Base:** In a bowl mix together flour, brown sugar, salt and orange zest. Using 2 knives, a pastry blender or your fingers, cut butter in until mixture resembles coarse crumbs. Press evenly into pan. Bake in preheated oven for 10 minutes. Place pan on a rack.

2. **Filling:** Sprinkle chocolate over hot base. Let stand for about 2 minutes or until chocolate softens. Using a knife, spread evenly over base.

3. **Topping:** In a bowl mix together flour, baking powder and salt. In another bowl, beat eggs, brown sugar and vanilla until blended. Blend in flour mixture. Stir in walnuts. Spread mixture evenly over chocolate. Bake 20 minutes longer or until top is firm and golden brown. Place pan on a rack to cool completely, then cut into squares.

MAKES 28 DIAMONDS

Greek Baklava Diamonds

Preheat oven to 350° F (180° C)
13- by 9-inch (3.5 L) cake pan, ungreased

Base		
3 1/2 cups	finely chopped walnuts	825 mL
1/2 cup	granulated sugar	125 mL
1 tsp	ground cinnamon	5 mL
2	packages (each 8 oz [250 g]) refrigerated crescent rolls	2

Glaze		
2 tbsp	butter *or* margarine	25 mL
1/4 cup	granulated sugar	50 mL
2 tbsp	lemon juice	25 mL
1/2 cup	liquid honey	125 mL

1. **Base:** In a bowl mix together nuts, sugar and cinnamon.

2. On a work surface, separate each package of dough into 2 long rectangles. Line bottom of pan with half, spreading 1/2 inch (1 cm) up the sides. Spread evenly with nut mixture. Place remaining dough on top, pressing down. Using the dough edges and the perforations in the dough as guidelines, take a sharp knife and score the dough 5 times lengthwise and 7 times diagonally to make diamond-shaped pieces.

3. **Glaze:** In a saucepan over medium-high heat, combine butter, sugar, lemon juice and honey. Bring to a boil. Remove from heat and spoon half evenly over top of the dough. Bake in preheated oven for 25 to 30 minutes or until golden brown. Spoon the remaining glaze over hot pastry. Place pan on a rack to cool completely, then cut into diamonds.

MAKES 30 SQUARES

Rainbow Gelatin Squares

13- by 9-inch (3.5 L) cake pan, greased

Clear Layers		
4	pkgs (4 servings each) gelatin dessert mix, assorted flavors	4
3 cups	boiling water, divided	750 mL
3 cups	cold water, divided	750 mL

Creamy Layers		
3	pkgs (4 servings each) gelatin dessert mix, assorted flavors	3
2 1/4 cups	boiling water, divided	300 mL
3/4 cup	cold water, divided	175 mL
1 1/2 cups	evaporated milk, divided	375 mL
4 cups	frozen whipped topping, thawed	1 L
	Sliced fresh strawberries (optional)	

1. **Clear layers:** In a bowl combine gelatin dessert mix with 3/4 cup (175 mL) boiling water, stirring until completely dissolved. Add 3/4 cup (175 mL) cold water and mix thoroughly. Pour into prepared baking pan and refrigerate for 35 to 40 minutes or until almost set.

2. **Creamy layers:** In another bowl, combine gelatin dessert mix with 3/4 cup (175 mL) boiling water, stirring until completely dissolved. Add 1/4 cup (50 mL) cold water and 1/2 cup (125 mL) evaporated milk; mix thoroughly. Spoon over chilled clear layer and refrigerate until almost set.

3. Repeat clear and creamy layers, making 7 in all, chilling each layer before adding another. (See photo opposite page 160 for color ideas.)

4. When all layers are completed and gelatin is set, cut into squares. Decorate squares with topping and garnish with sliced strawberries, if using.

MAKES 36 BARS

Butterscotch Pudding Bars

Preheat oven to 350° F (180° C)
13- by 9-inch (3.5 L) cake pan, ungreased

Base		
1 cup	all-purpose flour	250 mL
1/2 cup	chopped pecans	125 mL
1/2 cup	butter	125 mL

Filling		
1 cup	confectioner's (icing) sugar, sifted	250 mL
8 oz	cream cheese, softened	250 g
3 cups	frozen whipped topping, thawed, divided	750 mL

Topping		
2	pkg (4-serving size) butterscotch instant pudding mix	2
3 1/2 cups	milk	825 mL
1/4 cup	chopped pecans	50 mL

1. **Base:** In a bowl mix together flour and pecans. Using 2 knives, a pastry blender or your fingers, cut butter in until mixture resembles coarse crumbs. Press evenly into pan. Bake in preheated oven for 15 to 20 minutes or until lightly browned. Place pan on a rack to cool.

2. **Filling:** In a bowl, beat sugar and cream cheese until smooth. Fold in 1 cup (250 mL) of the whipped topping and spread evenly over baked base.

3. **Topping:** In another bowl, beat pudding mix and milk until blended and smooth. Spoon over filling. Chill for 15 to 20 minutes until set. Top with remaining whipped topping and pecans. Chill for 2 hours. Cut into bars.

TIP Plastic wrap will cling better to the rim of a bowl or pan if you moisten the rim with a few drops of water.

MAKES 24 SQUARES

Chocolate-Peanut Butter Coconut Gems

Preheat oven to 325° F (160° C)
13- by 9-inch (3.5 L) cake pan, ungreased

Base		
1 1/2 cups	graham wafer crumbs	375 mL
1/2 cup	butter or margarine, melted	125 mL

Filling		
1 1/3 cups	flaked coconut	325 mL
1	can (10 oz [300 mL]) sweetened condensed milk	1

Topping		
1/2 cup	smooth peanut butter	125 mL
1 1/2 cups	semi-sweet chocolate chips	375 mL

1. **Base:** In a bowl mix together crumbs and melted butter. Press evenly into pan.

2. **Filling:** Sprinkle coconut evenly over base. Pour condensed milk evenly over coconut. Bake in preheated oven for 20 to 25 minutes or until lightly browned.

3. **Topping:** In a saucepan over low heat, melt peanut butter and chocolate chips, stirring until smooth. Spread evenly over filling. Place pan on a rack to cool for 30 minutes, then chill thoroughly. Cut into squares.

TIP To prevent cakes from becoming soggy, always cool cakes in their pans, on a wire rack, so the bottom of the pan will be cooled by circulating air.

MAKES 36 BARS

Frosted Chocolate Nut Bars

2 cups	all-purpose flour	500 mL
1/2 tsp	salt	2 mL
2 cups	granulated sugar	500 mL
1 cup	butter or margarine, softened	250 mL
4	eggs	4
1 tbsp	vanilla extract	15 mL
2 cups	chopped walnuts	500 mL
2	squares (each 1 oz [28 g]) unsweetened chocolate, melted	2

Frosting		
1 cup	milk	250 mL
5 tbsp	all-purpose flour	75 mL
1 cup	confectioner's (icing) sugar, sifted	250 mL
1 cup	butter or margarine, softened	250 mL
2 tsp	vanilla extract	10 mL

Preheat oven to 350° F (180° C)
13- by 9-inch (3.5 L) cake pan, greased

1. In a bowl mix together flour and salt.

2. In another bowl, beat sugar and butter until smooth and creamy. Beat in eggs until incorporated. Stir in vanilla. Blend in flour mixture. Stir in nuts.

3. Set aside half the batter and spread remainder evenly in prepared pan. Blend melted chocolate into reserved batter. Spread carefully over the batter in the pan. Bake in preheated oven for 30 to 35 minutes or until a tester inserted in the center comes out clean. Place pan on a rack to cool completely.

4. **Frosting:** In a saucepan whisk milk and flour until smooth. Cook, stirring constantly, over medium heat, until thickened (about 10 minutes). Remove from heat and set aside.

5. In another bowl, beat sugar, butter and vanilla until smooth and blended. Gradually add milk mixture, beating until smooth and spreadable. Spread frosting over top of cake. Cut into bars.

Krispie Toffee Triangles

Preheat oven to 350° F (180° C)
8-inch (2 L) square cake pan, greased

Base		
1/2 cup	all-purpose flour	125 mL
1/4 tsp	baking soda	1 mL
Pinch	salt	Pinch
1/3 cup	butter or margarine, melted	75 mL
1/3 cup	packed brown sugar	75 mL
3/4 cup	crisp rice cereal	175 mL

Filling		
1/2 cup	butter *or* margarine	125 mL
1 1/4 cups	sweetened condensed milk	300 mL
1/2 cup	packed brown sugar	125 mL

Topping		
1/2 cup	semi-sweet chocolate chips	125 mL
1 1/4 cups	crisp rice cereal	300 mL

TIP After placing batter in your baking pan, bang the pan on the counter 2 or 3 times. This will get rid of any large air pockets which will create holes in the cake.

1. **Base:** In a bowl mix together flour, baking soda and salt. Make a well in the center. Add melted butter, brown sugar and rice cereal and mix until blended. Press evenly into prepared pan. Bake in preheated oven for 10 to 12 minutes or until lightly browned. Place pan on a rack.

2. **Filling:** In a saucepan over low heat, stir together butter, condensed milk and brown sugar until sugar is dissolved. Increase heat and bring to a boil, stirring constantly; boil for 5 minutes. Spoon evenly over baked base.

3. **Third layer:** In another saucepan over low heat, melt chocolate chips. Stir in cereal and mix until well coated. Spread evenly over filling. Chill for at least 3 hours, then cut into 16 squares. Cut each square in half diagonally to form 2 triangles.

MAKES 24 BARS

Glazed Boston Cream Bars

Preheat oven to 350° F (180° C)
9-inch (2.5 L) square cake pan, lightly greased

Cake		
1 1/3 cups	all-purpose flour	325 mL
1 1/2 tsp	baking powder	7 mL
1/4 tsp	salt	1 mL
3	egg whites	3
1/2 cup	granulated sugar, divided	125 mL
1/4 cup	butter or margarine, softened	50 mL
2 tsp	vanilla extract	10 mL
2/3 cup	skim milk	150 mL

Filling		
1 1/2 cups	skim milk	375 mL
1	pkg (4-serving size) vanilla instant pudding mix	1

Chocolate Glaze		
3 tbsp	granulated sugar	45 mL
2 tbsp	unsweetened cocoa powder, sifted	25 mL
1 1/4 tsp	cornstarch	6 mL
1/3 cup	skim milk	75 mL
1/2 tsp	vanilla extract	2 mL

TIP To determine whether an egg is fresh, immerse it in a pan of cool, salted water. If it sinks, it is fresh. If it rises to the top, it has passed its peak and is best discarded.

1. **Cake:** In a bowl mix together flour, baking powder and salt.

2. In a clean bowl, beat egg whites until frothy. Gradually beat in 1/4 cup (50 mL) of the sugar, until stiff peaks form.

3. In a large bowl, beat remaining sugar and butter until smooth and creamy. Stir in vanilla. Gradually blend in flour mixture alternately with milk, just until incorporated. Stir in 1/3 of egg white mixture, until well blended, then fold in remainder. Spread evenly in prepared pan. Bake in preheated oven for 35 minutes or until a tester inserted in the center comes out clean. Place pan on a rack to cool for 10 minutes, then turn cake out onto rack to cool completely .

4. **Filling:** Prepare pudding according to the instructions on the package but use 1 1/2 cups (375 mL) of milk. Chill for 30 minutes or until thickened.

5. **Glaze:** In a saucepan combine sugar, cocoa, cornstarch and milk. Bring to a boil over medium heat and cook for 1 to 2 minutes, stirring constantly, until slightly thickened. Remove from heat and stir in vanilla. Cool in refrigerator for about 20 minutes.

6. Using a serrated knife, cut the cake in half horizontally and place the bottom piece, cut side up on a plate. Spoon filling evenly over top. Top with second layer, cut side down. Spoon glaze over top, allowing some to drip down the sides. Chill for 3 to 4 hours, until glaze hardens, then cut into bars.

MAKES ABOUT 24 BARS

Old-Fashioned Butter Tart Bars

Preheat oven to 350° F (180° C)
9-inch (2.5 L) square cake pan, ungreased

Base		
1 cup	all-purpose flour	250 mL
2 tbsp	granulated sugar	25 mL
1/2 cup	butter or margarine, softened	125 mL

Filling		
1 1/2 cups	packed brown sugar	375 mL
1 cup	chopped walnuts	250 mL
1/2 cup	raisins	125 mL
3	eggs, beaten	3
3 tbsp	all-purpose flour	45 mL
1/2 tsp	baking powder	2 mL
1 tsp	vanilla extract	5 mL

1. **Base:** In a bowl mix together flour and sugar. Using 2 knives, a pastry blender or your fingers, cut butter in until mixture resembles coarse crumbs. Press evenly into prepared pan. Bake in preheated oven for 15 to 18 minutes or until golden brown. Place pan on a rack.

2. **Filling:** In another bowl, combine brown sugar, walnuts and raisins. Add eggs, flour, baking powder and vanilla and beat until well blended. Spread evenly over hot base and bake 20 to 25 minutes longer or until golden brown. Place pan on a rack to cool completely. (The filling may seem a bit jiggly at first but will become firm when completely cooled.) Cut into bars.

MAKES 16 SQUARES

Buttermilk Spice Squares

Preheat oven to 350° F (180° C)
8-inch (2 L) square cake pan , greased

2 1/2 cups	cake flour, sifted	625 mL
2 tsp	baking powder	10 mL
2 tsp	ground cinnamon	10 mL
1/2 tsp	baking soda	2 mL
1/2 tsp	ground cloves	2 mL
1/4 tsp	ground allspice	1 mL
1/4 tsp	ground nutmeg	1 mL
1/4 tsp	ground mace	1 mL
1/2 cup	butter or shortening, softened	125 mL
1 cup	packed brown sugar	250 mL
2	eggs	2
1 cup	buttermilk	250 mL

1. In a bowl mix together flour, baking powder, cinnamon, baking soda, cloves, allspice, nutmeg and mace.

2. In another bowl, beat butter and sugar until smooth and creamy. Beat in eggs until incorporated. Gradually blend in flour mixture, alternately with buttermilk, just until incorporated. Spread evenly in prepared pan. Bake in preheated oven for 45 to 50 minutes or until a tester inserted in the center comes out clean. Place pan on a rack to cool completely, then cut into squares.

TIP If you don't have any buttermilk, here's an easy substitute: For each cup of buttermilk needed, just add 1 tbsp (15 mL) lemon juice to 1 cup (250 mL) regular milk and stir well.

Coffee-Bran Squares

Makes 16 squares

1/2 cup	whole bran cereal	125 mL
1 cup	cold, strong coffee	250 mL
1 cup	granulated sugar	250 mL
1 cup	whole wheat flour	250 mL
1/2 cup	all-purpose flour	125 mL
1 tsp	baking soda	5 mL
1 tsp	ground cinnamon	5 mL
1/2 tsp	salt	2 mL
1/2 tsp	ground nutmeg	2 mL
1/4 tsp	ground cloves	1 mL
1/4 cup	vegetable oil	50 mL
1 tsp	vanilla extract	5 mL
1 tbsp	vinegar	15 mL

Preheat oven to 350° F (180° C)
8-inch (2 L) square cake pan, lightly greased

1. In a bowl mix together cereal and coffee. Let stand for 2 minutes or until coffee is almost completely absorbed.

2. In another bowl, mix together sugar, flours, baking soda, cinnamon, salt, nutmeg and cloves.

3. In a large bowl, whisk together oil, vanilla and vinegar. Stir in cereal mixture until blended. Blend in flour mixture. Spread evenly in prepared pan. Bake in preheated oven for 35 to 40 minutes or until a tester inserted in center comes out clean. Place pan on a rack to cool completely, then cut into squares.

TIP For a quick dessert, take 1 can of refrigerated biscuit dough and separate the biscuits. Dip each biscuit in melted butter, then in a mixture of 1 tsp (5 mL) ground cinnamon and 3/4 cup (175 mL) granulated sugar. Place biscuits in a greased cake pan, sides touching, and bake in a preheated 450° F (230° C) oven for 10 minutes or until golden brown. Place pan on a rack to cool completely, then cut into squares.

MAKES 24 BARS

Cinnamon Raisin Bars

3 cups	raisins	750 mL
1 1/2 cups	all-purpose flour	375 mL
1 tsp	baking soda	5 mL
1 tsp	salt	5 mL
1 tsp	ground cinnamon	5 mL
1 tsp	ground nutmeg	5 mL
1 cup	packed brown sugar	250 mL
1/2 cup	butter or margarine, softened	125 mL
3	eggs	3

Preheat oven to 350° F (180°C)
9-inch (2.5 L) square cake pan, greased

1. In a saucepan over medium heat, add sufficient water to cover raisins. Bring to a boil and cook for 5 minutes. Remove from heat and strain cooking liquid into a 1 cup (250 mL) measure. Add water, if required, to make 1 cup (250 mL) of liquid. Set raisins and liquid aside.

2. In a bowl mix together flour, baking soda, salt, cinnamon and nutmeg.

3. In another bowl, beat brown sugar and butter until smooth and creamy. Beat in eggs until incorporated. Gradually blend in flour mixture, alternately with reserved raisin liquid, until just incorporated. Stir in reserved raisins. Spread evenly in prepared pan. Bake in preheated oven for 35 to 40 minutes or until a tester inserted in the center comes out clean. Place pan on a rack to cool completely, then cut into bars.

MAKES 16 SQUARES

Scottish Cottage Pudding Squares

1 3/4 cups	all-purpose flour	425 mL
2 1/2 tsp	baking powder	12 mL
1/2 tsp	salt	2 mL
1/4 cup	shortening, softened	50 mL
1 cup	granulated sugar	250 mL
1	egg	1
1/2 tsp	vanilla extract	2 mL
1/4 tsp	almond extract	1 mL
1 tbsp	grated orange zest	15 mL
2/3 cup	milk	150 mL

Orange Sauce (optional)		
6 tbsp	granulated sugar	90 mL
3 tbsp	all-purpose flour	45 mL
1/4 tsp	salt	1 mL
1 tbsp	grated orange zest	15 mL
1 cup	orange juice	250 mL
1 tbsp	lemon juice	15 mL

Preheat oven to 350° F (180° C)
8-inch (2 L) square cake pan, greased

1. In a bowl mix together flour, baking powder and salt.

2. In another bowl, beat shortening and sugar until smooth and creamy. Beat in egg until incorporated. Stir in vanilla, almond extract and orange zest. Blend in flour mixture alternately with milk, until just incorporated. Spread evenly in prepared pan. Bake in preheated oven for 30 to 35 minutes or until a tester inserted in the center comes out clean. Cut into squares immediately and serve while still hot (or cool slightly and serve warm), with orange sauce.

3. **Orange sauce (optional):** In a saucepan mix together sugar, flour, salt and zest. Gradually add orange juice and cook, stirring, over low heat for 5 minutes or until sauce thickens. Remove from heat and stir in lemon juice. Serve hot or cool slightly and spoon over squares.

MAKES 16 SQUARES

Dutch Crumb Squares

2 1/2 cups	cake flour, sifted	625 mL
1/2 tsp	baking soda	2 mL
1/2 tsp	salt	2 mL
1/2 cup	butter or margarine, softened	125 mL
3/4 cup	packed brown sugar	175 mL
1 cup	seedless raisins, ground in a food processor	250 mL
1	egg, beaten	1
3/4 cup	buttermilk	175 mL
2 tbsp	granulated sugar	25 mL
Pinch	ground cinnamon	Pinch

TIP When working with a sticky or fluffy batter, wet your spatula, or hands, before patting or spreading the batter in the pan.

Preheat oven to 350° F (180° C)
8-inch (2 L) square cake pan, greased

1. In a bowl mix together flour, baking soda and salt.

2. In a bowl, beat butter and brown sugar until smooth and creamy. Gradually blend in flour mixture. Set aside 3/4 cup (175 mL).

3. To remaining mixture add raisins, egg and buttermilk, beating until well blended. Spread evenly in prepared pan. Sprinkle reserved crumb mixture evenly over top. Sprinkle sugar and cinnamon over top of crumb mixture. Bake in preheated oven for 20 to 25 minutes or until a tester inserted in the center comes out clean. Place pan on a rack to cool completely, then cut into squares.

Honey Cake Spice Bars

MAKES 36 BARS

2 tbsp	packed brown sugar	25 mL
1/4 cup + 2 tsp	vegetable oil	50 mL + 10 mL
1/4 cup	water	50 mL
1/4 cup	liquid honey	50 mL
3/4 cup	frozen apple juice concentrate, thawed	175 mL
2	eggs	2
1/2 cup	ground almonds	125 mL
2 1/4 cups	all-purpose flour	550 mL
1 1/2 tsp	baking powder	7 mL
1 tsp	ground cinnamon	5 mL
1/2 tsp	ground ginger	2 mL
1/4 tsp	ground allspice	1 mL

TIP For a decorative touch, use a sharp knife to gently score center of each bar before baking and place a whole, blanched almond in each. Bake as directed.

Preheat oven to 375° F (190° C)
13- by 9-inch (3.5 L) cake pan, lightly greased

1. In a saucepan combine sugar, oil, water, honey and apple juice concentrate. Bring to a boil and remove from heat. Set aside to cool. Add eggs and mix to blend.

2. In a bowl mix together almonds, flour, baking powder, cinnamon, ginger and allspice. Make a well in the center. Add apple juice mixture and stir until blended. Shape dough into a ball, wrap tightly in plastic wrap and chill for 2 hours.

3. Press dough evenly into prepared pan. Bake in preheated oven for 25 to 30 minutes or until golden brown. Place pan on a rack to cool completely, then cut into bars.

Swing Shift Squares

MAKES 16 SQUARES

1	orange	1
1 cup	all-purpose flour	250 mL
1 1/2 tsp	baking powder	7 mL
1/2 tsp	salt	2 mL
2	eggs, beaten	2
1/2 cup	granulated sugar	125 mL
3 tbsp	butter or shortening, melted	45 mL
3/4 cup	chopped walnuts	175 mL
1 cup	raisins	250 mL

Preheat oven to 325° F (160° C.)
8-inch (2 L) square cake pan, greased

1. With a sharp knife, peel orange. Remove and discard the bitter white pith. In a food processor, process orange and peel finely. Set aside.

2. In a bowl mix together flour, baking powder and salt.

3. In another bowl, beat eggs, sugar and butter until smooth. Stir in reserved orange mixture. Blend in flour mixture. Stir in walnuts and raisins. Spread batter evenly in prepared pan. Bake in preheated oven for 30 minutes or until a tester inserted in the center comes out clean and dry. Place pan on a rack to cool slightly, then cut into squares.

Spicy Oatmeal Bars with Citrus Glaze

MAKES 36 BARS

1 3/4 cups	all-purpose flour	425 mL
1 1/2 tsp	baking soda	7 mL
3/4 tsp	ground cinnamon	4 mL
1/4 tsp	ground nutmeg	1 mL
1/4 tsp	ground cloves	1 mL
1/2 cup	butter or margarine, softened	125 mL
1 cup	packed brown sugar	250 mL
2	eggs	2
1 tsp	vanilla extract	5 mL
1 cup	unsweetened applesauce	250 mL
1 1/2 cups	quick-cooking rolled oats	375 mL
1 cup	raisins	250 mL
1/2 cup	chopped walnuts	125 mL
Citrus Glaze		
1/2 cup	confectioner's (icing) sugar, sifted	125 mL
2 tsp	water	10 mL
2 tsp	lemon juice	10 mL

Preheat oven to 375° F (190° C)
13- by 9-inch (3.5 L) cake pan, greased

1. In a bowl mix together flour, baking soda, cinnamon, nutmeg and cloves.

2. In another bowl, beat butter and brown sugar until smooth and creamy. Beat in eggs until incorporated. Stir in vanilla. Gradually blend in flour mixture alternately with applesauce until just incorporated. Stir in oats, raisins and walnuts. Spread evenly in prepared pan. Bake in preheated oven for 30 to 35 minutes or until a tester inserted in the center comes out clean. Place pan on a rack to cool.

3. **Glaze:** In a bowl, beat confectioner's sugar, water and juice until smooth and spreadable. Drizzle glaze over top of warm cake. Cool completely, then cut into bars.

MAKES 24 BARS

Orange-Raisin Bars

Preheat oven to 350° F (180° C)
9-inch (2.5 L) square cake pan, lightly greased

Base		
2 cups	all-purpose flour	500 mL
1 cup	granulated sugar	250 mL
1 tsp	baking powder	5 mL
1 cup	butter *or* margarine	250 mL
1	egg, beaten	1

Filling		
1 1/3 cups	raisins	325 mL
3/4 cup	granulated sugar	175 mL
2 tbsp	all-purpose flour	25 mL
1 cup	boiling water	250 mL
1/2 tsp	orange juice	2 mL
Pinch	salt	Pinch

TIP For a more pronounced orange flavor, increase amount of orange juice in filling to 1 tsp (5 mL).

1. **Base:** In a bowl mix together flour, baking powder and sugar. Using 2 knives, a pastry blender or your fingers, cut butter in until mixture resembles coarse crumbs. Mix in egg just until dough forms. Form dough into a ball then divide in half. Press one portion into prepared pan. Set other aside.

2. **Filling:** In a saucepan over low heat, stir together raisins, sugar, flour and boiling water until sugar is dissolved. Increase heat and bring to a boil. Reduce heat to simmer and cook, stirring constantly, for 5 to 8 minutes or until thickened. Remove from heat. Stir in orange juice and salt. Set aside to cool slightly.

3. Spread filling evenly over dough. On lightly floured work surface, press remaining dough to make a 9-inch (23 cm) square and place over the raisin filling. (Disregard any small holes in the dough.) Bake in preheated oven for 25 to 35 minutes or until lightly browned. Place pan on a rack to cool completely, then cut into bars.

MAKES 12 BARS

Peachy Topped Bars

Preheat oven to 400° F (200° C)
8-inch (2 L) square cake pan, greased

Base		
1 1/2 cups	all-purpose flour	375 mL
1/4 cup	granulated sugar	50 mL
2 tsp	baking powder	10 mL
1/2 tsp	salt	2 mL
1	egg	1
3 tbsp	butter or shortening, melted	45 mL
1/2 cup	milk	125 mL

Peach Topping		
1 1/2 cups	thinly sliced peaches	375 mL
2 tbsp	granulated sugar	25 mL
1/2 tsp	ground cinnamon	2 mL

1. **Base:** In a bowl mix together flour, sugar, baking powde and salt. Make a well in the center.

2. In another bowl, beat egg, butter and milk until blended. Add to flour mixture and mix until just incorporated. Spread evenly in prepared pan.

3. **Topping:** In a bowl mix together peaches, sugar and cinnamon. Spread evenly over batter. Cover pan with aluminum foil and bake in preheated oven for 10 minutes. Remove foil and bake 15 minutes longer or until golden brown. Place pan on a rack to cool, then cut into bars. Serve warm or cooled completely.

MAKES 12 BARS

Pink Lemonade Bars

Preheat oven to 325° F (160° C)
8-inch (2 L) square cake pan, ungreased

Base		
2 cups	vanilla wafer crumbs	500 mL
1/2 cup	butter or margarine, melted	125 mL

Topping		
3/4 cup	water	175 mL
Half	can (12 oz [355 mL]) frozen pink lemonade concentrate	Half
48	miniature marshmallows	48
1 cup	whipping (35%) cream	250 mL

1. **Base:** In a bowl mix together crumbs and butter. Set aside 1/2 cup (125 mL) and press remainder evenly into bottom and halfway up the sides of pan. Bake in preheated oven for 15 minutes. Place pan on a rack to cool completely.

2. **Topping:** In a saucepan combine water and lemonade concentrate. Heat over low heat until lemonade thaws and mixture is hot. Stir in marshmallows until melted and smooth. Chill for 3 to 4 hours or overnight, until mixture is thick and syrupy.

3. In a bowl whip cream until stiff. Fold gently into marshmallow mixture until blended. Spoon into cooled base. Sprinkle remaining crumb mixture evenly over top. Freeze for 3 to 4 hours or until firm. Cut into bars. Allow to stand at room temperature for about 30 minutes before serving. Store covered in the freezer.

MAKES 16 SQUARES

Poppyseed Squares

Preheat oven to 350° F (180° C)
8-inch (2 L) square cake pan, greased

1 cup	poppyseeds	250 mL
1 cup	milk	250 mL
2 cups	all-purpose flour	500 mL
2 tsp	baking powder	10 mL
1/2 tsp	salt	2 mL
1/2 cup	butter or margarine, softened	125 mL
1 cup	granulated sugar	250 mL
2	eggs, separated	2
	Grated zest of 1 orange or 1/2 tsp (2 mL) almond extract	
	Confectioner's (icing) sugar	

1. In a bowl combine poppyseeds and milk. Let stand for 1 hour.

2. In another bowl, mix together flour, baking powder and salt.

3. In a third bowl, beat butter and sugar until smooth and creamy. Beat in egg yolks until incorporated. Blend in flour mixture alternately with poppyseed mixture, mixing just until incorporated. Stir in orange zest.

4. In a clean bowl, beat egg whites, until stiff. Fold gently into batter. Spread evenly in prepared pan. Bake in preheated oven for about 45 minutes or until a tester inserted in the center comes out clean. Place pan on a rack to cool completely. Sift confectioner's sugar over top. Cut into squares.

Plantation Marble Squares

2 cups	cake flour, sifted	500 mL
2 tsp	baking powder	10 mL
1/4 tsp	salt	1 mL
1/2 cup	butter or margarine, softened	125 mL
1 cup	granulated sugar	250 mL
2	eggs	2
1/2 cup	milk	125 mL
1 tsp	ground cinnamon	5 mL
1/2 tsp	ground nutmeg	2 mL
1/2 tsp	ground cloves	2 mL
2 tbsp	fancy molasses	25 mL

TIP If desired, frost with a Butter Frosting (see recipe, page 179), then sprinkle with nuts and/or raisins.

Preheat oven to 350° F (180° C)
8-inch (2 L) square cake pan, greased

1. In a bowl mix together flour, baking powder and salt.

2. In another bowl, beat butter and sugar until smooth and creamy. Beat in eggs until incorporated. Gradually blend in flour mixture alternately with milk, until just incorporated.

3. Divide batter into 2 bowls. Stir cinnamon, nutmeg, cloves and molasses into one of the bowls; spread mixture evenly in prepared pan. Drop batter from remaining bowl, by spoonfuls, over top. Run a knife through batters to create a marbling effect. Bake in preheated oven for 45 to 50 minutes or until a tester inserted in the center comes out clean. Place pan on a rack to cool completely, then cut into squares.

Bars Squares

No-Bake Bars and Squares

MAKES 18 LONG BARS

Chocolate Peppermint Bars

9-inch (2.5 L) square cake pan, greased

Base		
1/4 cup	butter or margarine, melted	50 mL
1 1/4 cups	vanilla wafer crumbs (about 28 wafers)	300 mL

Filling		
4 cups	peppermint-flavored ice-cream, softened	1 L

Topping		
2	squares (each 1 oz [28 g]) unsweetened chocolate	2
1/2 cup	butter *or* margarine	125 mL
3	eggs, separated	3
1 1/2 cups	confectioner's (icing) sugar, sifted	375 mL
1 tsp	vanilla extract	5 mL
1/2 cup	chopped pecans	125 mL

1. **Base:** In a bowl mix together butter and crumbs. Set aside 1/4 cup (50 mL) and press remainder evenly into prepared pan.

2. **Filling:** Spread softened ice-cream evenly over top of base, then freeze until solid.

3. **Topping:** In large a saucepan over low heat, melt butter and chocolate, stirring until smooth. Set aside to cool slightly, then beat in egg yolks. Stir in vanilla. Gradually add confectioner's sugar, beating until blended and smooth. Fold in nuts.

4. In another bowl, beat egg whites until soft peaks form. Gently fold into chocolate mixture until combined, then spread mixture over top of ice-cream. Sprinkle reserved base mixture over top and freeze. When ready to serve, cut into bars.

TIP Raw eggs can be a potentially dangerous source of salmonella. To reduce this food-safety risk, add egg yolk to butter and chocolate in Step 3 and cook over low heat. Use pasteurized egg whites in Step 4.

MAKES 24 BARS

Hawaiian Cheese Cake Bars

9-inch (2.5 L) square cake pan, ungreased

Base		
1 cup	graham wafer crumbs (about 14 wafers)	250 mL
1/4 cup	granulated sugar	50 mL
1/4 cup	butter or margarine, melted	50 mL

Topping		
1	can (20 oz [568 mL]) pineapple chunks packed in juice	1
1	pkg (4-serving size) lemon-flavored gelatin dessert mix	1
8 oz	cream cheese, softened	250 g

1. **Base:** In a bowl mix together wafer crumbs, sugar and butter until blended. Press evenly into pan. Chill until firm.

2. **Topping**: Drain pineapple, reserving juice. Cover pineapple and refrigerate until ready to use. Add water to the juice to make 1 cup (250 mL) and In a saucepan over medium heat, bring to a boil.

3. In a heatproof bowl, combine lemon gelatin and boiling liquid. Stir until gelatin dissolves. Set half aside. Add cream cheese to remainder and beat until smooth and blended. Spread evenly over base. Chill until set.

4. Arrange pineapple chunks over top and spoon reserved gelatin mixture over top of pineapple. Refrigerate until set, then cut into bars.

No-Bake Eatmore Bars

MAKES 36 BARS

3/4 cup	packed brown sugar	175 mL
3/4 cup	liquid honey	175 mL
3/4 cup	smooth peanut butter	175 mL
1/2 cup	unsweetened cocoa powder, sifted	125 mL
1 1/4 cups	quick-cooking rolled oats	300 mL
2 1/2 cups	crisp rice cereal	625 mL
1 cup	chopped peanuts	250 mL
1 cup	chopped, mixed dried fruit (such as dates, risins, apples, apricots, cranberries, etc.)	250 mL

13- by 9-inch (3.5 L) cake pan, lightly greased

1. In a saucepan over low heat, combine brown sugar, honey and peanut butter. Cook, stirring, until sugar dissolves and mixture is smooth. Stir in cocoa.

2. In a bowl mix together oats, cereal, peanuts and dried fruit. Add brown sugar mixture and mix until blended (mixture will be a bit crumbly). Press batter evenly into prepared pan. Chill until set, then cut into bars.

Ice-Cream Peanut Krispies

MAKES 12 BARS

1/2 cup	peanut butter (smooth or crunchy)	125 mL
1/2 cup	corn syrup	125 mL
4 cups	crisp rice cereal (cocoa flavored, if desired)	1 L
2 cups	chocolate or vanilla ice cream	500 mL

13- by 9-inch (3.5 L) cake pan, greased with butter

1. In a large bowl, beat peanut butter and corn syrup until smooth and creamy. Stir in cereal and mix until well-coated. Press evenly into prepared pan. Chill until firm. When ready to serve, cut cake into 12 large bars. Place a slice of ice-cream on half the bars, then top with remaining bars. Cut each bar in half. Store in freezer.

MAKES 24 BARS

The Ultimate Nanaimo Bar

9-inch (2.5 L) square cake pan, greased with butter

Base		
1/2 cup	butter, melted	125 mL
1/4 cup	granulated sugar	50 mL
1	egg, beaten	1
1/3 cup	unsweetened cocoa powder, sifted	75 mL
1 tsp	vanilla extract	5 mL
2 cups	graham wafer crumbs (about 30 wafers)	500 mL
1 cup	shredded coconut	250 mL
1/2 cup	chopped walnuts	125 mL

Filling		
1/4 cup	butter, softened	50 mL
2 tbsp	vanilla custard powder *or* vanilla instant pudding mix	25 mL
2 tbsp	milk (approximate)	25 mL
2 cups	confectioner's (icing) sugar, sifted	500 mL

Topping		
4	squares (each 1 oz [28 g]) unsweetened chocolate	4
1 tbsp	butter	15 mL

TIP Classic Nanaimo bars are made with Bird's Custard Powder. If you can't find it, substitute an equal quantity of vanilla instant pudding powder (sold in tins).

1. **Base:** In a bowl mix together melted butter, sugar, egg, cocoa and vanilla until blended.

2. In another bowl, mix together crumbs, coconut and walnuts. Add butter mixture and mix well. Press evenly into prepared pan. Chill at least 1 hour.

3. **Filling:** In a bowl cream butter. Beat in custard powder, milk and confectioner's sugar until blended. If mixture is too thick, add a few drops more milk. Spread evenly over base and chill for 30 minutes or until firm.

4. **Topping:** In a saucepan over low heat, melt chocolate and butter, stirring until smooth. Spread evenly over topping, then cut into bars. Store, covered, in the refrigerator.

Noble Napoleons

13- by 9-inch (3.5 L) cake pan, lined with wax paper

Base		
40	graham wafers	40
1	pkg (6 oz [170 g]) chocolate pudding and pie filling (not instant pudding)	1
2 cups	milk	500 mL
1 cup	whipping (35%) cream, whipped	250 mL

Topping		
2 tbsp	butter *or* margarine	25 mL
1 cup	semi-sweet chocolate chips	250 mL

Frosting		
1 tbsp	butter or margarine, softened	15 mL
1 tbsp	milk	15 mL
3/4 cup	confectioner's (icing) sugar, sifted	175 mL

1. **Base:** In prepared pan, place half of the graham wafers in a single layer, cutting end pieces to fit. Set aside.

2. Prepare pudding mix according to package directions, using 2 cups (500 mL) of milk. Place a layer of plastic wrap directly on pudding (to prevent a skin from forming) and chill. When pudding is chilled, fold in whipped cream. Spread evenly over wafers in pan. Cover with remaining graham wafers, cutting as necessary to cover top completely. Chill for several hours or overnight.

3. **Topping:** In a saucepan over low heat, melt butter and chocolate chips. Spread evenly over top layer of graham wafers. Chill until chocolate is firm.

4. **Frosting:** Mix together butter, milk and confectioner's sugar until blended and smooth. Using a cake decorator's bag, or any appropriate method, make a checkerboard design over top of chocolate. Chill until set. Before serving, leave at room temperature for about 15 minutes, then cut into bars. Store, covered, in refrigerator.

Puffed Wheat Bars

1/2 cup	butter *or* margarine	125 mL
1/2 cup	corn syrup	125 mL
1 cup	packed brown sugar	250 mL
2 tbsp	unsweetened cocoa powder, sifted	25 mL
1 tsp	vanilla extract	5 mL
1/2 cup	salted peanuts	125 mL
8 cups	puffed wheat cereal	2 L

13- by 9-inch (3.5 L) cake pan, greased

1. In a saucepan over low heat, bring butter, corn syrup, brown sugar and cocoa to a boil. Cook, stirring for 3 minutes. Remove from heat. Stir in vanilla. Stir in peanuts and puffed wheat. Press evenly into prepared pan. Set aside until firm, then cut into bars.

Blueberry and White Chocolate Squares

Base		
1/4 cup	butter or margarine, melted	50 mL
2 cups	amaretto cookie crumbs	500 mL

Topping		
1 1/2 cups	blueberries, fresh or individually frozen and thawed	375 mL
1/3 cup	whipping (35%) cream	75 mL
8	squares (each 1 oz [28 g]) white chocolate, finely chopped	8

8-inch (2 L) square cake pan, lined with foil, ends extending

1. **Base:** In a bowl mix together butter and cookie crumbs. Press evenly into prepared pan

2. **Topping:** Sprinkle blueberries evenly over base.

3. In a large saucepan, heat whipping cream to boiling. Remove from heat and add chocolate, stirring until melted and smooth. Spoon evenly over blueberries. Chill for 2 hours or until firm. Transfer cake, with foil, to a cutting board and cut into squares.

Honey Nut Chocolate Squares

1 cup	smooth peanut butter	250 mL
3/4 cup	liquid honey	175 mL
1 tsp	vanilla extract	5 mL
3 cups	crisp rice cereal	750 mL
1 cup	salted peanuts	250 mL
1 cup	semi-sweet chocolate chips	250 mL

8-inch (2 L) or 9-inch (2.5 L) square cake pan, greased

1. In a saucepan over medium heat, bring peanut butter and honey to a boil, stirring until smooth. Remove from heat and stir in vanilla. Add cereal, peanuts and chocolate chips and mix well. Press evenly into prepared pan. Chill for 1 hour until firm. Cut into squares.

RAINBOW GELATIN SQUARES (PAGE 141) ➤

MAKES 36 BARS

Base		
1/4 cup	granulated sugar	50 mL
1/4 cup	unsweetened cocoa powder, sifted	50 mL
1/2 cup	butter *or* margarine	125 mL
2 cups	graham wafer crumbs (about 30 wafers)	500 mL
1	egg, beaten	1
1 tsp	vanilla extract	5 mL
1 cup	flaked coconut	250 mL
1/2 cup	finely ground walnuts	125 mL

Topping		
1/4 cup	butter or margarine, softened	50 mL
3 tbsp	custard powder	45 mL
Pinch	salt	Pinch
2 cups	confectioner's (icing) sugar, sifted	500 mL
3 tbsp	boiling water	45 mL

Frosting (optional)		
6	squares (each 1 oz [28 g]) semi-sweet chocolate	6
1 tbsp	butter	15 mL

Coconut Custard Ice-Box Bars

13- by 9-inch (3.5 L) cake pan, ungreased

1. **Base:** In a large saucepan over low heat, stir together sugar, cocoa and butter, until butter is melted and sugar dissolves. Remove from heat and sprinkle graham crumbs over top. Let stand for 1 minute, then stir until blended. Stir in egg and vanilla. Stir in coconut and walnuts. Spread mixture evenly in pan. Chill until firm (about 30 minutes).

2. **Topping:** In a bowl, beat butter, custard powder and salt until creamy. Gradually add confectioner's sugar beating until mixture resembles coarse crumbs. Slowly add boiling water, beating until mixture is smooth and spreadable. Spread over base and chill 30 minutes longer or until topping has hardened.

3. **Frosting:** (optional) In a small saucepan, over low heat, melt chocolate and butter, stirring until melted and smooth. Drizzle over cake. Chill until chocolate is firm. Cut into bars.

TIP Raw eggs can be a potentially dangerous source of salmonella. To reduce this food-safety risk, use pasteurized egg in Step 1.

MAKES 30 SQUARES

1	pound cake (about 10 oz [300 g]), cut into 12 slices	1
1/3 cup	cranberry juice	75 mL
2 cups	fresh whole raspberries	500 mL
2	pkgs (each 4-serving size) vanilla instant pudding mix	2
2 1/2 cups	milk	625 mL
4 cups	whipped topping, divided	1 L

Raspberry Patch Shortcake

13- by 9-inch (3.5 L) cake pan, ungreased

1. Line pan with sliced cake. Drizzle cranberry juice evenly over top. Spread raspberries evenly over top.

2. Prepare pudding according to package directions, using 2 1/2 cups (625 mL) of milk for both packages. Fold in 1 cup (250 mL) of the whipped topping and spoon over the raspberries. Spread remaining topping evenly over top. Chill for at least 1 hour. Cut into squares.

◄ NO-BAKE CRISPY PEANUT BUTTER SQUARES (PAGE 163)

Luscious Lemon Squares

MAKES 12 LARGE SQUARES

13- by 9-inch (3.5 L) cake pan, ungreased

Base		
1/4 cup	butter or margarine, melted	50 mL
1 1/4 cups	graham wafer crumbs (about 18 wafers)	300 mL

Filling		
3/4 cup	boiling water	175 mL
1	large pkg (6 oz [170 g]) lemon-flavored gelatin dessert mix	1
1/4 cup	lemon juice	50 mL
1/4 cup	liquid honey	50 mL
1	can (14 oz [385 mL]) chilled evaporated milk	1
1 tsp	grated lemon zest	5 mL

1. **Base:** In a bowl mix together butter and wafer crumbs. Set aside 1/4 cup (50 mL) and press remainder into pan.

2. **Filling:** In a heatproof bowl, combine boiling water and gelatin, stirring until gelatin is completely dissolved. Add lemon juice and honey. Set aside to cool.

3. In another bowl, beat evaporated milk until stiff. Gently fold in lemon zest, then gelatin mixture. Spoon over base and sprinkle remaining crumbs evenly over top. Chill for 4 hours or until set. Cut into squares.

Chocolate Peanut Krispies

MAKES 30 SQUARES

13- by 9-inch (3.5 L) cake pan, lightly greased

2/3 cup	smooth peanut butter	150 mL
2 cups	semi-sweet chocolate chips	500 mL
3 cups	miniature marshmallows	750 mL
6 cups	crisp rice cereal	1.5 L

1. In a large saucepan over low heat, melt peanut butter and chocolate chips, stirring constantly until smooth. Remove from heat. Stir in marshmallows and cereal, mixing until combined. Press evenly into prepared pan and chill until firm, about 1 hour. Cut into squares and store, covered, in refrigerator.

MAKES 16 SQUARES

No-Bake Crispy Peanut Butter Squares

1 cup	smooth peanut butter	250 mL
1/4 cup	butter *or* margarine	50 mL
1/2 cup	packed brown sugar	125 mL
1/2 cup	corn syrup	125 mL
1 tsp	vanilla extract	5 mL
Pinch	salt	Pinch
2 cups	corn flakes cereal	500 mL
1 cup	crispy rice cereal	250 mL

8-inch (2 L) square cake pan, lightly greased

1. In a saucepan over low heat, stir together peanut butter, butter, brown sugar and corn syrup, until blended and smooth. Remove from heat and stir in vanilla and salt.

2. In a bowl mix together cereals. Add peanut butter mixture and mix well. Press evenly into prepared pan. Chill for 6 hours or until firm. Cut into squares.

MAKES 24 BARS

Pineapple Graham Bars

Base		
2 cups	graham wafer crumbs (about 30 wafers)	500 mL
1/2 cup	butter or margarine, melted	125 mL

Topping		
2 cups	milk	500 mL
60 to 70	miniature marshmallows (1 pkg [16 oz (500 g)])	60 to 70
1 1/2 tsp	lemon extract	7 mL
2 cups	drained crushed pineapple	500 mL
2 cups	whipping (35%) cream, whipped	500 mL

13- by 9-inch (3.5 L) cake pan, greased

1. **Base:** In a bowl mix together graham crumbs and butter. Set aside 1/2 cup (125 mL) and press remainder evenly into prepared pan.

2. **Topping:** In a saucepan over low heat, combine milk and marshmallows, stirring until melted and smooth. Remove from heat and stir in lemon extract. Set aside to cool, stirring occasionally.

3. When cooled, gently fold in pineapple, then whipped cream, until well combined. Spread mixture evenly over base, then sprinkle with remaining crumb mixture. Chill for 3 to 4 hours, then cut into bars. Store, covered, in refrigerator.

TIP Make whipped cream fluffy by adding 1 tsp (5 mL) of honey as you whip. Finish off by beating in some confectioner's sugar.

MAKES 16 SQUARES

Coconut Date Refrigerator Squares

8-inch (2 L) square cake pan, ungreased

Base

1/2 cup	finely chopped pitted dates	125 mL
1/3 cup	granulated sugar	75 mL
1/2 cup	butter *or* margarine	125 mL
1/3 cup	unsweetened cocoa powder, sifted	75 mL
1	egg	1
1 tsp	vanilla extract	5 mL
2 cups	graham wafer crumbs (about 30 wafers)	500 mL
1 cup	shredded coconut	250 mL
1/2 cup	chopped walnuts	125 mL

Filling

1/3 cup	butter *or* margarine	75 mL
2 tbsp	vanilla custard powder	25 mL
1/4 cup	milk	50 mL
2 cups	confectioner's (icing) sugar, sifted	500 mL

Topping

1 tbsp	butter *or* margarine	15 mL
4	squares (each 1 oz [28 g]) semi-sweet chocolate	4

1. **Base:** In a saucepan combine dates, sugar, butter and cocoa. Cook, stirring over medium heat, until butter melts. Remove from heat and stir in egg and vanilla until blended. Add crumbs, coconut and nuts and mix well. Press evenly into pan. Chill for 2 to 3 hours.

2. **Filling:** In a bowl cream butter. Beat in custard powder, milk and confectioner's sugar until blended and smooth. Spread evenly over chilled base. Chill for 30 minutes.

3. **Topping:** In a small saucepan, melt chocolate and butter, over low heat, stirring constantly until smooth. Spread over chilled layers. Chill until chocolate hardens, then cut into squares.

TIP Raw eggs can be a potentially dangerous source of salmonella. To reduce this food-safety risk, use pasteurized egg in Step 1.

Bars Bar Squares

Esther's Special Favorites

MAKES 30 SQUARES

Felicia's Apple Squares

Base		
2 cups	all-purpose flour	500 mL
1 cup	granulated sugar	250 mL
1 tsp	baking powder	5 mL
1/2 cup	butter or margarine, melted	125 mL
2	egg yolks, beaten	2

Topping		
9	medium apples, peeled and coarsely grated (about 3 lbs [1.5 kg])	9
2 tsp	brown sugar	10 mL
1 tsp	lemon juice	5 mL
2 tbsp	cold butter or margarine, cut into tiny chunks	25 mL
1 tsp	granulated sugar	5 mL

Preheat oven to 350° F (180° C)
13- by 9-inch (3.5 L) cake pan, greased

1. **Base:** In a bowl mix together flour, sugar and baking powder. Add butter and egg yolks and mix until crumbly. Set aside 1 cup (250 mL) and press remainder evenly into prepared pan.

2. **Topping:** In a bowl mix together apples, brown sugar and lemon juice. Spread evenly over base. Sprinkle reserved crumb mixture over top. Sprinkle with butter chunks, then sugar. Bake in preheated oven for 45 to 50 minutes or until golden brown. Place pan on a rack to cool completely, then cut into squares.

MAKES 24 BARS

Christine's Chocolate Nut Bars

1 cup	corn syrup	250 mL
1 cup	packed brown sugar	250 mL
1 cup	smooth peanut butter	250 mL
2 tbsp	butter *or* margarine	25 mL
1 tsp	vanilla extract	5 mL
Pinch	salt	Pinch
4 cups	crisp rice cereal	1 L
2 cups	peanuts	500 mL
	Chocolate frosting (see pages 179 to 181 for recipes)	

9-inch (2.5 L) square cake pan, greased

1. In a large saucepan over low heat, stir together corn syrup, brown sugar, peanut butter and butter until sugar is dissolved. Increase heat and bring to a boil; cook, stirring constantly, until melted and smooth. Remove from heat. Stir in vanilla and salt. Stir in cereal and peanuts until blended. Press evenly into prepared pan. Chill until firm. Frost with a chocolate frosting of your choice. Cut into bars.

TIP To prevent icings or frostings from running off your cake, try dusting the surface lightly with cornstarch before frosting.

MAKES 36 BARS

Betty's Sour Cream Chocolate Chip Bars

Preheat oven to 350° F (180° C)
13- by 9-inch (3.5 L) cake pan, greased

Base		
1 1/3 cups	all-purpose flour	325 mL
1 1/2 tsp	baking powder	7 mL
1 tsp	baking soda	5 mL
1 tsp	ground cinnamon	5 mL
Pinch	salt	Pinch
6 tbsp	butter or margarine, softened	90 mL
1 cup	granulated sugar	250 mL
2	eggs	2
1/2 tsp	vanilla extract	2 mL
1 cup	sour cream	250 mL

Topping		
1 cup	semi-sweet chocolate chips	250 mL
1 tbsp	granulated sugar	15 mL

1. **Base:** In a bowl mix together flour, baking powder, baking soda, cinnamon and salt.

2. In another bowl, beat butter and sugar until smooth and creamy. Beat in eggs until incorporated. Stir in vanilla. Blend in flour mixture alternately with sour cream, until just incorporated. Spread evenly in prepared pan.

3. **Topping:** Sprinkle chocolate chips evenly over top. Sprinkle sugar over chocolate chips. Bake in preheated oven for 30 to 35 minutes or until a tester inserted in the center comes out clean. Place pan on a rack to cool completely, then cut into bars.

MAKES 24 BARS

Felicia's Passover Mocha Nut Bars

Preheat oven to 350° F (180° C)
9-inch (2.5 L) square cake pan, greased

2	squares (each 1 oz [28 g]) bittersweet chocolate	2
1/2 cup	butter *or* margarine	125 mL
2	eggs	2
1 cup	granulated sugar	250 mL
1/2 tsp	salt	2 mL
1/2 cup	sifted cake meal (Passover)	125 mL
1 cup	chopped nuts	250 mL

TIP Try substituting carob for chocolate in some of your recipes. Carob is similar to chocolate in flavor, but is lower in fat and is caffeine-free.

1. In a saucepan over low heat, melt chocolate and butter, stirring until smooth. Set aside.

2. In a bowl, beat eggs, sugar and salt until blended and thick. Add cake meal and mix well. Blend in chocolate mixture. Stir in nuts. Spread evenly in prepared pan. Bake in preheated oven for 25 to 30 minutes or until a tester inserted in the center comes out clean. Place pan on a rack to cool completely, then cut into bars.

Colleen's 'Sex in a Pan'

I have no idea – and neither does Colleen – how this recipe got its name, but it has been around for a long time and it is delicious!

Preheat oven to 350° F (180° C)
13- by 9-inch (3.5 L) cake pan, greased

Base

1 cup	all-purpose flour	250 mL
1/2 cup	chopped almonds or pecans	125 mL
3 tbsp	granulated sugar	45 mL
1/2 cup	butter *or* margarine	125 mL

Filling

8 oz	cream cheese, softened	250 g
1 cup	confectioner's (icing) sugar, sifted	250 mL
2 cups	frozen whipped topping (thawed) or whipped cream, divided	500 mL

Topping

2	pkgs (each 4-serving size) chocolate or caramel instant pudding mix	2
1	pkg (4-serving size) vanilla instant pudding mix	1
4 cups	milk	1 L
	Grated chocolate, chopped nuts or cherries for garnish (optional)	

1. **Base:** In a bowl mix together flour, nuts and sugar. Using 2 knives, a pastry blender or your fingers, cut butter in until mixture resembles coarse crumbs. Press evenly into prepared pan. Bake in preheated oven for 12 to 15 minutes or until browned. Place pan on a rack to cool completely.

2. **Filling:** In another bowl, beat cream cheese and confectioner's sugar until smooth and creamy. Fold in 1 cup (250 mL) of the whipped topping. Spread evenly over cooled base.

3. **Topping:** In a bowl, beat puddings and milk until blended and smooth. Spread evenly over cream cheese mixture. Spread with remaining whipped topping. If desired, garnish with chocolate, nuts or cherries. Chill until ready to serve. Cut into squares.

TIP This recipe freezes well.

Pack sweetened whipped cream, flavored with vanilla, into freezer trays. Freeze until firm. Cut in squares and serve on warm cakes or pies.

MAKES 36 BARS

Cecille's Cookie Bars

Preheat oven to 350° F (180° C)
13- by 9-inch (3.5 L) cake pan, greased

Base		
1 1/2 cups	crushed corn flakes cereal	375 mL
3 tbsp	granulated sugar	45 mL
1/2 cup	butter or margarine, melted	125 mL

Topping		
1 cup	semi-sweet chocolate chips	250 mL
1 1/3 cups	flaked coconut	325 mL
1 cup	coarsely chopped walnuts	250 mL
1	can (10 oz [300 mL]) sweetened condensed milk	1

1. **Base:** In a bowl mix together corn flake crumbs, sugar and butter. Press firmly into prepared pan.

2. **Topping:** Spread chocolate chips evenly over base. Sprinkle coconut evenly over top. Sprinkle nuts evenly over top of coconut. Pour condensed milk evenly over nuts. Bake in preheated oven for 25 minutes or until edges are lightly browned. Place pan on a rack to cool completely, then cut into bars.

MAKES 30 SQUARES

Sima's Pineapple Squares

Preheat oven to 375° F (190° C)
13- by 9-inch (3.5 L) cake pan, greased

Topping		
3 cups	crushed pineapple, drained, 2 tbsp (25 mL) juice reserved	750 mL
1/2 cup	granulated sugar	125 mL
2 tbsp	cornstarch	25 mL
1 tbsp	butter	15 mL

Base		
1 1/2 cups	all-purpose flour	375 mL
2 tsp	baking powder	10 mL
Pinch	salt	Pinch
2	eggs	2
3/4 cup	granulated sugar	175 mL
1/2 cup	vegetable oil	125 mL
1/2 cup	orange juice	125 mL
1/4 cup	water	50 mL

1. **Topping:** In the top of a double boiler over simmering (not boiling) water, combine pineapple and sugar. In a small bowl, mix cornstarch with reserved pineapple juice. Add to sugar mixture along with butter. Cook, stirring frequently, until mixture thickens. Set aside.

2. **Base:** In a bowl mix together flour, baking powder and salt. Make a well in the center. In another bowl, beat eggs, sugar, oil, orange juice and water. Pour into well and mix until just blended. (Batter will be thin.) Set aside one-half of the batter and pour remainder into prepared pan.

3. Spoon pineapple mixture evenly over batter. Drop remaining batter, by spoonfuls, over pineapple, leaving spaces in the form of vertical and horizontal lines between the dollops of batter. Bake in preheated oven for 25 minutes, then reduce heat to 350° F (180° C) and bake 10 minutes longer, until golden brown. Place pan on a rack to cool completely, then cut into squares.

Baba Mary's Honey Diamonds

MAKES 36 DIAMONDS

2 cups	all-purpose flour	500 mL
1/2 tsp	baking soda	2 mL
1/2 tsp	ground cinnamon	2 mL
1/4 tsp	salt	1 mL
1/4 cup	butter or shortening, softened	50 mL
1 cup	packed brown sugar	250 mL
2	eggs	2
1/3 cup	liquid honey	75 mL
1/2 cup	milk	125 mL
	Butter Frosting (see recipe, page 179)	
1/2 cup	ground nuts	125 mL

TIP To soften brick-hard brown sugar, transfer it to a paper bag and place in a 350° F (180° C) oven until the bag is warm. Then crush with a rolling pin and spread out on a cookie sheet to cool.

Preheat oven to 350° F (180° C)
13- by 9-inch (3.5 L) cake pan, greased

1. In a bowl mix together flour, baking soda, cinnamon and salt.

2. In another bowl, beat butter and sugar until smooth and creamy. Add eggs and beat until incorporated. Stir in honey. Gradually blend in flour mixture alternately with milk, until just incorporated. Spread evenly in prepared pan. Bake in preheated oven for 35 to 40 minutes or until a tester inserted in the center comes out clean. Place pan on a rack to cool completely.

3. Frost generously with Butter Frosting, then sprinkle with nuts. Cut lengthwise into 6 strips; cut crosswise at an angle into 6 strips to make diamonds.

Arlene's Pineapple Cheesecake Squares

MAKES 16 SQUARES

	Base	
36	finely crushed graham wafers	36
1/4 cup	butter, melted	50 mL

	Topping	
1 lb	cream cheese, softened	500 g
1/2 cup	granulated sugar	125 mL
3	eggs	3
1 tsp	vanilla extract	5 mL
10	finely chopped maraschino cherries	10
1/2 cup	drained crushed pineapple	125 mL

Preheat oven to 350° F (180° C)
8-inch (2 L) square cake pan, lightly greased

1. **Base:** In a bowl mix together wafer crumbs and butter. Set aside 3/4 cup (175 mL) and press remainder evenly into prepared pan.

2. **Topping:** In a bowl, beat cream cheese and sugar until smooth. Beat in eggs, one at a time, until incorporated. Stir in vanilla. Stir in cherries and pineapple. Spread evenly over base. Sprinkle reserved crumb mixture evenly over top. Bake in preheated oven for 35 minutes or until just set. Place pan on a rack to cool completely, then chill for 4 hours, or longer, before cutting into squares.

Olga's Blueberry Cake Squares

MAKES 30 SQUARES

Base

2 1/2 cups	all-purpose flour	625 mL
1 tbsp	baking powder	15 mL
1/2 tsp	salt	2 mL
2	eggs	2
1 cup	granulated sugar	250 mL
3 tbsp	water	45 mL
1 tsp	vanilla extract	5 mL
1	can (19 oz [540 mL]) blueberry pie filling	1

Topping

1 tbsp	butter, softened	15 mL
2 tbsp	all-purpose flour	25 mL
1 tbsp	granulated sugar	15 mL
1	egg yolk	1

Preheat oven to 350° F (180° C)
13- by 9-inch (3.5 L) cake pan, greased

1. **Base:** In a bowl mix together flour, baking powder and salt.

2. In another bowl, beat eggs, sugar, water and vanilla until blended. Gradually blend in flour mixture. Set half aside and spread remainder evenly in prepared pan. Spread pie filling evenly over top.

3. On a floured work surface, divide remaining dough into 14 portions. Shape each into a rope, half to fit vertically across the cake and half to fit horizontally. Place over cake.

4. **Topping:** In a bowl mix butter, flour, sugar and egg yolk until mixture is crumbly. Sprinkle evenly over cake. Bake in preheated oven for 55 to 60 minutes or until golden brown. Place pan on a rack to cool completely, then cut into squares.

TIP Here's how to protect your frosted cake without having the plastic wrap stick to the frosting. Stick miniature marshmallows on the ends of toothpicks, then stick the toothpicks around the top and sides of the cake, then cover with plastic wrap. After the cake has been unwrapped, the marshmallows make a nice snack.

Wendy's Chocolate-Chip Cream Cheese Bars

MAKES 36 BARS

1	pkg (18 oz [510 g]) refrigerated chocolate chip cookie dough, softened	1
1 lb	cream cheese, softened	500 g
1 cup	granulated sugar	250 mL
2	eggs	2
1 1/2 tsp	vanilla extract	7 mL
1	pkg (18 oz [510 g]) refrigerated chocolate chip cookie dough, chilled	1

Preheat oven to 350° F (180° C)
13- by 9-inch (3.5 L) cake pan, greased

1. Spread softened cookie dough evenly in prepared pan.

2. In a bowl, beat cream cheese and sugar until smooth. Beat in eggs, one at a time, until incorporated. Stir in vanilla. Spread evenly over dough.

3. On a cutting board, cut chilled dough into very thin slices. Completely cover cream cheese mixture with thin cookie slices. (Place dough in freezer for 15 minutes to make slicing easier.) Bake in preheated oven for 40 minutes or until golden brown. Place pan on a rack to cool completely. Store in refrigerator, then cut into bars.

Christine's Frosted Strawberry Squares

Base		
1 cup	all-purpose flour	250 mL
1/2 to 3/4 cup	chopped walnuts	125 to 175 mL
1/4 cup	brown sugar	50 mL
1/2 cup	butter, melted	125 mL

Topping		
2	egg whites	2
1 cup	granulated sugar	250 mL
1 1/2	pkgs (10 oz [300 g]) frozen strawberries, partially thawed	1 1/2
2 tbsp	lemon juice	25 mL
1 cup	whipping (35%) cream	250 mL

TIP These squares can be made in advance and kept frozen for up to 2 weeks.

Preheat oven to 350° F (180° C)
Ungreased cookie sheet
13- by 9-inch (3.5 L) cake pan, ungreased

1. **Base:** In a bowl mix together flour, nuts, brown sugar and melted butter. Spread mixture evenly onto cookie sheet. Bake in preheated oven for 20 minutes, stirring often. Set aside one-third of baked crumbs. Spread remainder evenly in prepared pan.

2. **Topping:** In a bowl, beat egg whites until frothy. Gradually add sugar, beating until stiff peaks form. Fold in strawberries and lemon juice.

3. In another bowl, whip cream until stiff. Fold into strawberry mixture. Spoon evenly over base and top with remaining crumbs.

4. Freeze overnight. About 30 minutes before serving, remove from freezer and cut into squares.

TIP Raw eggs can be a potentially dangerous source of salmonella. To reduce this food-safety risk, use pasteurized egg whites in Step 2.

Shirley's Cornmeal Squares
(Malai Cake)

1 cup	all-purpose flour	250 mL
1 tbsp	baking powder	15 mL
1 tsp	salt	5 mL
1/2 cup	yellow cornmeal	125 mL
2 cups	water	500 mL
1/2 cup	butter or margarine, melted	125 mL
6	eggs, separated	6
2 cups	creamed cottage cheese	500 mL
2 cups	sour cream	500 mL
1/2 cup	granulated sugar	125 mL

TIP This cake is delicious when served warm with sour cream and strawberries.

Preheat oven to 350° F (180° C)
13- by 9-inch (3.5 L) cake pan, greased

1. In a bowl mix together flour, baking powder and salt.

2. In the top of a double boiler, combine cornmeal and water. Cook, over low heat, until mixture thickens. Stir in butter until melted. Set aside to cool.

3. In another bowl, beat egg yolks, cottage cheese, sour cream and sugar until blended. Blend in flour mixture, alternating with cornmeal mixture, just until incorporated.

4. In a clean bowl, beat egg whites until stiff peaks form. Fold into batter. Spoon into prepared cake pan, spreading evenly. Bake in preheated oven for 55 to 60 minutes or until golden brown. Place pan on a rack to cool completely, or cool slightly and serve warm. Cut into squares.

MAKES 16 SQUARES

Betty's Fruit Cocktail Squares

Preheat oven to 350° F (180° C)
8-inch (2 L) square cake pan, greased

	Base	
1 cup	all-purpose flour	250 mL
1 tsp	baking soda	5 mL
1/4 tsp	salt	1 mL
3/4 cup	granulated sugar	175 mL
1	egg, beaten	1
2 cups	fruit cocktail, partially drained	500 mL

	Topping	
1/3 cup	packed brown sugar	75 mL
1 tsp	ground cinnamon	5 mL

1. **Base:** In a bowl mix together flour, baking soda and salt.

2. In another bowl, mix together, sugar, egg and fruit cocktail. Blend in flour mixture. Spread evenly in prepared pan.

3. **Topping:** In a small bowl, mix together brown sugar and cinnamon. Sprinkle evenly over top of cake. Bake in preheated oven for 40 to 45 minutes, until golden brown. Place pan on a rack to cool completely, then cut into squares.

MAKES 30 SQUARES

Cecille's Walnut Squares

Preheat oven to 325° F (160° C)
13- by 9-inch (3.5 L) cake pan, ungreased

	Base	
1 1/2 cups	all-purpose flour	375 mL
1 tbsp	packed brown sugar	15 mL
Pinch	baking powder	Pinch
1/2 cup	butter *or* margarine	125 mL

	Topping	
1 1/4 cups	finely chopped walnuts, divided	300 mL
2	eggs	2
3/4 cup	packed brown sugar	175 mL
2 tbsp	all-purpose flour	25 mL
Pinch	baking powder	Pinch
1 tsp	vanilla extract	5 mL
	Butter Frosting (see recipe, page 179)	

1. **Base:** In a bowl mix together flour, brown sugar and baking powder. Using 2 knives, a pastry blender or your fingers, cut butter in until mixture resembles coarse crumbs. Press evenly into prepared pan. Bake in preheated oven for 15 to 20 minutes or until golden brown. Place pan on a rack to cool slightly.

2. **Topping:** Set aside 1/2 cup (125 mL) of the chopped walnuts. In a bowl, beat eggs and brown sugar until blended. Blend in flour, baking powder and vanilla. Stir in remaining 3/4 cup (175 mL) walnuts. Spread evenly over warm base. Bake 15 to 20 minutes longer, until golden brown. Place pan on a rack to cool completely. Frost with Butter Frosting and sprinkle reserved walnuts over top. Cut into squares.

Mama's Ice-Box Cake Bars

How this recipe got its name: The story is that an ingenious cook, a lady with a flair, created a reasonable facsimile of a cake by alternating layers of cookies with flavored whipped cream. This creation was placed in an old-fashioned ice-box to mellow – hence the name Ice-Box Cakes.

1	pkg (4-serving size) gelatin dessert mix, any flavor	1

Walnut Filling		
1 cup	graham wafer crumbs	250 mL
1 cup	finely chopped walnuts	250 mL
	Grated zest of 1 lemon	
1/2 cup	packed brown sugar	125 mL

Sour Cream Filling		
1 1/2 cups	sour cream	375 mL
1/2 cup	packed brown sugar	125 mL
2 tsp	lemon juice	10 mL
1 tsp	vanilla extract	5 mL

1	pkg (14 oz [400 g]) whole graham wafers	1

13- by 9-inch (3.5 L) cake pan, ungreased

1. Prepare gelatin according to package directions, allowing to set partially. Gelatin should be firm enough to spread.

2. **Walnut filling:** In a bowl mix together wafer crumbs, walnuts, zest and brown sugar.

3. **Sour cream filling:** In another bowl, mix sour cream, brown sugar, lemon juice and vanilla until thoroughly blended.

4. Line bottom of pan with half of the whole graham wafers. Spoon half of sour cream filling over top, spreading evenly. Place remaining graham wafers on top and spread evenly with remaining sour cream filling.

5. Spoon half the walnut filling evenly over cream cheese layer; spread evely with the partially set gelatin. Spoon remaining walnut filling over top, spreading evenly. Chill for 3 to 4 hours until cold and set. Cut into bars before serving.

Shauna's Cinnamon Apple Squares

Base		
1 3/4 cups	all-purpose flour	425 mL
2 tsp	baking powder	10 mL
Pinch	salt	Pinch
2	eggs	2
3/4 cup	granulated sugar	175 mL
3/4 cup	vegetable oil	175 mL
1/2 cup	cold water	125 mL
1	can (19 oz [540 mL]) apple pie filling	1

Topping		
2 tbsp	granulated sugar	25 mL
1/2 tsp	ground cinnamon	2 mL

Preheat oven to 350° F (180° C)
13- by 9-inch (3.5 L) cake pan, greased

1. **Base:** In a bowl mix together flour, baking powder and salt.

2. In another bowl, beat eggs and sugar until thickened. Beat in oil until blended. Gradually blend in flour mixture, alternately with water, until just incorporated. Spread a little more than half the batter evenly in prepared pan.

3. **Topping:** Drop spoonfuls of apple pie filling over top of batter. Spread remaining batter evenly over apple filling.

4. In a small bowl, mix together sugar and cinnamon. Sprinkle evenly over over top of cake. Bake in preheated oven for 40 to 60 minutes or until golden brown. Place pan on a rack to cool completely, then cut into squares.

MAKES 16 SQUARES

Lisa's Midas Squares

8-inch (2 L) square cake pan, ungreased

Base		
1 cup	smooth peanut butter	250 mL
1/2 cup	cane sugar syrup (golden syrup)	125 mL
1/2 cup	packed brown sugar	125 mL
2 cups	corn flakes cereal, lightly crushed	500 mL
1 cup	crisp rice cereal	250 mL

Frosting		
1/2 cup	packed brown sugar	125 mL
3 tbsp	milk	45 mL
1 tbsp	margarine, softened	15 mL
1 cup	confectioner's (icing) sugar, sifted	250 mL
1/2 tsp	vanilla extract	2 mL

1. **Base:** In a saucepan over low heat, stir peanut butter, syrup and brown sugar, until sugar dissolves and mixture is smooth. Stir in corn flakes and rice cereal. Press firmly and evenly into pan.

2. **Frosting:** In a bowl, beat brown sugar, milk, margarine, confectioner's sugar and vanilla until smooth and spreadable. Spread over base. Chill for 3 to 4 hours or overnight. When serving, cut into squares.

MAKES 30 SQUARES

Colleen's Fruit Cake Squares

Preheat oven to 400° F (200° C)
13- by 9-inch (3.5 L) cake pan, greased

1 1/2 cups	water	375 mL
1 1/2 cups	raisins	375 mL
2 tsp	baking soda	10 mL
3 cups	all-purpose flour	750 mL
1 tsp	ground cinnamon	5 mL
1 tsp	ground nutmeg	5 mL
1 tsp	ground ginger	5 mL
2 cups	granulated sugar	500 mL
1 cup	vegetable oil	250 mL
3	eggs	3
2 tsp	vanilla extract	10 mL
1/2 cup	chopped nuts (optional)	125 mL
1/2 cup	chocolate chips (optional)	125 mL

1. In a saucepan over low heat, stir together water, raisins and baking soda. Increase heat and bring to a boil. Cook, stirring occasionally, for 5 minutes. Set aside to cool.

2. In a bowl mix together flour, cinnamon, nutmeg and ginger. Make a well in the center.

3. In another bowl, beat sugar, oil, eggs and vanilla until blended. Stir in raisin mixture. Pour into flour mixture and stir just until incorporated. Stir in nuts and chocolate chips, if using. Spread evenly in prepared pan. Bake in preheated oven for 1 hour and 10 minutes or until a tester inserted in the center comes out clean. Place pan on a rack to cool completely, then cut into squares.

Jeanette's Filled Coffee Cake Squares

Base		
3 cups	all-purpose flour	750 mL
2 tsp	baking powder	10 mL
1/2 tsp	salt	2 mL
1/2 cup	butter or margarine, softened	125 mL
2 cups	granulated sugar	500 mL
4	eggs	4
1 tsp	vanilla extract	5 mL
1 cup	milk	250 mL

Filling		
1 cup	packed brown sugar	250 mL
2 tbsp	butter, softened	25 mL
2 tbsp	all-purpose flour	25 mL
1 cup	chopped nuts	250 mL
1 tsp	ground cinnamon	5 mL

Preheat oven to 350° F (180° C)
13- by 9-inch (3.5 L) cake pan, greased

1. **Base:** In a bowl mix together flour, baking powder and salt.

2. In another bowl, beat butter and sugar until smooth and creamy. Beat in eggs, one at a time, until incorporated. Stir in vanilla. Gradually blend in flour mixture, alternately with milk until just incorporated. Set half aside and spread remainder evenly in prepared pan.

3. **Filling:** In a bowl, beat sugar and butter until smooth and creamy. Blend in flour, nuts and cinnamon. Spoon half the filling over batter in pan. Spread reserved batter evenly over filling. Spread remaining filling evenly over batter. Bake in preheated oven for 40 to 50 minutes or until a tester inserted in the center comes out clean. Place pan on a rack to cool completely, then cut into squares.

Christine's Lemon Squares

Base		
1/2 cup	butter or margarine, softened	125 mL
1/4 cup	confectioner's (icing) sugar, sifted	50 mL
1/2 tsp	salt	2 mL
1 cup	all-purpose flour	250 mL

Topping		
2	eggs, beaten	2
1 cup	granulated sugar	250 mL
2 tbsp	all-purpose flour	25 mL
1 1/2 tsp	grated lemon zest	7 mL
2 tbsp	lemon juice	25 mL
	Confectioner's (icing) sugar	

Preheat oven to 350° F (180° C)
8-inch (2 L) square cake pan, lightly greased

1. **Base:** In a bowl, beat butter and confectioner's sugar until smooth and creamy. Beat in salt, then gradually blend in flour until a soft dough forms. Press evenly into prepared pan. Bake in preheated oven for 20 minutes or until lightly browned. Place pan on a rack to cool slightly.

2. **Topping:** In a bowl mix together eggs, sugar, remaining 2 tbsp (25 mL) flour, zest and juice until blended. Spoon evenly over warm base. Bake 20 to 25 minutes longer. Remove from oven and sift confectioner's sugar over top. Place pan on a rack to cool completely, then cut into squares.

Frostings and Glazes

Apricot Brandy Glaze

1	jar (12 oz [340 mL]) apricot preserves	1
1/4 cup	apricot brandy	50 mL

1. In a small saucepan over low heat, cook apricot preserves until very warm. Add apricot brandy and cook, stirring, for 1 to 2 minutes. Remove from heat. Strain through a fine sieve and allow to cool.

Banana Frosting

1/2 cup	butter or margarine, softened	125 mL
1/2 cup	mashed bananas	125 mL
3 1/2 cups	confectioner's (icing) sugar, sifted	825 mL
1 tbsp	lemon juice	15 mL
1 tsp	vanilla extract	5 mL

1. In a bowl cream butter and bananas until blended. Gradually add confectioner's sugar, lemon juice and vanilla and mix well. Chill until mixture is the right consistency for spreading.

VARIATION To make this recipe a banana filling, chop 2 bananas with a little pulverized sugar and lemon juice.

TIP If your frosting becomes hard or too stiff while beating, just add a little lemon juice.

Broiled Topping

1/2 cup	packed brown sugar	125 mL
1/4 cup	butter or margarine, softened	50 mL
3 tbsp	evaporated milk	45 mL
1/2 cup	desiccated coconut or chopped nuts	125 mL
1 tbsp	grated orange zest (optional)	15 mL

1. In a bowl mix together brown sugar, butter, milk, coconut and, if using, orange zest. Spread mixture evenly over cake before cutting into squares or bars, then put under broiler for 2 to 3 minutes or until topping is bubbly and golden brown.

TIP This is especially good with a butter, chocolate, orange, or carrot cake.

Brown Sugar Meringue

2	egg whites	2
1 tbsp	lemon juice	15 mL
1 cup	packed brown sugar	250 mL

1. In a small bowl with an electric mixer, beat egg whites until doubled in volume. Beat in lemon juice. Beat in brown sugar, 1 tbsp (15 mL) at a time, until meringue stands in firm peaks.

2. Spread over cake and bake in a 350° F (180° C) oven for about 10 minutes or until meringue is browned. Place pan on a rack to cool completely, then cut into bars or squares

TIP Meringues are often called "angel crust" because of its gossamer texture.

MAKES ENOUGH FOR A 13- BY 9-INCH (3.5 L) PAN

Butter Frosting

4 cups	confectioner's (icing) sugar, sifted	1 L
1/3 cup	butter, softened	75 mL
1 1/2 tsp	vanilla extract	7 mL
2 tbsp	light (5%) cream or milk (approximate)	25 mL

1. In a bowl cream butter. Slowly add about half of the confectioner's sugar, blending well. Beat in vanilla and gradually blend in the remaining confectioner's sugar. Add only enough cream to make the right spreading consistency.

VARIATIONS Chocolate Butter Frosting: When adding vanilla, also add 2 squares (each 1 oz [28 g]) unsweetened chocolate, melted and cooled, and mix to blend.

Lemon Butter Frosting: To creamed butter, add 1/2 tsp (2 mL) grated lemon zest. Replace light cream with lemon juice, only enough to make frosting the right spreading consistency.

VARIATIONS Mocha Coffee Butter Frosting: To creamed butter, add 1/4 cup (50 mL) unsweetened cocoa powder and 1/2 tsp (2 mL) instant coffee.

Orange Butter Frosting: To creamed butter, add 2 tsp (10 mL) grated orange zest, and replace light cream with 2 tbsp (25 mL) orange juice.

Pineapple Butter Frosting: Omit vanilla and light cream, and add 1/3 cup (75 mL) pineapple juice and 2/3 cup (150 mL) granulated sugar. Combine the butter, juice and sugar in a small saucepan and heat until sugar is dissolved. Remove from heat and gradually beat in the confectioner's sugar, just enough to give a good spreading consistency.

MAKES ENOUGH FOR A 13- BY 9-INCH (3.5 L) PAN

Caramel Frosting

1 1/2 cups	packed brown sugar	375 mL
1/2 cup	granulated sugar	125 mL
1 cup	milk	250 mL
1 tbsp	butter or margarine	15 mL

TIP For easier handling of icings and frostings when decorating cakes, use a squeeze bottle with a pointed tip, like your ketchup and mustard squeeze bottles.

For a different topping or spread, place caramel candies in the bottom of your baking pan before pouring in batter. Bake as usual, then invert the cake, spread melted caramel evenly over top of cake; cool and cut into bars or squares.

1. In a saucepan over medium-low heat, combine brown sugar, granulated sugar and milk; cook until sugar is dissolved. Increase heat and bring to a boil; cook until syrup forms a soft ball in cold water. Add butter and stir until melted. Remove from heat. Cool to lukewarm. Beat until thick and creamy and of right consistency for spreading.

MAKES ENOUGH FOR A 13- BY 9-INCH (3.5 L) PAN

Chocolate Chip Frosting

1 1/2 cups	granulated sugar	375 mL
1/2 cup	butter or margarine	125 mL
1/3 cup	evaporated milk	75 mL
1/2 cup	semi-sweet chocolate chips	125 mL

1. In a small saucepan over low heat, combine sugar, butter and milk until sugar is dissolved. Increase heat and bring to boil; cook, stirring constantly, for 1 minute. Add chocolate chips and stir until melted. Allow to cool slightly before using.

White Chocolate Butter Cream Frosting

1/4 cup	whipping (35%) cream	50 mL
6	squares (each 1 oz [28 g]) white chocolate	6
1 cup	confectioner's (icing) sugar, sifted	250 mL
1 cup	cold unsalted butter, cut into chunks	250 mL

1. In a saucepan over low heat, heat cream and chocolate, stirring constantly until chocolate is melted and mixture is smooth. Set aside to cool for about 15 minutes.

2. Pour cooled chocolate mixture into the small bowl of an electric mixer. Blend in sugar. With motor running, add butter a little at a time. Beat on high speed for 2 minutes or until smooth and fluffy.

Chocolate Velvet Frosting

1 1/2 cups	granulated sugar	375 mL
1/4 tsp	salt	1 mL
6 tbsp	cornstarch	90 mL
1 1/2 cups	boiling water	375 mL
3	squares (each 1 oz [28 g]) unsweetened chocolate	3
1/4 cup	butter *or* margarine	50 mL
1 tsp	vanilla extract	5 mL

TIP Need a garnish? Sprinkle bars or squares with sugar and spice, or glaze with a thin mixture of orange juice and confectioner's sugar.

1. In a saucepan over low heat, combine sugar, salt and cornstarch. Stir in the boiling water until well blended. Cook, stirring constantly, until mixture thickens.

2. Add chocolate and butter; cook, stirring until melted. Remove from heat. Stir in vanilla. Pour into a bowl and chill, stirring several times, until thick enough to spread.

Cocoa Frosting

3 tbsp	butter or margarine, softened	45 mL
1/3 cup	unsweetened cocoa powder	75 mL
2 cups	confectioner's (icing) sugar, sifted	500 mL
3 tbsp	milk	45 mL
1/2 tsp	vanilla extract	2 mL
1/4 tsp	salt	1 mL

1. In a bowl with an electric mixer, cream together butter and cocoa until smooth and blended. Stir in confectioner's sugar alternately with milk, blending until smooth and of the right consistency for spreading. Stir in vanilla and salt.

Coffee Frosting

1/2 cup	butter or margarine, softened	125 mL
2 cups	confectioner's (icing) sugar, sifted	500 mL
3 tbsp	coffee liqueur	45 mL
2 tbsp	milk	25 mL
1 tbsp	instant coffee powder	15 mL

1. In a small bowl with an electric mixer, cream butter and about half of the confectioner's sugar, until smooth and fluffy.

2. In a measuring cup, mix together liqueur, milk and instant coffee until blended. Add to the creamed mixture alternately with the remaining confectioner's sugar, beating until smooth.

No-Cook Fudge Frosting

1 cup	confectioner's (icing) sugar, sifted	250 mL
3 tbsp	milk	45 mL
1	egg	1
1 tsp	vanilla extract	5 mL
2	squares (each 1 oz [28 g]) unsweetened chocolate, melted and cooled slightly	2
3 tbsp	butter or margarine, softened	45 mL

1. In a bowl combine confectioner's sugar, milk, egg and vanilla, stirring constantly until blended. Stir in melted chocolate, then butter, beating well after each addition.

2. Chill for 10 minutes in refrigerator. Place bowl in ice water. Beat frosting over ice water until the right consistency for spreading.

TIP Raw eggs can be a potentially dangerous source of salmonella. To reduce this food-safety risk, use pasteurized egg.

Cream Cheese Frosting

6 oz	cream cheese, softened	180 g
1/2 cup	butter or margarine, softened	125 mL
2 tsp	vanilla extract	10 mL
4 1/2 cups to 5 cups	confectioner's (icing) sugar, sifted	1.125 L to 1.25 L

1. In a bowl, beat together cream cheese, butter and vanilla until light and fluffy. Gradually add 2 cups (500 mL) of the confectioner's sugar, beating well. Gradually beat in as much of the remaining sugar as required to make the right consistency for spreading.

Lemon Glaze

1 cup	confectioner's (icing) sugar, sifted	250 mL
4 tsp	lemon juice	20 mL

TIP To remove lumps from confectioner's sugar, press through a sieve, or sift until smooth.

1. In a small bowl, mix together confectioner's sugar and lemon juice until smooth and blended.

VARIATION Pineapple Glaze: Add another 1/2 cup (125 mL) confectioner's sugar and replace lemon juice with 1/4 cup (50 mL) pineapple juice.

Easy Orange Frosting

2	egg whites	2
1 1/4 cups	granulated sugar	300 mL
1/4 cup	frozen orange juice concentrate, thawed	50 mL
1 tbsp	light corn syrup	15 mL

1. In the top of a double boiler over simmering (not boiling) water, combine egg whites, sugar, concentrate and syrup. Cook, beating constantly with an electric mixer, on high speed, for about 10 minutes, or until frosting forms stiff peaks. Remove from heat. Cool slightly.

Penuche Nut Icing

1 cup	packed brown sugar	250 mL
1/4 cup	milk	50 mL
1/4 cup	shortening	50 mL
1/2 tsp	vanilla extract	2 mL
1/4 tsp	salt	1 mL
1/2 cup	chopped nuts	125 mL

TIP To keep frosting from hardening in the bowl, cover it with a damp towel.

1. In a saucepan over medium-low heat, combine brown sugar, milk, shortening and salt. Slowly bring to a rolling boil, stirring constantly, and boil for 2 minutes.

2. Remove from heat and beat with an electric mixer until lukewarm. Add the vanilla and beat until thick enough to spread. If too thick, add a little cream. Stir in nuts.

Pink Lemonade Frosting

1/2 cup	frozen pink lemonade concentrate, thawed	125 mL
3 1/2 to 4 cups	confectioner's (icing) sugar, sifted	825 mL to 1 L
2	egg whites	2
Pinch	salt	Pinch

1. In a bowl with an electric mixer, combine concentrate, confectioner's sugar, egg whites and salt. Beat, on high speed, until thick enough to spread.

TIP Raw eggs can be a potentially dangerous source of salmonella. To reduce this food-safety risk, use pasteurized egg whites.

Rocky-Road Frosting

2	squares (each 1 oz [28 g]) unsweetened chocolate	2
2 cups	miniature marshmallows, divided	500 mL
1/4 cup	water	50 mL
1/4 cup	butter or margarine	50 mL
2 cups	confectioner's (icing) sugar, sifted	500 mL
1 tsp	vanilla extract	5 mL
1/2 cup	chopped walnuts	125 mL

1. In a small saucepan, combine chocolate, 1 cup (250 mL) of the marshmallows, water and butter, over low heat, stirring constantly until blended. Remove from heat and cool slightly.

2. Slowly beat in confectioner's sugar, then vanilla. Beat until smooth and thick, about 2 minutes. Stir in the remaining 1 cup (250 mL) of marshmallows and the nuts; mix until well combined.

Praline Topping

MAKES ENOUGH FOR AN 8- OR 9-INCH (2 L OR 2.5 L) PAN

1 cup	chopped nuts	250 mL
1/2 cup	packed brown sugar	125 mL
1/4 cup	butter or margarine, melted	50 mL
3 tbsp	whipping (35%) cream	45 mL

TIP To keep cake crumbs from getting into your frosting, first spread cake with a thin layer of frosting and let it set. Then frost as usual.

1. In a small bowl, combine nuts, brown sugar, butter and cream. Mix together until well blended.

2. Spread evenly over a hot or cooled cake and broil about 3 inches (7.5 cm) from the heat for 1 to 2 minutes, or until pale brown.

Strawberry Butter Cream Frosting

MAKES ENOUGH FOR AN 8- OR 9-INCH (2 L OR 2.5 L) PAN

4 oz	cream cheese, softened	125 g
1/4 cup	butter or margarine, softened	50 mL
1/3 cup	mashed fresh strawberries	75 mL
2 cups	confectioner's (icing) sugar, sifted	500 mL

1. In a bowl with an electric mixer, cream butter and cream cheese until fluffy. Beat in strawberries. Stir in the confectioner's sugar and beat until the right consistency for spreading.

Vanilla Frosting

MAKES ENOUGH FOR AN 8- OR 9-INCH (2 L OR 2.5 L) PAN

3 cups	confectioner's (icing) sugar, sifted	750 mL
1/3 cup	butter or margarine, softened	75 mL
2 tbsp	milk	25 mL
1 1/2 tsp	vanilla extract	7 mL

1. In a bowl with an electric mixer, cream confectioner's sugar and butter. Stir in milk and vanilla and beat until smooth and the right consistency for spreading.

Vanilla Glaze

MAKES ENOUGH FOR A 13- BY 9-INCH (3.5 L) PAN

1 cup	granulated sugar	250 mL
1/2 tsp	baking soda	2 mL
1/2 cup	buttermilk	125 mL
1 tbsp	light corn syrup	15 mL
1/2 cup	butter or margarine	125 mL
1 tsp	vanilla extract	5 mL

1. In a saucepan over low heat, combine sugar, baking soda, buttermilk, syrup and butter. Heat slowly, stirring constantly, to boiling. Continue cooking for 2 minutes. Remove from heat. Stir in vanilla.

Date Frosting

1	pkg (8 oz [250 g]) pitted dates, chopped	1
1 cup	boiling water	250 mL
1 cup	granulated sugar	250 mL
1/2 cup	butter *or* margarine	125 mL
1/2 cup	chopped pecans	125 mL

1. In a saucepan combine dates, boiling water, granulated sugar and butter; cook over medium heat, stirring constantly, for about 20 minutes or until mixture is very thick. Remove from heat; stir in pecans. Cool to lukewarm.

Make-Ahead Whipped Cream Frosting

1/2 tsp	unflavored gelatin	2 mL
1 tbsp	cold water	15 mL
1 cup	whipping (35%) cream	250 mL
Pinch	salt	Pinch
1/2 tsp	vanilla extract	2 mL
1 tbsp	granulated sugar (optional)	15 mL

TIP This recipe will keep for up to 4 days in the refrigerator, without separating. Be sure to use very fresh cream.

VARIATION Chocolate-Dotted Whipped Frosting: Grate 1 square (1 oz [28 g]) semi-sweet chocolate (about 1/4 cup [50 mL]) and fold into frosting; cover and chill in refrigerator.

1. In a small bowl, sprinkle gelatin over the water. Set bowl in 1 inch (2.5 cm) of hot water in a saucepan. Let stand until gelatin dissolves. Remove and let mixture cool for 1 minute.

2. In a small bowl with an electric mixer, whip the cream until almost stiff, then add dissolved gelatin mixture, salt and vanilla, and sugar (if using). Continue beating until stiff peaks form. Cover and chill in refrigerator.

3. Before spreading, beat with a spoon to blend.

White Fluffy Frosting

2	egg whites	2
1/4 tsp	cream of tartar	1 mL
2 1/2 tbsp	water	32 mL
2 tbsp	light corn syrup	25 mL
1 1/2 tsp	vanilla extract	7 mL
1/2 tsp	lemon extract	2 mL
2 cups	confectioner's (icing) sugar, sifted	500 mL

1. In a bowl with an electric mixer, beat egg whites and cream of tartar until stiff peaks form.

2. In another bowl, whisk together syrup, water, vanilla and lemon extract. Add to the egg white mixture alternately with the confectioner's sugar, beating well after each addition, until creamy and stiff and easy to spread.

TIP Raw eggs can be a potentially dangerous source of salmonella. To reduce food-safety risk, use pasteurized egg whites in this recipe.

Index